About the Author

I grew up in Hartlepool, in north east England. I studied Modern History at Oxford University and Law at the College of Law, York. I became a solicitor in the City of London. I advised banks and shareholders on large-scale infrastructure projects for twenty years, until I realized that I was appalling at it. My long-term passion is to be a writer – of very silly, but uplifting comedy.

Dear Adam,

Middle-Class Hell and How to Cure It

Thank you for so much 'fun' over the years :)

If there is anything you want to change in your life, Part 3 of this book tells you how to do it.

With lots of love,

Mark Hanlon +++

Mark Hanlon

Middle-Class Hell and How to Cure It

Olympia Publishers

London

www.olympiapublishers.com
OLYMPIA PAPERBACK EDITION

A CIP catalogue record for this title is
available from the British Library.

ISBN: 978-1-78830-062-9

First Published in 2018

Olympia Publishers
60 Cannon Street
London
EC4N 6NP

Printed in Great Britain

Dedication

Dedicated to all the wonderful people in my life, including family and friends, who have given me encouragement and support. And to the Old Lady, for silly messages when we are supposed to be "working", and for creating comic absurdity from the mundane.

Also dedicated to Terrance Dicks, a marvellous writer without whom I would not be able to read, and Mark Jones, for much help and encouragement early in life.

Part One
Working-Class Hell

Hartlepool

I shouldn't knock Hartlepool too much.

I currently live in Catford, in south east London, whose claim to fame – and there are many, most of them sensibility-shocking – is a large, black fibreglass cat, hanging off the edge of a building, "welcoming" all to a brutalist shopping centre. But it has a slightly wicked grin, threatening to fall off its perch and flatten you if you mock it.

Hartlepool feels strangely similar, in that both places seem to have been utterly impervious to gentrification. Both places are also represented by animals: a cat and a monkey.

And Hartlepool is the right place to start this journey, a very Working-Class town in the North East of England, where I was born, and, from there, up and away into the sunny uplands of "Middle-Class Helldom".

A curious place, the Middle-Class, to which many aspire, yet which is mad and frustratingly funny at one and the same time. But if taken seriously, it's "Hell".

This story plots my journey from a Working-Class background, to a Middle-Class one, with some observations on life in both along the way, which will be relevant to all of you. Plus, it offers some tips on how to fix what we don't like. Really, it does. And they work as well. Really. It could end

Working-Class Hell and Middle-Class Hell for good. Honestly. Well, maybe... but plough on, dear reader.

But first, how could one best describe Hartlepool to those who have never been there?

Before being installed as the town's new MP in the early 90s, Peter Mandelson, in an article for the *Hartlepool Mail*, the local rag, described Hartlepool as being, "Surrounded by an arc of beautiful Anglo-Saxon villages..." And then it stopped.

The article didn't go any further. It wasn't clear whether the printing presses ground to a halt in horror before describing what was in the centre of the arc, or whether Mandelson simply couldn't bear to go on. I looked puzzled when I read that article, and wondered why it went no further. I turned the paper upside down, back to front, and shook it, to see whether the rest of the town would emerge from the article, like a mutant birth.

It never did. I'm sure the article went on to literary brilliance, but not in the copy I possessed, which just mysteriously stopped.

So let me tell you about Hartlepool, on the assumption that Mandelson's article is never, ever seen again.

As nowhere else, fifty per cent of the population seems to consist of angels, the nicest people you could meet. I recall teachers being encouraging, going well beyond the call of duty in giving up their free time, their lunch hours, overworked and wide-eyed suicidal, to educate me. And there were legions of people like that, thousands of kind little mad old ladies wandering around, being nice to everybody, yet strangely clueless, without any idea where they were or what was going on. This is the kind of bliss to which I now aspire. I just seemed to attract them. Grannies with bosoms that would heave every time they saw me. Grannies might like having heaving bosoms. But how would I know?

I'm not a Granny.

And then there was the other fifty per cent. Well, you can guess by comparison; but I don't think I've ever observed that phenomenon elsewhere, of an exact fifty/fifty split between angels and the not so angelic.

Another couple of curious "facts". The people of Hartlepool were alleged to have hung a monkey. Lots of you may know about this already. But for those who don't, the tale goes thus.

During the Napoleonic wars, or possibly hundreds of years either side, no one knows or cares, the survivor of a ship-wreck was washed ashore a Hartlepool beach. It was a monkey. And the good people of Hartlepool tried to interrogate the poor unfortunate primate (not Primark), which, in modern depictions in a nod to historical accuracy in the eighteenth century, is wearing a Hartlepool United football top, and drinking a pint of locally brewed lager out of a modern tankard.

For some unfathomable reason, the stupid animal failed to co-operate under interrogation or to give coherent answers, with detailed precision, on French invasion plans.

The Hartlepudlians, not having met a Frenchman or woman before, assumed that it was a French spy, and hung it.

After looking at the percentage of Leave voters in the 2016 Euro referendum for Hartlepool, the bit about their not knowing what the French look like is entirely plausible, both then and now.

And on to more curious tales: this one is less well known. Some drunk in a pub, who told me he was a Lord (probably Lord Mandelson, but I was too focused on watching a woman trying to suck the innards out of fish batter with a plastic straw), said that during a solar eclipse in 1911, the fishwives of

Hartlepool ran out *en masse* into the garden and buried the pots and pans.

Quite why, nobody knows.

This, ladies and gentlemen, is my genetic stock.

It does have its upsides. One lady was interviewed by Jeremy Paxman about the German bombardment of Hartlepool in 1914. She was there at the time, and she said she thought that the sound of the bombardment was caused by one of the neighbours beating the carpet. What a totally understandable and practical point of view, I thought.

Yet something even more curious emerges from all these tales.

Apart from the bombardment carpet-banger lady, these tales aren't actually true.

Yet everybody believes they are.

People believe they are true, despite not having answers to simple logical questions: (i) why were the French there in the first place? (ii) why did they have a monkey? (iii) how did it survive the ship-wreck when no one else did? (iv) where was it going? (v) what was it going to do when it got there?

And why, God preserve us, would: (i) a load of women be hypnotically affected by an eclipse; and then (ii) bury all the pots and pans in the garden?

Someone must have sat there and made all this up. And when people heard it, they said, "Oh my word, that makes perfect sense, it really must have happened." And thus it is repeated as unquestioned fact.

Because, if you've lived in Hartlepool, you will know that simply nothing is implausible, as these pages will go on to demonstrate.

Another curious thing about Hartlepool is the weather. If you want a laugh, just focus on Hartlepool during any weather forecast, and see what's going on. Whatever Azores high hangs over the rest of the country, permitting all of us to bask in something marginally over minus three in July, Hartlepool has its own curious little weather bomb going off. It is the only place I know, anywhere in the world, where, as summer hauls itself into view, people say, "It's summer," and then proceed to put more warm clothes on.

It just seems to get colder in the summer.

I remember my Granny, as December turned into the first of May, hurtling down the front path of her council house, pinny flapping, shelf bosom heaving, nostrils flaring, head down as the heated rollers transformed into the chariot wheels from Ben Hur, as she ploughed herself headlong through the hedge desperate to reach the gas fire. Her slippers and panty-girdle would catch alight as she mounted it, like a vast sexually uncontrollable hippo, pinny incandescent, wrestling with the gas fire controls like some World War II aircraft pilot. And with a final heave and a semi-orgasmic blast, she finally turned the temperature control of the gas fire from "maximum" to "nova", and then to a set of off-the-scale symbols, desperate to get the heat up. Just as the outside air temperature plunged fifteen degrees in the middle of the day, heralding the arrival of the British summer in Hartlepool.

And so it stayed like that, for months, the whole national gas grid creaking under the strain to heat Hartlepool in summer until, in some utterly perverse leap of logic, people would turn the gas fires back down as summer ended and things "got back to normal".

The fascinating thing about Granny, of course, and about so many people in Hartlepool, is that their social aspirations were to be in the "right" section of the "Working-Class".

To Granny, the Middle-Class, the subject of this book, were viewed with suspicion. "Southerners." And, God forbid, Tory voters (Hartlepool did have a Tory MP in the 1950s, apparently, but he turned to drink). To the extent that the Middle-Class existed in Hartlepool, they lived behind "West Park".

"West Park" was a place to which people aspired, certainly, but it was also viewed with suspicion, and some resentment too, because it was out of reach. It almost seemed like a closed, exclusive world. If one ventured there, one had to fake a posh accent, and pretend that one wasn't waiting for a clapped-out old smoke-filled hissing and wheezing ramshackle Corporation bus back to the rest of the town, when one weepingly left this one oasis of apparent civilisation.

Granny's whole narrative, particularly when I was growing up in the '80s, was, "What was happening to the Working-Class?" That was a subject of manic obsession.

And to be in the "right" section of the Working-Class counted for everything.

So her council house had to be pristine. Windows washed daily – or more often. Steps and paths scrubbed. The sofas smoothed down.

And it was all rather pointless, on one level. The house stood underneath Steetley chimney, a magnesium chemical plant, which seemed to belch out constant noxious fumes that smelt of rotten eggs.

Then, the house next door was a dilapidated wreck, with waist-high grass in a never-tended garden. And the whole area was gradually sinking down, as what might be called the "respectable" Working-Class moved on to buy their own homes and the "others" moved in. The "others" being those who weren't the "right" sort of Working-Class. In Granny's eyes, at least.

It was a losing battle for respectability. But it was the fight to maintain it that counted, even if the odds were as grim as Steetley chimney.

Perhaps that, at the end of the day, lies behind all class distinction. It is the fact that one "tries to be better", despite the comical things that intervene to undermine our hubris.

But it wasn't just outside factors that made the battle for constant cleanliness a losing one.

Granny also chain-smoked Players Full Strength inside the house. Most days, you could just make out a pair of eyes and a pinny, leering out of the smoke-filled gloom. The interior walls were strangely globulated, as if someone had thrown pepperoni pizzas at the walls and they hadn't fallen off. At some point, which can only be guessed at, probably in the 1950s, protruding patterned wallpaper had been slapped up on every wall that could be found. Nicotine stains from the Players Full Strength required that this be painted over every six months. So often had it been painted over that the original pattern was indistinguishable. The walls looked like a large ribbed condom covered in three decades of cracked paint.

Added to which, the internal décor seemed very dark so that, despite its being spotlessly clean, its energy felt oppressive.

The interior design, too, was a strange affair. The house had a pantry, and then a large dining room, with a wall full of kitchen cabinets. Off from that was the kitchen, which was impossibly small. It could barely be found on a floor plan of the house. In fact, it could barely be found on a floor plan of itself.

Yet the strangest feature of that whole arrangement was a row of kitchen cabinets in the dining area containing nothing but... tea bags.

No food, no utensils, no pans, pots, knick-knacks... nothing... just shelves of boxes of PG Tips tea bags.

Counting the tea boxes, all stacked from the back to the front of the cupboards, and from the base to the top of the cupboards, was an impossible task. Rather like painting the Forth Bridge, it was never-ending. Someone tried, and he came away muttering something about the kitchen cabinets of infinity, that extended beyond this universe and into the next. He emerged from the house, blinking and stumbling into the daylight, and was never seen again.

No one quite knew why the cabinets were full of boxes of PG Tips, and the house contained no food. There was mention among the family of the possibility of a nuclear holocaust and the necessity to hoard tea, and that the kitchen cabinets were really a nuclear shelter. In Granny would clamber, at the first sound of a nuclear siren, to emerge unfazed at the devastation, heated rollers unmoved.

Granny was indestructible.

She seemed to survive on tea, Players Full Strength and nothing else. Nothing.

However, the teapot was always full, and visits by anyone required a gargantuan force-fed consumption of tea. They would eventually leave the house, bursting in agony.

And of course, as Granny took each box of PG Tips out of the cupboard, she would look at the picture of the monkey on the front (for in those days PG had a picture of an actual monkey on the front of the box) and, with some race memory of her ancestors' allegedly having hanged a monkey suddenly kicking in, she would scowl, "The bloody French. They should hang them!" Forgetting, of course, that her ancestors had apparently tried, but that it had all gone horribly wrong.

On top of the tea was the Players Full Strength.

She regaled this astonishing tale of a surgeon who had once said to her, "Now Mrs Granny, don't smoke anything with a filter on, it will kill you. I smoke Players Full Strength, no filter. Now look at me: fit as a fiddle! The filter kills you, but full strength, with no filter, is absolutely fine," as he rolled off his chair, dead. Let us be thankful that he didn't work in a sexual health clinic, and apply the same logic there.

So, among all that tosh, it was a losing battle to keep that house clean. The stench of the industrial chimney, the stench, gradually, of the wrong sort of neighbours moving in, the stench of the Players Full Strength, the stench of the constant flow of tea, and the bizarre painted ribbed condom that adorned every wall, was enough to defeat anyone with any sanity.

But not Granny!

Appearances had to be met!

Part of that was the daily communion, for the sake of appearances, with the woman over the road, Mrs Holroyd. But due to Granny's not being able to pronounce her name when taking tea and fag simultaneously, she became Mrs Haemorrhoid.

Mrs Haemorrhoid never batted an eyelid at this name slip. She was too busy stealing Granny's fags and anything like a name slip was excusable in the face of such easy theft.

And the daily communion was too good to miss when there was juicy gossip about next door's not paying the electric bill, and installing a petrol generator and a donkey in the back garden. The donkey would "eeeeorrrrrr" right on cue when there was a point to be made about how awful the neighbourhood was becoming.

"Ohhh the noise, Mrs Haemorrhoid!" said Granny, "The stench and the fumes," as the two of them chain smoked their way back to the industrial revolution.

As the illegal generator next door belched into gear, Granny would scratch her pussy, raise a tea cup, and nod indignantly at the clothes line in the garden as her panty girdles and pinnies became charred beyond recognition in the generator fumes. She didn't realise that these were usually scorched already as a result of the summer gas fire incident, yet the fumes from the generator added to their final denouement, like some grizzly flame-filled execution in the reign of *Bloody Mary*.

As the panty girdles went out in a blaze, these communions went on for hours...

Every day.

The same stories. Every day.

Neither of them could clearly remember what they'd been on about the day before, and so every day it started again. From about ten a.m. until four p.m.

Yet, each day, Mrs Haemorrhoid would lap it up. My grandfather would pour tea for six hours. He was allowed a vocabulary of two words in every situation – "Yes, Freda."

Granny and Mrs Haemorrhoid did not move for six hours, they did not stop talking for six hours. School holidays were purgatory as they meant six weeks of this every day, if I was with Granny that time.

The one brief respite was when they would decide to phone in together to a radio talk show, usually if the subject matter was Prince Philip, because he was Greek. They would babble senselessly at the presenter and not realise that they'd been cut off at about ten thirty, and they'd still be talking into the phone at about two p.m. with the odd interjection of, "Now did your viewers get that?"

Of course, when they did get through and they were on air, they were listening to themselves on the radio as they spoke down the phone, and the feedback loop of having them speaking down the phone and having the same nonsense come through the radio at the same time, in an endless loop of the babble of infinity, was simply too much.

And finally, after several young universes had aged and died, Mrs Haemorrhoid would haul herself up, tea dribbling from her gaping face as her tea-inflated carcass was about to spray her cardigan buttons in all directions, and she'd slosh out the door with, "Well, I only popped in for five minutes; I'll bring you some fags tomorrow, Freda."

As she went, Granny's face would cloud after she slammed the door on her, "She nicked all me bloody fags... the impitent bugger."

"Impitent" was the favourite word. No one knew what it meant, but it was used constantly.

And, of course, the next day, Mrs Haemorrhoid would turn up to say she'd forgotten the fags, steal some more, and then the tea ritual would start all over again.

The respite between four p.m. one day and ten a.m. the next day was needed not for basic essentials like sleep, or anything else, but to see whether some new piece of gossip could be gleaned. If a fight could possibly happen with the neighbours during those hours, that gave material for the next sixty years.

Occasionally, one would tune in to the discussion with Mrs Haemorrhoid, if one was feeling that there was no hope in the world and that this was the best there was. I would do this regularly over the years, waves of information hitting me about getting tits caught in the mangle when wringing out a panty-girdle, sagging bosoms, the life and habitat of a donkey, the Department of Health and Social Security, Prince Philip, and how to present oneself at the door in a pinny if the insurance man called. Oh that poor man, the insurance bloke! He came for a two pounds a week insurance premium, yet he was a Mrs Haemorrhoid substitute, and he would get the whole six hours if she was away on holiday. He would emerge battered and broken.

Even if one had heard it all before, the tale could become quite gripping, rising to a crescendo, with drama-filled cliffhangers. But all talk would stop as they realised that the teapot was empty, and had to be refilled before they could plunge senselessly on.

Yet over the years, out of all this nonsense, one strange fact emerged through the smoke and babble-filled gloom. Listening to talk on political issues one day, my jaw suddenly dropped. My God, I reflected, as I heard one view after another, in between panty-girdles and the joy of twin-tub washing machines... My Granny is a Nazi...

...And so she was, if all the dots were joined and everything she said were taken literally. But she voted Labour, of course!

This is typical, I have found, in many Working-Class households. Granny is really a Nazi. It was my first introduction to Working-Class Hell.

And then another fascinating thing happened. I ran up to Granny one day at the school gates, and I said something inspiring like, "Hello Granny," only to be given an evil look as she heaved herself off.

I should have realised. There was something not right about the pinny. It was darker somehow, with a hint of danger. It had an unmistakeable air of... menace... something not quite right about it, like accidently falling into a parallel universe to discover that all your female friends have beards (mine all do!), but not quite working out that there is something wrong with this... which there isn't, of course.

Yet this is exactly what had happened.

My Granny had an evil twin. She wasn't a doppelganger. She was a real evil twin sister. One who was not spoken of, but I'd just met her.

And my jaw dropped further... if Nazi Granny was the good one, what the hell was the evil twin like...?

I had to find out...

Middle-Class Hell

The art of cliffhanger chapter-endings is not to resolve them straight away, but to drag them out as long as possible, switch scene, maybe even introduce another strand of narrative or plot, and return to the cliffhanger later.

It's a common trick of writers, to make their audience think, "Ahhhh, that's clever, the writer is making me wait for a resolution to this incomprehensible and implausible melodrama, by first switching scene."

No, it's not clever.

In reality it just annoys the reader, who doesn't think it's clever at all, and who quite rightly wants to know what happens quickly and get on with their life.

I acknowledge that it's annoying.

And, for this reason, that's exactly why I'm doing it.

The strung-out cliffhanger, and inevitably naff resolution, is simply another aspect of Middle-Class Hell that comes from reading any book or following any melodrama. I'm just easing you into how far Middle-Class Hell has progressed into every area of our lives. It really is everywhere.

On the subject of Middle-Class Hell, it might have become obvious that Grannies, pinnies, panty-girdles, Hartlepool, more Grannies, more pinnies, evil twin Grannies, evil pinnies, and vast amounts of tea on North East council estates is not very Middle-Class.

Because to be Middle-Class, as Granny would tell you, was a vague, distant dream, in those communities but, if one became Middle Class, everything would be amazing.

It would be better than amazing. It would give you the ability to look down on everyone you'd left behind, stop struggling, and have a bountiful life where everything worked smoothly and you just glided along, being admired and envied by everyone, and most importantly, you shopped in nice shops.

Like John Lewis.

The reality – as I eventually became Middle-Class – is somewhat different.

Rather than everything gliding along smoothly, it can, and does, become its own form of Hell.

Perhaps those born Middle-Class haven't experienced this. They are just used to it, maybe.

But coming from a Working-Class background, there was an expectation, a hope perhaps, that life would be easy once Middle-Class status had been achieved.

But no. Middle-Class Hell, at its root, seems to be a fatal combination of over-expectation, added to complexity, which ends in absurdity.

Take the example of a wind chime.

On the surface, it's a lovely, Middle-Class thing. I bought one after I acquired my second flat in London, which had some outside space, on a bend of the River Thames.

I thought it would be gorgeous to come home to, and to sit and listen to, after an easy Middle-Class day lounging in the office (in a proper office, not at a desk), doing very little but being told I was wonderful by management and customers alike and earning a fortune, to glide home in a taxi (not the Tube), no traffic, and to sit outside with a glass of chateau de-something 1945 or, even more Middle-Class, a vastly overpriced English sparkling wine from some vineyard with about three grape vines and a vat of old gooseberries to make up for the lack of anything approaching a grape.

You turn up in these English vineyards and are usually met by a tour guide in a pair of wellies with a brolly, looking over a rain-lashed muddy field about the size of a small car park, and are given a cheery introduction. "Well, we had a terrible summer again this year, and everything just got washed away. We threw the whole grape crop out again, but we have a lovely bottle of sparkling gooseberry in our shop, £50, bargain. This is our show vineyard; our real working vineyard, where most of our grapes come from, is in a prime location."

"Where?" someone would ask.

The guide's face would collapse. "Hartlepool."

The Middle-Classes are far more badly affected by bad summers than the Working-Classes, you know.

The Middle-Classes go to fantastic lengths to enjoy the summer; they slave away in the garden in the autumn and again in the spring to achieve perfection, and buy things like garden furniture sets and parasols and barbecues, only to find that it all goes tits-up in the inevitable washout next summer season.

The Working-Classes, by comparison, recoil at the idea of opening the curtains when the sun shines and, when it does, up goes the heating, as we have seen.

Granny had this curious thing of not opening the curtains sometimes during the heady Hartlepool summer. And turning up the gas fire, as we have seen.

Regarding the closed curtains, on asking why, "Zombies," she would reply. "They look in and have designs on my mangle, panty-girdles and twin tub washing machine." So the curtains stayed shut, and the gas fire roared even more as the sun came out.

But about the wind chime: I would look at it and gaze into the distance as I sat there thinking of sipping sparkling English gooseberry – now £75 a bottle, and we suckers fall for it – and there it would be in the background, tinkling away in a gentle breeze, creating a spa or zen-like Japanese garden atmosphere, as I would contemplate whether I could be even more lazy in the office the next day, yet still wonderfully productive.

So I got it home and started to put the wind chime up, drilling holes in the wall.

Inevitably, the drill bit broke.

At work for several days, so can only go to B&Q at the weekend for more drill bits.

Trip to Old Kent Road (London) B&Q on Sunday.

No drill bits. Everything, absolutely everything else, but no drill bits.

Most of Sunday afternoon gone.

No time in the week to go, as back at work.

Trip to B&Q next Saturday.

No drill bits. Most of Saturday gone. Told to go to Greenwich, they have them there.

Off to Greenwich B&Q on Sunday.

No drill bits. Told they have them in Old Kent Road.

Aargh…

2 weeks have now gone by.

Fed up with B&Q. Order them off Amazon.

Don't turn up. Order them again. Wrong ones turn up.

Eventually, take a trip miles out of London, but it takes all day as there are engineering works on the railway line, but find drill bits. At last. Hooray.

Drill hole successfully in the wall, but then the whole brick falls out.

Find another spot and drill holes in the wall. Success. But the plastic screw holder falls apart as I put a screw in it, so need to go to B&Q for plastic screw holders.

Go to both Greenwich and Old Kent Road branches of B&Q.

Full of drill bits, both stores. Bursting, overflowing with drill bits; there is an offer on due to over-stocking. Why couldn't this have happened weeks ago, when I needed drill bits?

But no plastic screw holders in either store.

For weeks.

Spring has now turned to autumn, and the gentle breezes of April have now turned into the howling gales of October, before I finally get the wind chime up.

I lie back, waiting for the sweet melody to reach my ears.

Only for it to emit the most awful crashing, clanging, jangle from Hell, as the latest howling October blast smashes into it at three a.m. in the morning, like a thousand metal dustbin lids being banged together by the worst school orchestra in history.

At four a.m., the entire block of flats has been woken, and is banging on my door demanding that the torture end. Resident after resident threatens ASBO after ASBO, as I explain how lovely the building sounds with its new wind chime.

"It will be lovely when the wind dies down... sometime next year. You'll be tinkled off to sleep by its sweet melody, I promise you."

But it doesn't. The gales go on night after night, the residents are red-eyed in the lift every morning, until, finally, one gust releases all from their misery as the wind chime is lifted off its moorings, taking part of the wall with it, and hurtles headlong into the River Thames, with a final dying clang before it hits the water, to be carried off to Tilbury, and is never seen again.

That is Middle-Class Hell.

The best of intentions, an expectation of peace, ease, calm, and tranquillity, a twinkly wind chime, but, instead, the resulting pain and disaster and, above all, a waste of bloody time.

I have decided that it is time to examine it, this Middle-Class Hell thing. It is time for serious examination of this vital theme in so many of our lives, because it stares us in the face, like some big fat red Baboon arse, yet we don't understand it. This book is inspired by the need to undertake this serious examination of all the key aspects of this crucial subject. And to recognise it in our lives, and to deal with it. For it must be destroyed! Middle-Class Heaven and Working-Class Heaven must return!

But first, now that I've calmed down, how did I ever get there? How did I reach my own Middle-Class Hell? To discover that, I must drag you back to Working-Class Hartlepool... to more Granny, a mad dog, an insane headmaster, and a lady with a house full of knickers, before the elevation to the ranks of the Middle-Classes and then, finally, in Part Three... ascension. But ascension to what?

More Hartlepool

The origins, life and times, and indeed, probably, death of the evil twin (mutant) Granny remain a mystery.

For, eventually, we knew that she existed, but she was spoken of so little.

It seemed impossible that such a town could contain two identical neo-Nazi Grannies, stomping around in pinnies, fags in hand, cursing all before them, without somebody remarking on this... But it was never noticed.

To be fair... there was a lot of it about, as fair maids would one day transform in the space of a few hours from demi-goddesses into exact replicas of Granny, without any intervening period, a fag and pinny just somehow seeming to morph from them.

And how the twin Grannies avoided each other was a mystery; but rather like cats, they patrolled their territory at different times, so as not to bump into each other and hiss and screech at each other over the pinny counter in Marks & Spencer.

Besides, such a thing could NEVER be done in M&S... it was a cut above, and so was hallowed ground.

A blazing row in public anywhere else was fine though. But not in M&S.

So, despite the obvious issue of close physical proximity in a place like Hartlepool, they managed to avoid each other so that, to all intents and purposes, it seemed as if they didn't exist.

But the story of evil twin Granny did emerge one day. Granny had a coal shed in the garden full of... well, it was a tea overflow shelter, and, one day, Mrs Haemorrhoid was caught trying to break in and steal some supplies of tea.

An almighty row erupted, and Mrs Haemorrhoid was banned, with a cry of, "You impitent, thieving bugger," as she was head-butted out of the house.

So Granny sat there one day while I was there in the school holidays, alone, with no Mrs Haemorrhoid to drone at.

It was just the two of us, and so a pot of tea for two was required.

She began the preparations. Twelve tea bags were hauled out of the PG Tips box. The usual rule of one tea bag per person and one for the pot was lightweight horror to Granny. It was four tea bags per person and four for the pot. And even that was a bit of a delicate brew. Hardly flavoursome.

So in twelve tea bags went, and, as the pot groaned under the strain and they threatened to leap out, the difficult bit began. It began with an apology, "This is not for your eyes, but I've got to fist the teapot. Keep these impitent buggers in," as she'd scowl at the tea bags. And she'd turn away, not exposing the awful spectacle, as if she was necking a chicken in front of a vegan.

And off she went. Fisting the teapot. She tried desperately to get the tea bags stuck in. She did break a teapot from time to time; a handle or spout would explode off under the strain. The death of a teapot was usually a cause of days of flared tempers, tantrums and mourning, until she broke in the new one with a vigorously good fisting.

Once the tea bags were well and truly fisted in, the kettle would be boiled and the water would go into the small amount of free space left in the teapot. It would brew for a few minutes, and out would come liquid blobs of tannin-loaded sludge.

She'd raise it to her lips, tut "bit weak today", and maybe another tea bag would get flung in.

And in that day of no Mrs Haemorrhoid, it was my turn. So I had a massive tea cup thrust in front of me, and the tale of the evil twin Granny began.

I recounted the tale of meeting the evil twin outside the school gates, and asked to know what it was all about.

She inhaled deeply, lined up three fags, made sure the teapot was full, adjusted her panty-girdle, smoothed down the pinny, checked her rollers were still in (she had no hair left), sucked in to see if her teeth hadn't fallen out, and heaved her tits up off the dining table as she was clearly about to launch into a major epic that would go on for some time. And then she began...

I once didn't say a word to Granny in two whole years – I didn't dare stop her continuous flow.

"Well, Mrs Haemorrhoid..." she said to me.

She hadn't noticed that it was me sat in front of her, not Mrs Haemorrhoid. She was always getting confused about who she was addressing. She'd bitch about you to your face for hours without realising, as she thought she was talking to someone else. Eventually, Mrs Haemorrhoid was allowed back into the fold, but only because Granny got confused, and thought she was me.

"It all started during the War..."

It really was going to be an epic.

The divine feud between the twin Grannies began when they were in domestic service together to a Russian princess, or some such, in Knightsbridge or somewhere. It was a dangerous time and death was all around, as it was the War. Not sure which one though.

Granny's solution to an air raid was to wander round with an umbrella up. They'd try and drag her into air raid shelters for her safety, and she'd cheerfully commit assault and battery on the poor souls, refusing to be dragged in; and as they'd run for their lives into the air raid shelter, she'd wave her brolly in their direction screeching, "The bombs won't get me, I've got this umbrella," as incendiaries went off all around her. And with that, she'd skip off merrily down the street like a potty Mary Poppins, as most of London exploded and crashed into ruins. Indestructible, you see.

Well, it turns out that the whole thing with the evil twin came to a head because the evil twin had apparently stolen some money and sewn it up in a jacket.

It took simply hours to get to that point, and as the sun eventually set on a mid-summer evening, she finally wound up with, "Well, we don't talk about it."

I tried to press it: "Whose money? But how did you know? How did you know the money was sewn into the jacket?"

I had visions of her randomly tearing off family members' clothing, ripping it to pieces, to find a stash of dosh in the lining, with a fist waved menacingly at their face, "You impitent thieving bugger."

And being correct in the accusation, every single time some family member was violently disrobed.

But how could she possibly know where the stash was?

At that point, she had transcended, transmuted, from Granny, into Miss Marple, or more likely Inspector Columbo in an oversized pinny, with a special Granny cigar. She tapped her rollers knowingly, she nodded, and then her face turned to steel.

"No, we don't talk about it... Well, I think that's it for today, Mrs Haemorrhoid; no, we don't talk about it," and off she shuffled, head held imperiously high, the pinny soaked in sweat at such an exertion of remembrance.

I have visions of this having been a major family epic, along the lines of the Borgias but set in Hartlepool, on a bus, or in a discount shoe shop.

This feud had, of course, gone on for forty years. And they hadn't spoken since.

That is the wonderful thing about Working-Class family feuds.

Middle-Class bust-ups usually involve a raised eye-brow, a caustic remark, a Christmas present NOT from John Lewis. Above all, they are quiet.

I once bought someone a nail file one year as a Christmas present, after a particularly bad argument that involved no more than a haughty sniff in reaction to an egregious snub. A 49p nail file is a brutal insult, but it was given with the intention of sending a subliminal message to continue sharpening her nails. Like buying your mother-in-law a Venus flytrap for Mother's Day; it said everything.

But Working-Class family bust-ups: they are vast, noisy, involve screeching in the street, in public, for the whole world to see; they are total, they endure for decades. They evoke Churchill's, *"We shall fight on the beaches, we shall fight on the landing grounds, we shall fight in the fields and in the streets, we shall fight in the hills; we shall never surrender... against a monstrous tyranny never surpassed in the dark, lamentable catalogue of human crime."*

And, like any good war that's gone on for a while, no one can actually remember what it's about. So it was, I suspect, with

Granny and the evil twin Granny. It started over something, no one knows what, but just went on and on...

I suppose one aspect of the Working-Class Hell was its tribalism.

But in any event, the march to Middleclass Dom had started, as life moved along in Hartlepool.

For my parents decided to buy their own home, in a street called Dorchester Drive.

"Buy your own house!" Granny puffed. "That will end in disaster!"

The street itself was unremarkable. It would be hard to say in which period the houses were built, maybe at some time from the 1940s onwards, and they were of standard square brick construction: not dissimilar to the standard council house design in the North East at that time, but on a private estate.

What made the street were the people.

It seemed to be a street of soul mates.

Neighbours who met there in the 1970s are still friends now, forty years later, even though nearly all have moved away.

Everyone's door was open.

And people just wandered in. Nobody knocked. They just wandered in. A loud, "Hello," usually announced a presence, and sometimes not even that. It was not unusual to come down the stairs and find that half the street had wandered in and set up a coffee morning in your lounge, without announcing it.

The friendliness didn't just end with parents and neighbours, but whole families in the street of all ages just... seemed to get along.

You could stand and look out into the street and watch as visitors left one house, pondered, and then walked into another, and thirty minutes later they all came out again and crisscrossed each other in the street, as they decided to visit somebody else.

It would have been unspeakably unsociable to have locked one's doors and windows. You would have been considered very odd to have done so. Locking the front door came in during the 1980s, but before then, in the 1970s, definitely not.

To visit the place now, it would probably seem unremarkable. Just square block houses. But then, its atmosphere was idyllic.

I recall only summer, light and warmth. Which, as we know, was a very rare occurrence in Hartlepool.

The exception to that, of course, were the bonfire nights.

Bonfire night was traditionally hosted in one couple's garden, as they had the largest garden in the street. The preparation was painstaking. Everyone brought fireworks, and homemade wine. "Fig and Rosehip" was a favourite, simply because, after one glass of the stuff, it could only be pronounced, "Friggin' Rosehip".

The bonfire was always vast. It would be lit, and a huge clearance of earth was made in front of it so that people could put deck chairs and stools around the fire.

I recall that 1978 was a classic night for the bonfire. The place was packed, and good-natured. The fire was bigger than ever that year, and the "Friggin' Rosehip" had had a marvellous season. There were gallons of it, and the whole street was hammered within minutes.

That night never seemed to end, so big was the fire and so bountiful was the "Friggin' Rosehip". It went on in a blur, until someone noticed that the fire had raged so long and intensely that the chairs and stools, and their inhabitants, around the fire had actually sunk into the ground as the fire seemed to melt the earth around it, helped no doubt by intense rainfall several days before. I recall that Granny turned up, saying, insistently, "I have to sit down at my age," looked at some stool in the ground, and saw that one seat protruded about an inch out of the ground higher than everyone else's. She looked pleased, and sat down, very self-satisfied, with a superior look on her face, knowing that she had a chair that was above everybody else's.

Eventually, the fire died down, but no one wanted the night to end.

But crisis!

There was no more wood. But the show had to go on.

There were cheers from the seated legless (in every respect) crowd around the fire as things were thrown on to the fire, and away it blazed, back into life again.

Every twenty minutes or so, something else would go on to the fire, to another cheer, as the night continued, and everyone was happy.

But mysteriously, folk kept disappearing out of the garden and then re-appearing.

Something was clearly going on...

And then one observer, slightly less drunk than the rest, peered into the fire and said to someone else, "That looks awfully like your coffee table on there," to which the response would be, "That looks awfully like your TV cabinet on there, too," until everyone around the fire turned around to the garden gate to witness a whole production line of comings and goings, as more furniture was being carried from the street into the garden and hurled onto the fire.

Occasionally there were gasps of, "That's not my dining table on there, is it?" followed by a shrug of the shoulders and more "Friggin' Rosehip".

Eventually, the fire died, and the residents of Dorchester Drive staggered back home.

The next day, there were many wanderings from one house to another to peer inside, and then move on to the next one.

The whole street had decided to make an inventory, to see whether anyone had any furniture left.

Nobody had.

Nobody minded.

Everyone was complicit in having raided everyone else's houses, and in setting light to everything they could get their hands on. Looking back, the street was full of pyromaniacs, and no one noticed.

But it had been a good bonfire night.

Coffee mornings were a bit awkward after that, as mugs had to be placed on the floor and dinners eaten with plates on knees, or on the floor as well.

Otherwise, life carried on as normal in Dorchester Drive.

At the end of the day, the beauty of it was, no one cared.

And as the great fire of Hartlepool ended, and its embers died out, our time in Dorchester Drive had ended too.

Perhaps it was one of the last of the years of plenty for a while, and finances were good. It was Working-Class Heaven, for a period.

For it was time for the family to take its first foray into a Middle-Class lifestyle, and move house.

It was to be the start of a long journey…

And it was to be the first taste, at my young age, of Middle-Class Hell…

Because it would all go horribly wrong…

The Middle-Class Interregnum

Ahhhh, Ocean Road, Hartlepool!

The first foray into Middle-Classness.

It was a lovely road. Huge, handsome houses with vast gardens. Some of them had horses that trotted around paddocks, quite content.

Our new house was a dormer bungalow, and had an amazingly large front and back garden.

Dorchester Drive had been cosy, but this was much grander. It felt huge, somehow, with big windows in each end of the house overlooking large gardens, back and front. To get to the house, one walked up a large driveway, up a very steep slope, and, at the top of the slope, the house itself seemed to be slightly recessed into a hollow. None of us thought anything of that. It was to prove lethal, and comic.

But at first glance, it seemed idyllic.

From the front garden, a patch of sea could be seen in the distance. It was a short walk to the beach, a good sandy beach as well. There were large concrete bunkers on the beach, which I've always assumed were look-out posts as, after one German bombardment in World War One, it was assumed that they would try again in World War Two. Though it's a fair assumption that the Nazis might have been more bothered about taking mainland Europe and Russia than conquering Hartlepool. They tried that before when they bombed Hartlepool in World War One, and it seemed a bit pointless really. As we know, the good people whom they were invading mistook the bombardment for a Granny having a good carpet beating session.

Quite why anyone would want to conquer Hartlepool is a question worth pondering. It only makes sense if you wish to acquire endless lines of discount shoe shops, chip shops, and a fine wench of a Granny (plenty of choice there).

The battle for Hartlepool would no doubt rage for years, and the casualties would be enormous, like the siege of Monte Cassino or Moscow. It would be a seminal battle in any war, the battle for Hartlepool.

So, in anticipation of this, we had concrete bunkers on the beach, that no one seemed to want to remove. Everywhere else had beach huts. But Hartlepool, no. Wartime concrete beach bunkers. Anywhere else and they'd turn them into Middle-Class second homes.

Although the beach was sandy, there was the slight eyesore of Steetley chimney in the distance, which, as you will recall, loomed over Granny's house. Even now in 2016, a beach guide says this: "The dilapidated Steetley Pier is all that remains of the old magnesite works, *but the cliffs still glow yellow* with magnesium limestone."

I'm sorry, but a beach guide saying, *"but the cliffs still glow yellow..."* Who is this meant to attract?

If this wasn't enough, Hartlepool also has a nuclear power station, just a few miles down the coast.

We knew someone who worked there, who reacted in horror when he saw pictures of us swimming in the sea. "I

40

wouldn't do that," he said, "not after what we put in it." He chuckled darkly.

I once did a school trip to the nuclear power station, and our tour guide wore an impossible amount of make-up to cover her two heads, and a mutant tail.

She insisted that the nuclear power station was totally safe, and involved the destruction of no wildlife. Then we were taken to this pit that was used, I recall, as a sea water store or entry tank – frankly I'm at loss to remember.

We all peered over the edge.

Inside the bottomless pit were piles and piles of dead and semi-dead fish, the last survivors thrashing around as they experienced their last bit of consciousness before death. She smiled and her hand made a great swooping gesture over the edge, "See, nothing in here at all, completely free of wildlife," as a desperate fish flipped several feet into the air, to make one last attempted escape from the pit of death, only to fail miserably and to splat back down on top of the mile-high pile of the quite dead, or nearly dead, Pisces representatives.

Somebody asked, "Can I feed them, miss?"

And, of course, the Teesside industrial complex was also pumping all sorts of things into the sea as well, on top of everything else.

But we carried on regardless, and frequently sent our dog into the sea every day on a walk, but somehow failed to join the dots as to why our dog was becoming increasingly insane.

Yet this beach is now number thirteen (not remotely unlucky) in the nation's best beaches, according to the Daily Telegraph. If only we had known.

And a disused railway line was also close at hand several yards from the house that, when overgrown, became strangely beautiful and led to a secret, hidden dene, with amazing chalk cliffs, that accompanied a stream out to sea, and when the sun shone, the stream and the rocks became misty, and almost prehistoric-looking. It seemed a world away from panty-girdles, excessive tea, de-industrialisation and the other Horrors of Hartlepool at that time. It was amazingly beautiful.

The house seemed, in short, amazing. And I adored it, despite the strangeness of the beach experience.

But then... disaster struck the Middle-Class paradise!

Given the nature of this book, it seemed inevitable that it would happen at a wee, tender age, as I wasn't even ten at that stage.

I might as well get used to it.

For as soon as the family seemed to be progressing up the class-system strata, several disasters hit: (i) the house was haunted; (ii) we got a cute family Labrador/Golden Retriever cross breed that turned out to be the hound from hell; (iii) the neighbours were insane; (iv) the winters turned Siberian; and (v) the economy crashed, interest rates spiralled out of control, mortgage repayments doubled, and then redundancy hit.

But apart from that everything was fine.

To take each disaster in turn, my Mother never took to the house. I could never understand this, but some of it might have been that it was always freezing, and became a massive economic burden to heat and sustain – especially when mortgage rates doubled.

But she became convinced that the house was haunted. So did my sister. So did the ferocious dog that we managed to pick up. My sister lived in the bedroom in the loft, and it had an eerie atmosphere.

It was a loft conversion, with tiny windows, which were so high up the wall that nothing could be seen out of them, and very little light was let in. The room had pine built-in wardrobes, with a huge space behind as they were built into the large restricted height area that followed the slant of the roof. As this was so steep, the space behind the wardrobes was vast, but it just seemed to be inhabited by darkness. You could climb in, and it felt oppressive. The wardrobe doors also just opened and closed randomly, on their own, in the night. The dog that feared nothing simply refused to go up there. Other people would go up there, and then come back down again, shaking. My mother kept seeing things, including a ghostly image of a young boy who she thought was me, and in fact wasn't. She kept having weird dreams about being trapped in the house and running down darkened corridors with doors slamming, being pursued by... what?

I noticed absolutely nothing, of course.

I was, in any event, too busy being savaged by our new pooch, and was constantly dosed up to the eyeballs on tetanus injections as the mad lump took yet another bite out of me.

On the subject of the pooch from purgatory, we were at Granny's one day, being bored to death by the inevitable hundredth iteration of the neighbourhood's latest disaster – this one was about having a horse trot down the street, which then jumped on top of my uncle's car – oh, and then, after jumping on it, it just sat on it.

This really is true. A horse did trot down the street and sit on top of my uncle's car.

Mrs Haemorrhoid was stealing biscuits at the time, and trying to stuff them surreptitiously into the kangaroo pouch in her pinny, when my father was dragged in by this enormous – but then only six months old – Labrador/Golden Retriever cross-breed.

It was even well-disposed to Mrs Haemorrhoid (it was the only thing on earth that was) as it sniffed out her stolen biscuits in her pinny pouch, to Granny's fury at yet another theft, and again she banished her, Granny shouting out the door, as she was thrown out, "I've got a dog to savage you now - impitent thieving bugger." But Mrs Haemorrhoid was back the day after.

If the dog had stayed like that it would have been fine, but it got progressively madder.

We called it "Ben".

Despite its coming from two breeds, both with a reputation for having a placid, docile temperament, what emerged was the canine equivalent of a thuggish gang leader that was enthralled by violence.

He became uncontrollably vicious around other dogs. If there was another dog, he had to start a fight. He had to win. He had Thatcherite tendencies.

His reputation started to grow. He had a particular fondness for the postman's mail bag, which was once snatched from him and torn to pieces. I left the door open one day after coming home from school, totally accidentally, and, moments later, walked back out to find that the bin men, who were in the street, had jumped in the back of the bin wagon, and that another of them had climbed up a telegraph pole, as Ben had bounded down the driveway towards them.

I later discovered that we named him Ben, not after some kindly thing called Ben, like, "Ben" Obi Wan Kenobi. I seem to remember that the characters in *Star Wars* called Obi Wan Kenobi "Ben" for no apparent reason. Why not Bernard Obi Wan Kenobi? Or Colin Obi Wan Kenobi? Or Farquhar Obi Wan Kenobi?

No, I recall that we named the dog after the enormous, murderous, flesh-eating rat out of the film called… "Ben"

Here is a summary of the film I found on Wikipedia:

"Ben is a 1972 American horror film, about a young boy and his pet rat, Ben.

A lonely boy named Danny Garrison befriends Ben, the rat leader of the swarm of rats. Ben becomes the boy's best friend, protecting him from bullying, and keeping his spirits up in the face of a heart condition.

However, things gradually take a downward turn, as Ben's swarm becomes violent, resulting in several deaths. Eventually, the police destroy the rat colony with flame throwers, but Ben survives and makes his way back to Danny. The film closes with Danny, tending to the injured Ben, determined not to lose his friend".

After that completely bizarre set-up, it was hardly surprising that the dog turned out to be a complete headcase.

As an aside, I really must watch that film. Becoming best friends with a large protective violent gangster rat, whilst having a heart condition, sounds no more implausible than the rest of my life.

Eventually he had to go. The dog, not the rat.

The day Ben was to be taken away, a very rough character came to the door to take him. Ben looked at this guy, who had even more cuts and bruises and scrapes and holes in his head than he did. He just got up and walked away with him, without looking back. He decided to go with him, he'd found his soul mate.

We never heard about him ever again.

If Ben wasn't quite the fluffy family pet doggie we had imagined, the neighbours were even worse.

We got into what might be described as a "noise war" with them. I think it might have started with the gentle tinkling of a bath running but, like the outbreak to World War One, once the tensions had started, they escalated to boiling point, and soon it was all-out war; nobody had any idea what it was actually about, but it had to be continued at all costs, and to be pursued to total annihilation.

A genuine Working-Class Hell feud.

Our neighbours upped the volume of the dispute, and sent an inspector round to determine the amount of noise we made. It didn't help that our psycho dog could be heard somewhere in the house, growling and gnashing away, or tearing something to pieces as its final death scream pierced the neighbourhood, and the inspector's noise detector went off the scale.

As part of the escalating noise war, we played *The War of the Worlds* on the record player at full blast. This came out, I recall, in 1978, based on the HG Wells novel, and it was full of terrifying whoops and whooshes (for the time), and a gurgling noise, as the Martians pottered around the countryside with a giant spider, sucking everyone's blood, before finally perishing of man flu because they were foolish enough to invade during a particularly frosty patch of weather.

But it suited the neighbourhood feud perfectly, as it was indeed *The War of the Worlds* between the two houses on Ocean Road.

I don't think we appreciated, with any irony, that it was the perfect soundtrack for our situation – the same lack of ironic appreciation that dictates that if you name your pet after a violent psycho, it will probably end up being one.

The neighbours retaliated with gorgeous classical music, which wasn't quite the same as the weirdness blaring out of our house.

I recall on the Sunday before we finally moved out of the house, the neighbours, as their parting blast, treated us, for the whole day of the house move, to humanity's greatest classics at the loudest volume they could manage. We waltzed and glided around the house packing things to *Ad Dominum cum Tribularer* by William Byrd, and the *"Lark"* quartet by Joseph Haydn. Simply delightful.

With a rabid foaming lunatic dog and *The War of the Worlds* blaring out down the street, we were probably the chav family from hell, three decades too early, but it all seemed charming from where I was.

At least there wasn't the sight of a single panty-girdle on Ocean Road, so things had, for a while, looked up.

Until the Winter of Discontent in 1979...

Strangely enough, though I say it, the Winter of Discontent, though miserable, wasn't as much of a disaster for us as it was for everybody else.

For those readers who are unfamiliar with this, basically the whole country went on strike that winter, which also coincided with the worst winter weather for many a year. It was one of the coldest winters that century. The whole country, for several weeks, ground to a snowy and icy strike-bound halt.

I remember that, from late December to February, we had freezing temperatures for weeks, and blankets, then drifts, then mountains, of snow.

It was Siberian.

You might recall that the house was at the top of a slope, with a long driveway, and slightly recessed in a ditch at the top. So, when the snow came, it was impossible either to get up the drive or to get down it.

We were stranded.

We had no central heating. We managed to move into a house powered by a coke fire alone, which simply refused to light; even if we managed to set the rest of the house on fire, it would still sit there, unlit.

We were always, always freezing.

Gradually, as the snow set in we ran out of coke. And we couldn't get out to stock up on food supplies.

Then, without warning, one day the electricity went off.

We were marooned in a haunted house, freezing, nothing to eat, with a mad dog, and mad neighbours.

The neighbours seemed to be fine, as they had a lower-sloped drive so they could get in and out, and they had central heating. But they were quite happy to watch us freeze to death, or starve, or be munched by the dog, or preferably a combination of all three.

We were besieged.

Could such a combination of events strike one family at the same time? I look back and conclude that we were all paying off karma at a vastly accelerated rate.

Granny's opinion was, "It wouldn't have happened if you'd lived in a council house! It's your fault the country has ground to a halt; it's colder than a witch's titty, and the bin men are on strike, you've brought it all on," she shrieked up the driveway one day, before wandering off in her insulated pinny.

Then salvation happened.

We discovered a Wendy House.

I think my sister had it in a cupboard, somewhere in the haunted bedroom, and we found it one day at the height of the Winter of Discontent. The wardrobe door was flung open by some ghoul who couldn't take any more, and was desperate to escape both us, the house, and Hartlepool. There, at the entrance to the Gateway to Hell, in a wardrobe in Hartlepool in 1979, was our salvation. A Wendy House.

It was about the size of a large shopping bag, big enough for two children, was made out of polythene and held up with plastic sticks, and had a little flap on the front for a door. So a family of four climbed in there, with a rabid, out of control dog.

48

We might also have picked up a cat at some point as well, so that came in too.

It enabled us to survive.

As no one saw us for days, word got round. Where were we?

A friendly neighbour on the other side of our house, whose house was at a slightly higher level than us, was able, at a push, at the right angle, to throw chicken legs through the window.

We'd open a window in the lounge, crawl out of the Wendy House, and wait expectantly for a chicken leg to come flying through.

And despite everything, it was actually fun.

We eventually had a party, when some of the snow partially thawed and the power came back on. It was a riot, especially in the Wendy House. However, no one got down the drive at the end of the night without injury. Quite how they got up it in the first place remained a mystery.

The whole saga finally ended when the power came back on.

But it was a false dawn of hope.

As the snow thawed, economic disaster struck.

My father was made redundant; the factory he worked in closed, as the early 1980s de-industrialisation gripped the North East, and, to control the wage inflation unleashed by the Winter of Discontent pay claims, interest rates doubled to fifteen per cent. The mortgage became impossible to pay.

It was time to downsize, to put it mildly.

Granny, naturally, adored the misery of it all.

Life wasn't worth living, she said, unless it was miserable. She thrived on misery.

That, and hatred of the neighbours.

Not just her own. Everybody's neighbours.

Christmas Day was always the peak of misery.

A family member would be recovering from a life-shattering event, a recovery that had taken years before they were approaching the point of normality once again. Finally, they would emerge from the gloom and despair of whatever had befallen them, and become a new person.

And in would walk Granny for Christmas lunch.

She'd sit next to them and lay her hand on their arm, and gently say, "That thing that happened to you... wasn't it terrible... eeeeeeee, it destroyed you; and for years, we thought we'd lost you."

Then she'd pause, lean forward, and, like a vampire sucking blood, she'd light up and draw so much energy that her cheeks would flush with excitement, and she'd say, "Tell me about it again. Every last detail..."

And if you didn't, she would.

She would start on a monologue, and recount every last detail to everyone around the dinner table, for hours.

And just at the point of despair, and the return of a nervous breakdown for the poor victim concerned, she'd harumph and, with an enormous tit-heave, say, "Well, it's nothing like as bad as what happened to me," and she'd start on yet another terrible epic that had happened to her, until the crack of doom.

No one could say a word. You'd reach for the brandy bottle to set fire to yourself, and to hell with the pudding.

My father's redundancy, therefore, and the family downsizing, was of enormous joy and fascination for her.

Thus, Ocean Road was the first foray into Middle-Class Hell.

It hadn't gone quite to plan.

But following any failure, there must be a new beginning. We might be downsizing, but it was still a new beginning.

In Hartlepool terms, we ripped up everything and went for a complete new start. Yes, we sold the house from hell, the dog from hell had now gone, the neighbours from hell had gone, and also, crucially, the Middle-Class Hell had gone.

On the day we moved house, I went to school as usual.

I left Ocean Road, that morning after breakfast, as my parents started the big house move.

All my school friends, and even the teachers, were amazed at the exciting undertaking we were engaged in.

Such a bold move, they said. Amazing. How could we be so brave to make such a radical change.

I left school at about midday, and went to the new house for lunch. Chicken soup I remember.

We had moved a total of two streets away.

To this day, people still haven't recovered from the shock of this radicalism. "Two whole streets away!"

Some people died of shock. And they are still dead.

Descent

What has become evident, in the tales of Granny and Mrs Haemorrhoid, is the obsession with underwear in Northern Working-Class communities.

With Granny and Mrs Haemorrhoid, it was panty-girdles, topped off by an immaculately ironed pinny, but with much tugging throughout the day and breathing difficulties, as the panty-girdle tightened its grip; but the pain had to be endured for the simple fact that it was a panty-girdle.

It was rather like one of those monks who whips themselves silly every day, and then shuffles about wearing a habit and underwear made out of a cheese grater. The constant chafing in the nether regions, and the worst jogger's nipple imaginable, has to be endured for the sake of a higher purpose. Have you ever lifted a monk's habit and seen the wreckage underneath? I've had to do it, and it's not a pretty sight.

It's the same with a panty-girdle, so Granny once said.

Agony. But necessary. All for a higher purpose. But she wasn't sure what this "higher purpose" was.

Why not wear an ordinary pair of knickers instead of an agonizing panty-girdle, I thought?

I've asked that question of Granny, nuns, and monks.

In Granny's case, I was given a filthy look and kicked under the sideboard. "Do not question the panty-girdle!" she boomed.

For a while, in Ocean Road, I thought I'd escaped all that. But as we downsized, I discovered that, in the North East, the underwear obsession is simply inescapable.

And as for Working-Class Hell, we were now firmly back in it. Like panty-girdles, that was now inescapable too.

We moved to a smaller house, living next to a main road where cars used to scream by at a speed much greater than the speed limit of forty miles per hour.

The house was double-fronted, of course. Things hadn't fallen that far. Whilst that sounds gorgeously lush to those used to living in a shoe box in London, or somewhere pricey, this is what you get in the North East even when your whole life has crashed.

In this frame of mind, at the age of eleven, or something like that, I contemplated starting at the local comprehensive school.

I used to do the school walk every day of term, and it involved starting off for school at some stupid hour of darkness, going to someone's house, and picking up one or two kids from one house and going along to the next to pick up more... it turned into a flood of screaming children, and, before too long, there was a gang of about forty of us, trying to pack ourselves into tiny houses, to pick up more strays on the way to school.

Houses would start to look like trains in India or South East England, as children would cram into every available corner, or hang out of windows, or even clamber on to the roof, before picking up another little Johnny.

As it was Hartlepool, it was always raining, and freezing, and the kids who couldn't fit into the houses along the way usually got drenched and froze outside, and would go back home and throw a sickie. They left for school every day, but never quite got there.

As this gang normally picked up every urchin in the area, by the time it bundled itself through the school gates, it was normally lunchtime.

We all lived about two streets away from the school gates, but it still took all morning to get there.

One house we went to had the door thrown open to us every day by this lady with her knickers on display.

It didn't matter what she was wearing, they were always clearly visible. It wasn't as if she was harassed and hadn't had time to dress, she was perfectly composed, but out of the top of whatever she was wearing was an incredibly large amount of knicker. Come to think of it, an absolutely enormous amount of knicker as they were HUGE, yet she was very thin and almost non-existent. She opened a door once, and so thin was she that her arm fell off with the strain.

But back to her knickers. She would wear a pair of trousers or track suit bottoms, and the knickers would explode out of the top, usually taking in most of her upper body, her long flowing hair meeting the knicker elastic in perfect union.

Skirts didn't help, it was exactly the same.

She was once seen going to the opera in a single-piece flowing ball gown, the picture of elegance, until she turned around and her ball gown lifted up at the back, tucked into her knickers, which were an explosive pair of bloomers.

And the house was full of them. Before we could all get to the kitchen diner, the hallway was strewn with damp knickers from yesterday's wash, steaming on the top of radiators, the air full of damp knicker "perfume". The rest of the hallway was barely visible through the steam haze, but all that could be made out were knickers drying over the edge of the bannisters; the hallway telephone desk was covered in them; the receiver of the telephone had a pair draped over it; and even the umbrella stand had become devoid of umbrellas, but had, instead, turned into a knickers clothes-horse.

The main lounge was off the hallway, and that was covered in them, too; not an inch of sofa was visible under the expanse of VAST panty infinity before one finally escaped into the kitchen diner, where sat the washing machine with laundry baskets overflowing with knickers in front of it, waiting to force-feed it.

The poor machine groaned under the strain of yet another enormous knicker wash, smashing from side to side into kitchen cabinets, desperate to escape the house and rattle off down the street to find a place to die. It was a rusting knackered affair; its knobs and dials had fallen off under the strain long ago, but still it went, whipped and thrashed into service every day, force-fed on washing powder and knickers. For some, that might be heaven. For this washing machine, it was hell.

It was a poor beast to witness; its death was imminent, and it had led a horrible life, but everyone around it was oblivious to its desperate desire to expire. I recognized its pain, because it wore exactly the same expression as one of Granny's teapots, desperate to die as a result of having been vigorously stuffed and fisted just too many times in one day.

There is only so much a washing machine and a teapot in Hartlepool can take.

And then the family pet would shuffle in. No one knew what it was. It was covered from head to paw in a different pair of knickers every day. No doubt it was freed from the knickers at some point, but, in a moment of animal excitement, it probably ran into another pair dangling from somewhere, and got itself entangled again. So, as we arrived each morning, it would run in to say hello, completely blinded by knickers, bang into something, knock itself senseless, before eventually falling asleep and, no doubt, being freed at some point in the day; and then the whole thing started again.

It seemed in no obvious distress. But neither I nor anyone else who visited actually saw what the animal was. Dog? Cat? Badger? Aardvark? Perhaps it was something long extinct, invaluable, the last of its kind, hidden from all humanity under a pair of knickers. It had feet, and it moved, but that was all we could see, and all that could be said about it.

And yet knicker lady was the only woman in the house, with a husband and three boys. I once asked the eldest son, "Just what is going on with all those knickers?"

He looked at me, blank and genuinely puzzled.

"What knickers?" He was totally sincere in his denial.

I'm sure you will all have met someone like knicker woman. Such an experience resonates with us all, I'm sure.

It was around this time that I progressed from junior school to senior school, the local ramshackle comprehensive.

It seemed to be a very long, two-storey, flat-roofed construction, that was obviously thrown up on the cheap, and made out of cardboard.

It seemed very delicate and it wasn't pretty. All it took was a malnourished waif stepping on to a staircase to cause the whole construction to wobble and creak alarmingly.

The corridors were also too narrow and it was obvious that, after they had built the classrooms, they had run out of money, and couldn't afford a corridor between them. The result was a corridor so narrow, and so cheap, that it was no wider than a National Trust footpath dangling alongside a lethal cliff edge, and about as safe. The whole school ground to a standstill after every lesson as three hundred bodies tried to move from one end of the school to the other in that tiny corridor, to get stuck in the middle as the interior "walls" inevitably buckled under the stain. Often, the electrical system failed, so the corridors were plunged into darkness as everybody crushed in. The only thing that did work was an acoustic echo so, as people disappeared into the gloom, and screamed, seconds later, the echo of every perfect cadence of agony could be heard multiplied a thousand-fold in the darkness.

The school was located in one of the roughest council estates, on a field so windswept that parts of the school would regularly get blown off.

There was no car park, just a mound of debris that had formerly been the school.

It was an obvious design flaw to have built a school out of cardboard in a rain-lashed windy field. I recall a scene in the *Wizard of Oz* where there is a wind storm, and a witch on a bicycle flies past going in the wrong direction. It happened there regularly.

Occasionally, contractors would come along, scaffolding would go up, the debris would be collected from the car park, the school would be stuck back together, repainted, the scaffolding would be dismantled, the whole building would be signed off as safe and robust (?), and everyone would leave happily, only for a slight whiff-ette of a breeze the next day to cause the whole thing to come crashing down again.

It seemed a rather bizarre place. It clearly couldn't go on any longer. In response to its dilapidation, someone tried to burn it down, but, as the building was so accustomed to failure, even that didn't work.

There was a rumour that someone then tried to blow it up – a kind of Hartlepool Guy Fawkes, dressed as a monkey – but somehow that plot descended into incompetence as well. There was some tale that they used the wrong explosive, so this barrel of stuff just sat there festering in a basement or in the kitchens, failing to ignite; but it took about a decade before anybody noticed it.

The school refused to go out in a blaze of glory. It just decided that it wanted to fall apart in a long and protracted manner. It refused to burn, it refused to explode, it refused to be repaired. It just wanted to let itself go. It wallowed in its own vandalism, and gloried in its own self-harm, whilst defiantly continuing its existence.

The Headmaster, rather like Granny, foolishly tried to go against the grain of the inevitable decrepitude.

On my very first day, the female teachers huddled around in corduroy and beards – the male teachers looked the same – and the Headmaster swept grandly into the packed assembly hall. He wore a full gown and mortar board, cloak flowing in all directions, and proceeded to talk ever so poshly about the school and its reputation, and how we must enjoy ourselves in its "cloisters" – these were, of course, the impossibly narrow cardboard corridors that everybody got stuck in. He clearly didn't quite fit the place.

In his grandiloquence, he was trying to turn it into Hogwarts before its time, though, to be fair, the geography of the school did change regularly, like Hogwarts' geography, simply because, in this case, some part of the school would fall off in front of you and, hey presto, another wall had disappeared and, oh, look, there goes another staircase.

He went mad, of course.

One day, we all turned up for a school assembly and, rather than have this ornate figure of a Headmaster gliding around like an imperious Roman emperor in a black toga, the Deputy Head, who was a shambling, scruffy old wreck, lurched forward to take assembly.

He barely washed, hadn't changed his shirt for five years, the soles had fallen off both shoes, and the occasional toe nail poked through a decaying sock like a talon emerging from a coffin. He clearly hadn't had time to prepare, or wash, and he mumbled incoherently at assembly for months on end, before some inquisitive child asked him where on earth the Headmaster had got to.

He had, of course, been missing without word, for months.

The Deputy Head looked startled.

He peered through the haze of flies that constantly hovered around him. He inhaled deeply, drawing breath to answer the question, sniffing his BO as he was about to give an answer to the question on everyone's lips, and then he just shrugged his shoulders and didn't say a word.

He kept shrugging his shoulders, shaking his head in disbelief to plumes of dandruff, and looked utterly helpless; and then moved on to the next topic, which was school repairs. And he ran off the stage out of the assembly hall.

He suited the school perfectly, of course.

As with some dogs and their owners, they gradually come to resemble one another. But, at the end of the day, he was there and provided a form of stability. After a fashion.

Just as well, because it emerged that the previous Headmaster had, indeed, gone completely insane, and had had to be wheeled off the premises in his gown and hat.

He was clearly Middle-Class, and Hartlepool had just got to him.

They should open a lunatic asylum in Hartlepool purely for the Middle-Classes who can't cope.

It's hardly surprising. The school was hopeless. The only way to survive it was to adopt an air of ennui and shrug one's shoulders, as another piece of cardboard masonry dislodged itself and smashed into the ground below to plumes of plaster, and say nothing about it or something like, "Whoops, there goes another bit". It was rather like that closing scene out of *Carry On Up The Khyber* where they have a dinner party, and pretend to ignore that the place is being blown to pieces by The Khasi of Kalabar, and his henchmen, the Burpa tribesmen.

On the whole, it was just as well that none of us turned up before lunchtime, and that we were detained on the way in the houses of mad people with too many knickers. It was a kind and gentle distraction.

For, indeed, a low point of the descent in my fortunes had been reached, and it was undoubtedly that school that was at the centre of the curse.

Five years of it. It's just worth putting this into perspective.

It was like living through a world war. They went on for about the same length of time.

I also seem to remember that, after 1984, there wasn't a decent summer for about five years. The summers between 1985 and 1988 just seemed to pass by in a blur of horizontal rain and gale-force winds.

And the rest of the time, it was cold and bleak, and we were encased in a cardboard school.

My abiding memory is of a local shop that used to sell fruit cordial drinks, frozen in a plastic cup.

In January. Not in the summer, but made and sold in January. In the summer, they were nowhere to be seen.

They were utterly inedible, as they forgot to add water but just poured in fruit cordial, so the blast, if you were mad enough to suck on one, sent you through the roof.

So they were bought purely for the purposes of throwing around and using as frozen missiles. Great big, burly thugs would buy a load of them, and lie in wait in nooks and crannies at the school. As we have noted, the school was not well designed, so the entrances to the building were down long funnels of tarmac, with high walls on either side, perfect for entrapping targets and taking them out.

That is my abiding memory, of just looking up into the sky as more fruit missiles whizzed overhead. Everyone got hit by them once or twice, so it was common to miss a lesson due to severe concussion, and to spend the rest of the day wrapped in bandages, stumbling around. The teachers were very understanding if we missed lessons due to injury as they often used to hang out of windows, watching the trench warfare down below go on, usually egging it on for a laugh, with fake compassion for the fallen.

A shortage of fruit cordial missiles at the local shop one week caused people to make their own. There was one posh chap who used to make his frozen cocktail missiles out of lemon barley water, as that was slightly posher than Asda e-number own-brand orange juice.

So being bombarded every day for five years, in the freezing cold, was exactly like trench warfare, as the missiles pounded into school, layering the cardboard with pockmarks, like an old ship after a battle.

There were distractions. I took up playing the trombone, joining the school band, but characteristically of this period, it ended in comic disaster.

One of the most commonly mumbled bits of nonsense is "Practice makes perfect" It didn't. I got worse with practice.

Miraculously, the school allowed us to get out of lessons to go and learn a musical instrument.

I look back and consider that this is extremely enlightened in many respects: to get out of Maths or Home Economics, to contribute to the cultural health of the nation.

Getting out of certain lessons was definitely a boon.

In Home Economics, we were once taught how to knit a pinny, or a 1920s swimming costume.

Out of wool…

The pinnies were perfectly functional, but they would get awfully hot in the summer with the gas fire on.

But the swimming costumes, usually knitted for an absolutely identical version of Granny, in every case were a howling failure.

They were all finished in the same week, in the "summer" month amusingly known as June.

Hundreds of Grannies that weekend, with their new knitted costumes, would waddle delightedly down to the beach, desperate for a dip in the North Sea in their new Hartlepool couture knitted beachwear, banged together by little Johnny in Home Economics.

They were knitted in grey with a pink midriff, so every Granny looked like an enormous hippo.

On the beach, each Granny would scramble into one of the World War Two anti-Nazi concrete beach bunkers to change from pinny and panty-girdle, to emerge as a picture of elegant, vast corpulence, and roll and bounce down the beach, to hit the sea with a tsunami splash. They'd flop around in the sea for about a minute (the fish jumping into the fishing boats to end it all), and would then emerge, shivering, the costume inflated to the size of the R101 hot air balloon that had crashed in the 1930s. The whole thing simply took hours to drain, usually in the back of the car on the way home, each Granny's false teeth chattering to the refrain, "Yes, it's lovely; please do me another one." So getting out of that was a relief. I could get out of knitting or sewing or learning to wash up, and, instead, do something even more destructive, with a trombone.

I would sit in a room, and toot and parp tunelessly on the thing for an hour, and walk away extremely satisfied at having made such a deafening racket in the name of art and beauty.

The music block, naturally, was sectioned off from the rest of the school in its own cardboard enclave, in order to protect the rest of the school from the wretched cacophony that used to blast out of its walls.

The music block was, however, close to the Headmaster's office. As you will recall, he went quite insane, shortly after I started at the school, and at about the time when I attended trombone lessons in the music block.

The "music suite" – so genteel a name for a building from which sounds of Beelzebub regularly emerged – was next to a load of council houses. They were full of Grannies like mine, the panty-girdles stuck on clothes lines drying in a minus five breeze, huge icicle penises hanging off them at an appropriate entry point. All of these Grannies lived there in a state of complete wide-eyed shell shock and terror, at the sounds of the Antichrist that emerged from the building next door.

Ear plugs were no defence.

The only words residents close by could mutter was, "What... what... what... who are you... what...what...?"

One Christmas, we all felt sorry for them and, on a community outreach programme, delivered a load of old-fashioned rusty brass ear trumpets to them as compensation for having deafened them. That was totally destructive as, once they plonked the things into their ears, they could suddenly hear the almighty din from the music suite once more, and would have to relive the terror all over again. Usually, after this second assault on their hearing, their lunacy was complete.

My contribution to this was an old knackered rusty trombone with a droopy flaccid bell end. With age, sadly, that happens to us all.

The slight problem was that, at the age of eleven, it was impossible to carry my bell end around.

Stood on its end, it was taller than I was. And it was far too heavy actually to lift, carry, and practice on.

Plus, when one had to navigate the impossibly narrow corridors in the school, it would get jammed, stuck in one part of the passage, one end against one wall, the other end against the opposing wall, blocking all ingress and egress. A huge push of bodies would ram against it, trying to force this enormous member out of the way, but so huge was it that it was simply immoveable, and a huge heaving pile of bodies, thrust by everybody behind it, would eventually trip over it into a writhing mass on the floor. As more and more bodies pushed forward with pounding exertion, so the walls of the school would creak, and the staircases would wobble once more, but the bell end would be immovably wedged against it all.

The first time I went to the music suite to pick up this monstrosity, I was greeted by my music teacher.

I expected a delightful batty old thing, male or female, with a good vibe and who was generally cultured and lovely, preferably in tweed.

Instead, I was greeted by a battered old red car, screaming into the car park next to the music block, with such an ear-shattering screech that the local Grannies – those with any hearing left – looked into the air, contentment on their faces: the sweet honey of screeching tyres, so much better than the usual audible car crash from the music suite.

And then this thing lurched out of the car.

This music teacher was known, unaffectionate, as "Pickle Head". He had a head like a pickled onion, but it was permanently red.

He was always outraged, like some old Mr Angry Army Major, and so his face and head were always one shade of red or another.

He lunged menacingly at me, and his first words were, "In the boot of my car is a trombone. Fetch it."

My first mistake was to go to the car and bring a violin or a penny whistle, I can't remember which.

From that day, I was marked.

Pickle Head was an absolute terror.

All that could ever be heard outside his room was, "Get the right fucking note."

The madness in the music suite did not end there, as the Head Music Teacher was always legless on whisky. Every Tuesday evening, we would meet for a band practice and he'd flop in, too drunk to conduct, shirt buttons popping under the strain after so many years of hard drinking while teaching, and he'd take his cue from Pickle Head, and yell at the school band, "Get the right fucking note."

He did remain sober at the school concert once, which Granny attended, and we all got our own back on him as he missed his cue conducting and, at the tender ages of eleven to fifteen, thirty of us shouted back at him, "Get the right fucking note," in front of two hundred parents.

We never had another concert after that.

Hitting the right fucking note was not easy for me, as I could only play three notes and, after practice with Pickle Head, I got worse, and that went down to two notes.

The problem was that neither of my two fucking notes were required in any of the pieces we played. And in the end, three trombone players went down to one – me.

In any piece, especially a trombone-heavy piece, I just played two notes.

I started at the beginning of the piece; I couldn't read music, so I just trumped these two notes out from the beginning to the end, whether they were wanted or not, irrespective of whether anybody else had a solo or a duet. I just carried on, bellowing away for about an hour.

They were the dullest notes imaginable, and the look of pain on Pickle Head's face, or on the Head Music Teacher's face, before he passed out from drink, did genuinely induce pity in me.

There was no point yelling, "Get the right fucking note," as, by then, I was unteachable, partly because I simply couldn't carry the vast trombone anywhere to practice in the first place, plus, after the mad dog Ben, we had acquired another mad dog... a Doberman... and the Doberman simply refused to let me practice.

Getting a Doberman might have seemed a bad idea, after the mindless savagery of the last mutt.

But it was as soft as rags. A gentle sneeze would lead to its running for cover. It used to sit next to me every time I got the trombone out, and it would howl along. Simply howl.

It wasn't in pain when I played, though everyone else was.

It seemed quite content to sit beside me, and howl away as it suddenly discovered the joys of singing.

The combination of my attempts to wring notes out of the trombone and the howling of the new mutt, inevitably drew complaints from the neighbours, so my practicing had to stop.

So any practice I could get in, sadly, slowed to a trickle.

As virtually no one else in the band turned up to lessons anyway, often it was me and someone equally hopeless, usually with a triangle or a rattle, doing a full symphony between the two of us, with a total range of about four notes in total.

Then, by accident, I snapped the bell end of the trombone during one band practice.

It just snapped under the strain, like the woman's washing machine that lived with all those knickers, or a Granny teapot; it just couldn't handle any more.

I held it together and kept blowing into it, and it made the most awful noise, as I struggled incompetently through the rest of band practice. But suddenly, Pickle Head and the Head Music Teacher looked up at me, startled, and said, "Well done, that's almost passable," as my bell end nearly dropped off.

I ran back home, fearing the most terrible retribution if they ever found out that I'd wrecked the trombone.

Fortunately, we knew a local plumber who welded the remains of the trombone back together. The only problem was the slide no longer extended to its full length at either end.

This meant I could now only manage one note. One note.

I dreaded the next encounter with Pickle Head, who was bound to enquire why my encore would be even more limited.

Fortunately, I was pulled out of the school band as it affected my school work in other areas. And Granny was furious that she hadn't got a knitted swimming costume, despite their causing hypothermic death on a plague-like scale.

I took my resignation letter from the school band, hastily scribbled on the back of a copy of Beethoven's ninth symphony, to the Head Music Teacher in his office. I gave it to him just after he'd started drinking Johnnie Walker at ten a.m. on a Monday morning.

"I haven't been sober for nearly twenty years," he slurred. "It's the tunes, the tunes... I can't get them out of my head," he said, as he waved a tambourine around, its little cymbals jangling as if he was on a Hare Krishna dance down Oxford Street. All he needed was to wear orange and shave his head, and the picture would be complete.

His eyes were wide with madness, and he got aggressive. "And it's all you lot... you spotty load of adolescents, with all your pimples and your piles... you lot, who massacre the music of Chopin and Mozart and Schubert, and all that's left is this noise... this awful noise..." he wailed, as his eyes rolled, and he cackled like a naughty warty witch coughing up a hand grenade.

He waved helplessly at the bottle of whisky. "Only this stops it all... I wave my arms around, and people think I'm conducting an orchestra, but really I have no idea... I have absolutely no idea what is going on... I wave my arms because I'm trying to grab the bottle... and all you give me back is this wall of audible carnage."

And then he slumped back in his chair. His head crashed onto a large mounted cymbal next to him, and his feet hit a gong, which swayed back and forward violently. He flung an arm back until it hit a load of old bells on a table, until the whole lot swayed just a little too violently, and everything crashed on to the floor, with all the gentility of a sonic boom ripping through a two- minute silence for the dead in a convent.

And he sat there, amid the mess and the dying sound of the instruments hitting the floor, finally at peace.

Strangely, all that clanging and crashing was the most beautiful sound to have emerged from the music block in decades, so bad was the rest of the din. For the first time in ages, he smiled in contentment.

When I told Pickle Head that I was leaving, his head went a bright shade of purple with affront. Have you noticed how, when you are utterly incompetent at something, and everyone wants you to leave, they still get angry when you do?

Apparently, the head of Pickle Head went molten white with anger one day, and never changed back. It just made him look even more like a pickled onion.

Yet out of the gloom came a glimmer of light, like a beautiful white crocus emerging from shining white snow on a brilliant winter day.

I suddenly clicked with a history teacher and, out of the blue, got a decent grade.

Descent had finally turned into decent, and the end of my period in the school fast approached. Things had to get better. They just had to. And they did. But not for one moment did they approach normality.

Ascent

My father escaped yet another period of unemployment by getting a job as a manager of a newsagent in Hartlepool shopping centre.

He was terrible at it. He was the most bad-tempered, foul-mouthed, grumpiest newsagent in history.

A gypsy once wandered into the shop he ran, took one look at him and said, "You're not right for this, you should have been a farmer." She was bang on right of course, he is a wonderful gardener, but he looked thoughtful for a moment, before exploding and responding with the inevitable, "Bugger off."

Yet it saved our bacon.

At the time, Hartlepool shopping centre was a grey concrete jungle, built in the late sixties, that was condemned about a decade or two later. I understand that it replaced a traditional Victorian high street, which would have been gorgeous now if retained. I rather liked the concrete jungle, though, as it had a big circular ramp in the centre that was steep enough to roll down. It was open air, so, in the freezing weather from August to the following July, Grannies would tumble over in the snow and roll down it.

It was such fun.

The newsagent was part of a national chain, which had the incredibly courageous policy of charging London prices in Hartlepool, and thinking that the hard-up and sensible people of Hartlepool would pay.

It, predictably, wouldn't have lasted long, but for one amazing, unforeseen draw.

My father hated the place with such a passion that he was vile to everyone, especially customers. And they loved it.

Customers managed to do everything wrong: (i) they would arrive before the newspapers turned up, and they would tut and strut with indignation that their paper wasn't available before six thirty a.m., and so my father would explode; (ii) they arrived with the wrong change, usually a twenty-pound note (then worth something) when no change was available in the till, so my father would explode; (iii) they would ask for packets of crisps out of empty boxes, so my father would explode, and then usually throw the empty cardboard box across the shop floor; (iv) they would complain about the prices, and then my father would explode; (v) there would be no customers for hours, then suddenly, as my father was closing the shop, they'd all turn up, and then my father would explode.

Then the Area Manager would turn up, flash his car and bigger salary in his face, and my father would explode.

Gradually, this got noticed, especially on particularly bad days, when there would be lots of till slamming, or boxes of things would fly out of the shop door into the central parade of the shopping centre. Even a good mood was usually met with the buttons on the till being fisted, rather than pressed.

A tale started going around that this shop simply had to be visited, because it was run by the most bad-tempered and grumpy old Arkwright.

When, eventually, sky-high racketeering prices forced the shop to close, there was genuine bewilderment, a sense of loss, as people walked along the shopping parade. It was quiet. There was no shouting, swearing, yelling, and it was safe to walk past, as the risk of missiles flying out of the door had gone. It had become a normal, decaying concrete shopping centre and was suddenly depressing, without life, apart from Grannies rolling down the ramp.

Word got round that he'd finally exploded with such a rage that he'd combusted.

And so the world moved mournfully on.

No one knew what was really happening. A plan was afoot.

My life-long Labour-Party-supporting father, facing redundancy yet again, decided to turn us into Thatcherites, and opened his own shop. It transformed everything, as, within days, we all looked like her, complete with bouffant hair-do, and pearls.

It proves the maxim advocated by some: when you do something you hate, carry on doing it. After hating being a newsagent, he decided to invest everything into becoming one again. It made perfect sense (but see Part Three).

So, he acquired a gorgeous Victorian shop; after a brief period of refurbishment, the family piled in on the opening day to help out.

I awaited our first customer, along with my mother, with baited breath.

Hours went by without anybody coming in, as people wandered past the shop front, looking in with a total lack of interest, then snorting and striding off, looking disgusted.

Then she came, riding round the mountain... our first customer.

She was... how can I put this delicately... large-framed.

72

The shop front was newly painted, including a beautiful Victorian door.

That was flung off its hinges, and the shop frontage creaked alarmingly, as she tried to heave herself through. The electronic alarm that announced a customer arriving with a "beep" screamed in protest at the never-ending enormity of the vastness surging past its sensors.

The shop door was at one end of the room, and the cash register (and us) at the other, so there was clearly some distance to traverse, and the floor started to shake as she started to wobble herself forward. She emitted a huge wheezing noise, and so she resembled some gargantuan prehistoric "wheeze-zilla" looking for a well-hung King Kong to grapple with on top of a building.

She was unable to walk in a straight line, and so lurched alarmingly left; she crashed into a magazine rack full of newly-purchased stock, then with a loud "whoooaaaaaaa" wheeze, lurched over to the right, before hitting a fridge full of ice cream. And then, with another startled look, she managed to upend herself, move marginally forward, and careered to the left again, head-butting a stand full of greetings cards, before, finally, she dived headlong and hit the counter with a massive thud.

She wheezed herself upright, and placed a smouldering fag on the newly installed counter top, next to the till, the smoke rising unending into the air.

"Yes, dear," my mother asked politely, without batting an eyelid.

"How can we help you? A purchase perhaps?" She waved her arms at the remains of the newly-purchased stock in the remains of the newly-refurbished shop. The place was trashed beyond recognition.

The fat lady couldn't speak, but instead she gasped for breath. Her face was bright red, and resembled a large dumpling soaked in a vat of summer pudding.

She clutched her throat and waved her hands, as if about to speak.

Finally, as the counter started to smoulder under the lighted fag she had placed on it, she rasped, "Have you got change for 20p?" And she waved 20p in the air.

"Can we tempt you with anything, madam? You are our first customer, and very welcome you are," said my mother.

There followed an enormous rasp, followed by a gasping chesty cough that caused the surrounding countryside to rattle. "No!" she fog-horned back. "I only want change for 20p."

"Well, I'm awfully sorry," said my mother, completely unruffled, "we have just opened, and we don't have any change. But my husband has just gone to the bank to get some, and will be back presently. Are you sure there isn't anything else we can help you with? Cough mixture? It sounds as though you have a slight respiratory tickle…" as a hack from hell burst forth from her chest.

She shook her head, turned on her pair of puddings, and attempted to exit the shop. It was hoped that she'd hit the same things on the way out so as to minimise the damage, but, alas, she crashed from side to side, causing carnage at the only sites presently undamaged by her entrance.

Then, as the counter started to smoulder under her still-lit cigarette, we all panicked, and worried that the shop might catch light at any moment.

Realising that she had forgotten her fag, she tornadoed her way to the counter again, picked up her fag, and, with something resembling a nuclear blast, exited the shop in a mushroom cloud, as the remains of the beautiful Victorian door gave up on its hinges.

I learned later that she was a ballroom dancer.

"Oh dear, this shop lark isn't going to go very well," I thought. "If that's our first 'customer', we're doomed."

Fortunately, my father's temper came to the rescue.

Gradually, word spread round the town.

"The bad-tempered old git has just opened his own shop in Church Square. He's his own boss; there's no restraint on him now!"

And so scores of his old victims returned for the abuse once more.

It became a mark of pride in the town to be insulted, and, if you weren't, you'd not had a good visit.

And being his own boss, there really was no restraint on the till-slamming, abuse, and objects kicked or flung through the air.

And after he'd abused everyone who walked in and interrupted his day – "Why don't you all bugger off?" – five minutes later he'd be outside the shop door, surveying the area, waving at an empty street, desperate for customers to come in.

When one finally did, they would be greeted with, "Why the bloody hell do you have to come in now? Can't you see I'm trying to do stock control, now bugger off until I'm finished... A fiver, what makes you think I've got change for that? Bugger off!"

It saved our bacon, as the customer numbers swelled, desperate to catch sight of the gorilla throwing another paddy. We were solvent again.

If my father could be explosive, it was my uncle who was "artful".

During the 1992 General Election, the Liberal Democrat candidate stuck loads of fenceposts around the town with his "My Vote" campaign slogan nailed to them.

My uncle's wife was nagging him to build a new fence, so, naturally, the Liberal Democrat electioneering posts came in handy.

This caused a huge rumpus in the town centre one afternoon. The Liberal Democrats accused the Tories in the town centre of stealing the Liberals' fence posts. This was denied, and a fist fight broke out, just at the point at which my uncle nonchalantly walked past, having heard the whole exchange, chuckling about how nice his new fence looked.

While I don't condone such behaviour, this Tory/Lib Dem fracas in Hartlepool town centre set the scene for British politics from 2010-2015.

At about this time, I managed to pull decent GCSE grades out of the hat at the last minute, and I started to go to the local sixth form to do A-levels. It was a world away from the cardboard comprehensive. A state school, it had taken over a large manor house, and it was grand! It had wonderful, wide oak staircases that didn't move when you jumped up and down on them. The teachers were all brilliant, and it had a wonderful air.

Then, one of the history teachers took me to one side one day and started talking about which university I should start thinking about.

Following some of my suggestions, he shook his head, and said that we should try for Oxford University.

Wow! This seemed totally implausible, but I decided to take a shot at it.

I worked like crazy, and pitched up to the interview at Oxford in a freezing November, 1990.

It seemed that Mrs Thatcher was about to fall from power (she did, in a matter of days), so the whole of Oxford was buzzing with excitement. They'd expressed their dismay about her many times, so all around was an air of anticipation that she would actually fall.

I expected a Conservative bastion, but it really wasn't.

The Oxford I wandered into was not what I had expected. The culture shock was enormous, as you would expect. A taxi driver wanted to talk to me about Chaucer.

I was puzzled. Which was the real world? This one, or Hartlepool?

I'm still not sure of the answer.

But I was struck by the ease of the place.

And by how liberal, well-meaning and unstuffy it was.

Also, I wasn't looked down on for being from a state school. This was not what I had expected.

Others might have had different experiences, but if this was the Establishment, it was actually rather nice, and very well-meaning. Not a common view, but I have to speak as I found. My college was very state-school-orientated, and they took a high number of state school pupils, but I found people in other colleges to be the same.

My tutors were, and simply are, wonderful.

However, the entrance interview was nerve-wracking. My prospective history tutor put me at ease, and smiled kindly as he greeted me at the top of the stairs outside his study. I was the last to be interviewed, after my interview was swapped round with someone else. I wore my father's jacket, which was far too big; a few of the buttons had flown off in some rage or other in the shop.

I couldn't see much of my future tutor though.

His jumper and tie were covered in gravy.

I then looked up to find that most of his face was covered in gravy too.

He looked like he'd been blacked-up to play an ethnic role in some politically incorrect film from the 1950s.

All I could see were a pair of teeth peering out from a face covered in gravy. Even his glasses were smeared with it. He couldn't see, of course, but, as his voice was so loud, it bounced off things like sonar, so, like a bat, he navigated his way around simply by talking to himself and identified his position by the bounce back.

"May I thank you for your forbearance in waiting for such an elongated period," he enunciated.

"My colleague and I will be delighted to see you presently, after your not inconsiderable exertions in traversing such a distance in such inhospitable climatological conditions. But first, we must converse with another of your contemporaries on the vigour of his intellectual calibre and suitability for the endeavour for which he has so humbly submitted himself."

"Ta," I answered. ("Ta" is North East for "thanks"). "See ye in like an 'our?"

I still had my Hartlepool accent which involves dropping the "h" at the start of a word.

So, "Hartlepool" must be pronounced "'Artlepool". And David Cameron's famous, "hug a hoodie" is phonetically pronounced, "ug a udie".

Good. I'm glad you agree that that all makes perfect sense.

He nodded politely, clearly not understanding a word. Just as well, because I couldn't understand him either.

A nice start to the most important interview, at that stage, of my life.

When I finally got in, we spent the next hour not understanding each other.

He couldn't understand my accent, and I couldn't make out a word in one of his Sir Humphrey orations. Fortunately, another tutor was interviewing me and, bless, I think I might have got a point across.

But otherwise, it was astonishingly confusing.

Imagine my surprise, a few days later, when an offer came through.

I was gobsmacked.

I hadn't got especially good GCSE grades.

I thanked my parents, and a large number of teachers who had helped make it happen.

And in October 1991, I left Hartlepool, "for the last time..." as Mrs Thatcher had said just recently, when she had left Downing Street. Of course, it was a load of old twaddle, as we both went back.

But Working-Class Hell was over.

Well and truly over.

After some false starts, now the true Middle-Class quest was about to begin.

Or so I thought. At around that time, Oxford erupted into riots. It was less dreaming spires, and more screaming tyres...

And Now for a Word

I've mocked Hartlepool terribly, especially its Grannies.

I know the town well, so I can see it now, they will be outraged. And others of you might be outraged too.

And in some senses rightly so, because they have actually had a hard time.

And as I've noted, there are lots and lots of wonderful people there, and they and the town don't deserve the hand that fate has dealt them.

But what I do know is that the town has a tremendous sense of humour – they elected Peter Mandelson.

They also elected a guy as the town's mayor who dressed up as a monkey during the mayoral election campaign. With a pledge of free bananas for the town's children, they elected him several times. In fact, I think he might be the longest serving mayor in the UK.

With that sense of humour, they'll get the spirit of this, and hopefully they will recognise it is more affectionate than malicious.

There is a lot to be proud of where they live.

There are some amazing houses, a fantastic beach, and it is surrounded by National Parks in every direction: Northumberland to the north; the Lake District to the west; and

Yorkshire to the south has two of them, all a very short drive away.

And who could resist all those Grannies...

It really is as crazy, awful, and also as wonderful, as I've described it... no offence intended, I'm just having fun, as one should do in life.

Part Two
Middle-Class Hell

Uni

A two-carriage push-me-pull-you pacer train left Hartlepool railway station in October 1991: a gloomy day, the train almost touching the low hanging clouds as it bounced up and down on the rails, due to a combination of bad design, no suspension, and knackered, barely-maintained tracks.

The old trains in the 1970s were nice. They had character, big comfy seats, first class (even in the North East!) and you could sit at the front, and, due to no one's giving a toss about security then, you could watch the whole journey through the driver's window, and exchange knowing winks with him every time he went through a red signal.

Then, in the 1980s, they introduced cheap pacer trains that were basically a bus stuck on top of a pair of train wheels. No suspension. People groaned every time one crawled, but also bounced, into the station, like an under-powered hamster with depression. They knew they had the most awful journey ahead of them.

The train was full of Grannies, naturally, who had bought cups of tea from the station café. With every bump of the train, the tea was flung out of the cups, up into the air, and then rained down onto head scarves, rollers, and special out-door "on location" pinnies, worn religiously for a thirty-minute long distance trip out of town, as the train was bound for Middlesbrough where one went to shop, but invariably just found more Grannies. But the Grannies of Hartlepool would inevitably return home from the shopping trip empty-handed, as the stuff in the shops in Middlesbrough, though in the same chain store and at the same price, "wasn't the same" as the stuff they could buy in Hartlepool. Anywhere that far out of town was "foreign" country, so who knew what you might pick up.

With so much tea flying around, they were in Heaven, though one Granny, putting on her lipstick, cursed as the train hit another bump, and the lipstick ran straight across her face, up into the air and across the carriage. The "gash" made her resemble a particularly terrifying clown, but there was plenty of tea flying across the carriage, on the walls and running down the windows, and she washed her face in it.

The station café was to be celebrated, as it closed in the 1970s, I recall; but its re-opening in the early nineties was heralded as a massive regeneration project, but it was really just a shoe box with a wobbling tea urn and a particularly irritable kettle.

But that day, on that bouncy uncomfortable train, I was flushed with pride, as I thought of my ultimate destination.

I was off to study "Modern" History at Oxford University – which, wait for it, starts in 575 AD.

I told Granny that Modern History started in 575 AD, and she paused, put down her cup of tea, pondered, and then said in all sincerity, "Now I remember that... I was there... it was round about then that I said to Mrs Haemorrhoid..." She simply couldn't be outdone, and I concluded at that point that she was indeed immortal; she really was there in 575 AD, because evil never dies.

Forgetting completely the lessons of The Middle-Class Interregnum, I was hoping that this would be easy and plain sailing, a new beginning and up and away through the class system.

Oh dear...

Though Oxford was a tremendous opportunity, I had a hard time clicking with the place, and always seemed to be running against the current. Some love it, and there is much to love, but it was hard work. And in many ways, quite right that it should be tough; but I also should have been having the time of my life.

Middle-Class Hell – the expectation of liberation, throwing caution to the winds, expanding horizons, after so many years of restriction, but, oh dear, that isn't quite what happened.

In this case, I was expecting to arrive in some large, liberated party that would fit me like a glove. But on arriving at the halls of residence on my first day, I was stuck with a religious fundamentalist nutcase... for about three whole years.

I couldn't really get away from him as, in the first year, he was just across the corridor from me.

Then, suddenly, one Friday night, I was dragged into what was supposed to be a party in his room, and found it was a Bible-reading class. A Friday night! I could have been out getting completely smashed, and getting into adultery, fornication, debauchery, greed, envy, jealousy, alcoholism, theft, bearing false witness, coveting pretty much everything, and then not going to bed, and then more fornication, more debauchery, more adultery, more alcoholism... and, basically, just *sin*...

I was there to be educated, after all.

But no, this was a Bible-reading class, on a Friday night. Just above the street outside, where I watched revellers having a good time, wearing false inflatable bosoms.

I didn't know what the plan was until I got into the room, but, by then, it was too late.

I did eventually get out of it, but by that point they'd got their teeth in!

Suddenly, I was the target for religious conversion by every single religious fundamentalist in Oxford.

One of them let slip that there was a price on my head for conversion, so I would get accosted in the street, in cafes, libraries, at the bus station, anywhere, by some random individual whom I'd never seen before, walking up and saying, "Ahhh, I know who you are, welcome to the Kingdom of Heaven, this way. I can see that you are afflicted with Satan this morning. There's a Bible class and service for you which we have just organised around the corner," and they'd try and drag me off, until I could give them the slip.

"No thanks, I don't want to be converted," didn't deter them, it just made them more determined.

My life became a covert "escape and capture" routine, everywhere I went. I lived in a kind of bonkers spy film in which some poor innocent is fearful of being taken out in broad daylight by an assassin with a particularly pointy shoe. Whereas everyone normal I knew was wandering round in shag and alcohol induced hazes, I was on high alert, adrenaline constantly pumping through me like a wild animal, desperate to avoid getting captured, and munched to death, by fundamentalist predators.

They all studied Theology, of course, and had lousy grades. They wanted to be marked based on their level of fundamentalism, and not on the fact that the whole point of the subject was the academic exercise, and not an assessment of the integrity of their street corner "fire and brimstone" rant-a-thon.

The only sane one among the lot was the college Chaplain. All Oxford colleges have a chapel in their grounds. On one particularly scary occasion, when I was being chased around the quadrangles by a group of them, I banged on the chapel door, desperately seeking sanctuary in the House of God from... well, God, actually.

I had a long chat with the Chaplain, and it was evident that he found them all a rabid, tiresome lot. He used to give lovely sermons on a Sunday in the chapel; I never went, but apparently he used to put up newspaper clippings on an overhead projector, and chatted about them. God used to get a brief but subtle mention if He was lucky, but otherwise, it was a rambling chunter about anything he fancied a gossip about. The fundamentalists didn't go, as it wasn't fundamentalist enough. Then it was off to tea with lots of old ladies for the afternoon, which quickly turned into vast quantities of sherry. The day ended with a gaggle of lost, smashed old ladies propping each other up as they staggered about, trying to get out of the college, back to wherever they had come from.

These old ladies were delicate little things, and not what I was familiar with.

They were very polite, thin, and wore floral dresses, spoke posh, and were not at all like the pinny-armoured enormous battle Grannies of Hartlepool.

The Chaplain got made redundant in the end, so I heard.

Quite how you get made redundant in the Church I will never know.

None of this is to bash any organised religion; it's just that this particular band of followers were absolutely off their rocker.

Plus, my tutorials with the gravy stained tutor, who never got any cleaner, weren't getting far, as neither of us could understand the other, and the Carolingian Renaissance was, frankly, alien. There was a King called Charles the Fat, and then Charles the Bald, and I suddenly realised two things: (i) putting strange people in charge is not confined to Hartlepool; (ii) humanity has always been mad, and really isn't getting any better.

And Middle-Class Hell has always existed.

So my first year was a little unexpected.

I returned ready to start my second year, with a new spring in my step; everything would be different this time round, I assured myself.

This year, I'd be a complete hell-raiser. I could go all goth, dress like a vampire, and chase the fundamentalists down the street instead. Perfect symmetry.

As we were moving out of halls of residence into private housing, I'd get away from the religious nut by moving into private residences out in town. Whilst we had been in close proximity in my first year, just across the halls of residence corridor, hopefully he'd end up in one house, and I'd be miles away from him, in another house.

What could possibly go wrong? Especially as housing allocation was to be determined by a random and utterly impartial housing ballot.

When the housing ballot was published, I looked at the list expectantly. I kept scanning for his name and mine, as my eyes moved down the list. Hopefully they would be far apart. That meant that we would be in different houses. Then I got to the bottom of the list. My name and his were both next to each other, right at the bottom of the list.

But being next to each other on the list, and not being able to trade my place with someone further up the list, we were in the same house.

For a year.

A whole bloody year.

Damn. It was so much easier for them now to pursue the quest of religious conversion, if the fundamentalists could all descend on the house and hold candle-lit vigils outside my bedroom door.

This was pretty much what they did.

It was like being held prisoner in the Tower of London for a year, in some quasi-religious/political conspiracy: being tortured daily, and being offered the chance to recant the apostasy, whilst having a shaking finger waved at me and being menaced by a dirty bishop.

What should one do? How the hell was I to get out of that?

The easiest thing to do was to recant. Go along with it and pretend to be converted and, hopefully, they would ease off, and then I could carry on with living the life I wanted to lead.

That's exactly what I did.

It worked a treat.

It's an old trick; it probably started in the dark ages, gained traction in the middle ages and has worked for hundreds of years, every time the official religion changed. The fundamentalists fall for it every time. Just recant, and then carry on as before. They won't notice. Really! Religious fundamentalists, of whatever faith, really don't learn.

It got them off my back for a while. I'd beam from ear to ear every time I saw one, with a cheery, "What a lovely conversion I had... how was yours? So nice not to be burning in the everlasting fires of Hell today. Right, I'm off to the café for a glass of Holy Water," before nipping down the pub and necking down a few pints.

I got away with it for a while.

Then we came to the third year, and I looked expectantly towards the housing ballot. Finally, I could probably get away from him and his crowd of witch-burners.

I wandered into the college reception before the start of the third year, to look at the housing ballot list and see which house I had been allocated to, and with whom.

I reacted in horror to see that I'd come bottom of the list, with the head fundamentalist again. Oh My God (literally), another bloody year with him. They had suspected that I had relapsed after I'd fallen asleep in Teddy Hall graveyard wearing inflatable bosoms and a wimple, so they were after me again. I can't remember why I was dressed like that, but I do remember that it was appropriate for the occasion.

Fortunately, I found a way to deal with it. It was so startlingly simple.

I bought a poster with forty-four types of condoms on it, and stuck it on my bedroom door, facing the kitchen in the house we ended up in.

They wouldn't go near it!

So they left me alone.

I could now get on with learning things. And in the third year, it all started to come together. I started to enjoy Oxford. In fact I now loved it.

I was now studying Neville Chamberlain and the coming of the Second World War, with a delightful crumpled old tutor who was about to retire, and was known as the last of the aristocratic tutors. He was hopelessly dotty, and tutorials were so much fun, as he was quite, quite potty.

He had a wonderful turn of phrase, and my favourite was his description of the Second World War as, "Nothing more than a bit of a fuss," with a languid wave of the hand.

And then he'd continue, "Of course, what you have to realise, young man, is that Chamberlain's policy of appeasement of Hitler was not from a position of weakness, he knew that Hitler was as mad as a lettuce, but he wanted to keep the British Empire intact, and knew that a war would destroy it, unlike Churchill who never understood this… zzzzzzzzzz."

He was of a considerable age, so would usually doze off about five minutes after the start of the tutorial.

He had written a book about Chamberlain and appeasement from the source materials which we were using, and it came out in the very term that my group was studying his subject. He plugged his new book mercilessly in every tutorial, until, eventually, I went out and bought it. It was wonderful. It summarised in three hundred pages the several thousand pages we had to read.

Our grades all shot up, to his astonishment. And the gentle old duffer never twigged that we'd all followed his advice, gone out and bought his book, and weren't doing any work other than reading one forty-page chapter a week. The essay titles in the final exams all came from chapters in his book and, again, he never twigged that we'd actually gone and read it.

Everyone studying this subject had to turn up to a round table discussion for two hours every week. These were such fun. We'd get Cabinet papers from that period and had to read them in readiness for the round table discussion. They had "Top Secret" still stamped on them, which everybody thought was cool.

We'd meet in a large oak-panelled room, with an enormous mahogany table in the centre. A real fire crackled away in the corner. And the first thing the tutor would say was, "In Cabinet meetings in the 1930s, everybody did what I'm about to do." It was a cold November day and he'd shuffle over to the window in his enormous crumpled dandruff-infested pullover. There'd be much decrepit groaning and huffing, as he finally flung the window open and pulled, with even more huffing and puffing, on a long price of string that would ascend up from outside the window.

The object at the end of the string was a bottle of champagne. There were several strings hanging down so we were obviously in for quite a session if they each had a bottle of champagne dangling down. That they did.

It did worry me that these bottles were hanging out of the window over a busy street below, so, if the string snapped, there would be quite a mess if they fell and hit someone. And what a waste of good champagne.

As he dragged the bottle through the window he announced, "They always had champagne in Cabinet Meetings in the 1930s. Chamberlain of course used to remark that the First Lord of the Admiralty, Duff Cooper, was always legless at Cabinet Meetings on champagne and drank far too much of the stuff, but that never stopped the rest of them."

To my amazement, when doing my mocks, there was an exam question one year, "Was Duff Cooper underrated?"

"He was always pissed," I was tempted to write as the opening salvo. I did note that despite being drunk for years, Duff Cooper made a number of very good calls that turned out to be accurate. He resigned over Munich in 1938, and, while everyone was fretting about the cost of rearmament in the late 1930s, Duff just used to sit there in Cabinet, drunk, and slur, "Don't worry about the cost, the Americans will come in eventually and sort it all out."

That's pretty much how it turned out. He was right, of course, despite being drunk. Drunks, in my experience, take a long-term view, because they don't know what's going on in the present.

The tutor's eyes would glint as he magically produced some champagne glasses for us, and he poured the champagne with glee. "I found these old bottles in the college wine cellar... I'm retiring soon, so I'm helping myself. And I don't care..."

This happened every week. It was fine when we had an evening Cabinet meeting. It was a slight issue if we met at nine a.m.

We would discuss Cabinet papers every week, with one of us taking the role of a Cabinet Minister. We had some almighty rows on matters of foreign policy; then, as the champagne kicked in, we were really quite mellow about the onset of war, and tended to the Duff Cooper view that we'd do nothing and leave it all to the Americans.

By the end of the Cabinet meeting, we really didn't give a toss, as we got to the tenth bottle.

As we staggered out, it did strike me that this was a novel way to teach and a fascinating look at how Government works. If this lot were hard drinkers, could one actually survive the process of getting into Churchill's mindset, given his gargantuan capacity for drink whilst conducting the art of statecraft?

It's really those two memories I have taken away from Oxford, among many other wonderful memories: (i) three years of religious fundamentalism, and how to dodge it; (ii) Cabinet ministers guiding the nation at crucial points in its history are usually drunk. So, with a heavy heart, after three years of my degree, and getting a decent grade, it was time to leave Oxford.

There was to be one sting in the tail though.

I knew that I would never see the religious nut ever again. My life would be my own, without judgement.

But how was I to handle the graduation ceremony?

I looked at the dates and avoided the obvious ones in the summer months, just after exam results were announced, as they were always packed, and the vast majority of people went for those dates. The fundamentalists were bound to go for those days; it was easier to set fire to people in the summer months, as they were drier. So I plumped for a date in January, to which, commonly, no one turned up. The college secretary confirmed to me that I was the only person going, with one other. I was bound to be safe. The statistical chance of the religious nutter, the house mate and leader of the fundamentalists, being there on the same day were near zero, especially as we didn't even study the same subject.

Yes, out of a college with a lot of undergraduates in my year, he was the only other person there from my college on that day.

Isn't that bloody typical? Was there no escaping him?

At university, you expect liberation, and the chance to explore infinite boundaries once you are free from all parental restrictions. Yet you end up being surrounded by religious fundamentalists.

Middle-Class Hell.

So I asked the obvious question – where would I have the most freedom and what should my career be, I asked? "London" and "Law" came back as the answers.

If there was a Middle-Class profession, this was it… the quest for Middle-Classness continued…

But first I needed to go to Law School, and that meant a return to the North, to York…

Law School

Without doubt, Law School was two years of utterly stupefying tedium.

I'd come from drinking champagne, and being so smashed that I thought I was the First Lord of the Admiralty, to the equivalent of two years of memorising telephone directories.

The workload was punishing. Some said that the Common Professional Examination, which is basically a Law Degree rolled into one year, was one of the hardest courses around, after the NASA astronaut's course.

At least they went into space.

The only way to get through this was to be spaced.

The setting was also totally dysfunctional.

"Law School" was a disused primary school on the outskirts of York that they'd picked up on the cheap, because it was in the middle of nowhere, and was even more flimsy than my old comprehensive school in Hartlepool.

Consequently, because it was a disused primary school, everything was designed for five-year-olds.

Washbasins, the dining hall, staircases, the lot.

The whole place just seemed to operate in miniature. The desks, though slightly larger, were still not quite the right height for strapping twenty-odd-year-olds, and every time you sat down, your knees were higher than the desk, so it got lifted, wobbling, into the air.

The whole place affected the tutors' attitude towards us, too, and regressed us, in their eyes, to primary school kids. And so they treated us as such.

We, the future lawyers of the UK, Officers of the Supreme Court and all-round drunks, were regularly berated with: "You're a naughty boy," and, "You bad, bad, girl," and, "What a dirty lot you are," or even, "What you need is a jolly good smacked bottom!"

It was incredibly erotic.

Apart from the madness of the building I went to every day, I hadn't escaped the lunatic housemate syndrome.

It got repeated, yet again.

When one ascends to the Middle-Class, one hopes that one will just acquire reasonable, nice people around oneself. Surely at Law School everybody would be sensible?

Middle-Class Hell says, "No!"

You still keep attracting complete nutcases. And an institution which is supposedly full of sorted, ambitious people is, sadly, just the sort of place where you are going to find more of the lunatics.

It doesn't matter how high you get in life, how much you make, which circles you try to move in, Middle-Class Hell says that you are going to come across a ton of nutters.

This time, after the religious fundamentalists, I made sure that meeting new housemates would be on my terms. No more dodgy housing ballots; I'd assert control this time.

I got off to an early start, and decided to be the first through the door in renting a house, so that I would have control over who I sublet to. I wasn't being nasty, just protecting myself.

So I tipped up one day in June (term started in September) and rented a room in the closest house to the college I could find.

Most people left it right to the last minute to look out for a house, usually a week before term started. I made sure I was already in, and could screen out any potential fruitcakes a mile off.

I'd worked out a little trick to scare off bonkers headcases. I hit upon this genius method when I was assaulted one day in the street by one of those bunch of charity workers who accost you, asking for donations.

You know them... there are several of them, they find the longest street they can, they position themselves about thirty seconds apart, so that even if you escape one, there is always another ready to grope you about thirty seconds away down the street... they smile at you sweetly, so you smile innocently back, and then they pounce! After groping and poking you, they then make you feel guilty for not making a donation.

If you need to walk the whole length of the street, that's it; forget owning your salary. The fact that you have seen one, and have given everything you own, is not going to deter the rest from pursuing you relentlessly so that they hit their sales targets for that week, and you are a financial wreck.

But I discovered a cunning stunt...

It happened quite by chance.

I met one of them at the top of an impossibly long street one day, and we ended up in conversation as I had nothing better to do. He asked me how I was, and, in my naivety, I decided to tell them about my escapades with the religious fundamentalists at Oxford, my Granny's latest trauma with Mrs Haemorrhoid (who'd run off with a Harrods teapot), and the sudden revelation which I had just had about Neville

Chamberlain's foreign policy, and the role of Duff Cooper in saving the world, while he was drunk.

All perfectly sensible points, and by now you understand why these might have been on my mind. It never occurred to me that he just wanted money, so I rambled away for a good old age, and when he'd aged twenty years, he couldn't take any more. He staggered off and, for sweet mercy, begged a smelly old tramp who was sitting there, festering away in an old Vivienne Westwood shawl, to sign a direct debit form. The poor tramp had nothing (apart from the shawl) and had no idea what he was signing, but charity man was just desperate to have any excuse to get away from the academically brilliant points I was making about the role of lesbian nuns in eleventh-century feminism, or labour relations in the Dutch margarine industry in 1864.

I had survived years of Granny, you see. Anyone who knew her had built up resistance, listening to years of rambling nonsense. If you used your time well, you could listen to Granny and tune out at exactly the same time, to organise your whole life, meditate, produce a work of fiction in your head, or a timeless symphony, while nodding at just the right moments to convince her that you were consciously still in the room, and listening. The odd nod of the head and a repeat of certain random words she'd used, like "teabag… insulated slipper… bin bag… hedge… rolling pin… dirty panty-girdle", enabled you to get through a whole morning of rambling, without taking any notice of anything that was said. Also, and this is a curious fact, other people around her would start to pick up her habit of talking total nonsense without pause for hours on end. You became infected with it. So everyone who knew her, in the end, became adept at talking the same infinite tedium, without pause, to some shell-shocked companion, for simply days on end, without any consciousness of the destruction of the other person's sanity which they were causing. They suffered it, then they subconsciously dished it out. But it never occurred to me that no one outside Granny's immediate circle could cope when subjected to this for the first time, and that I'd picked up a little bit of Granny along the way.

But this is what I'd done to that poor charity worker. Watching him descend into gibbering made me realise just how lethal Granny really was. I had no idea that he only wanted cash. I had assumed, like Granny, that people who stand around in the street with a clip board and a pen, simply want to know everything that's going on in my life. Granny would have kept him there for days, so, in a way, he was lucky.

Yet I also discovered something remarkable in my assassination of this chap's mental health: these charity worker types communicate with some form of telepathy, because as soon as one of them thinks you're mad, the rest of them all the way along the street do as well.

It's astonishing how they just avoid you as you wander down the street from then on. I got to the end of the Tottenham Court Road financially viable, whereas grown men were weeping at the end of it after having given everything away. Not to mention what the Church of Scientology, or a brush with Catholicism, had done to them along the way.

I was being completely normal that day. But if you want to scare these people off from accosting you, just pretend that you're a raving loony by talking about your own life. It works every time, and leaves you free to donate as you wish. It makes the Middle-Class Hell of being accosted in the street a touch more bearable.

But I'd worked out that, if I could scare someone off at eleven paces by just chatting about my life, then I'd learnt an invaluable skill. It meant I could scare any nutter off at a mile. What a gift Granny had given me! The years of torture had produced a very well-disguised boon.

So what could possibly go wrong? I had this new place in York covered. I was there first, I could vet them, and scare off any potential loonies well in advance.

At first, this was a success. Two people decided to move in. They were "normal".

The curse was defeated.

Then, just after they moved in, they disappeared. They were both checked in at the college, but then the staff at the college didn't know where they had gone. They stopped turning up. They just disappeared into the night.

To this day, I don't know where they ended up or why they ran off.

After they'd gone, the landlady breezed in one day and said, "I've found a house mate for you..." She'd heard of my travails with house mates at Uni, and said, "Don't worry, this guy is a gem. You will get on famously."

"Fantastic!" I exclaimed, now excited to meet my new housemate.

He was a complete maniac.

When he walked in, I saw that he was covered head to foot in something black; from the top of his head downwards, no features could be seen as they were obscured by this black shiny covering.

I tried to be upbeat. "Nice burka!" I exclaimed.

"It's my hair," he replied.

And so it was.

He had this black mop that started at the top of his head, and continued over his eyes, and extended down, beautifully straight and flowing, to reach, apparently, floor level. At a distance, it did resemble a rather lush and expensive shiny burka.

He never tied his shoelaces, and, because of the impossibly long fringe that came over his eyes, he was constantly falling over. I'd be woken frequently in the night when I heard this crash, as he fell down the stairs (again); or I'd walk into the lounge or the kitchen, and find a new hole in the wall, or the remains of kitchen units that he'd fallen into.

He used to ride a bike, and his shoelaces would get caught in the gears and chain, and off he was flung. If he did manage to ride in a straight line without getting his shoelaces caught, his fringe (which was long enough to suck, and he did!) would ensure that he couldn't see what was ahead of him, and he would smash into cars, pedestrians, anything that was in his way.

I never knew where he was from, as I never got to see underneath his hair. For those who remember *The Magic Roundabout*, he was just an enormous, upright Dougal. There was no religious reason for it, and I certainly wouldn't judge on that basis, he just liked his hair like that.

Studying law was a strain for him, as the only way he could read a book was to shove it up underneath his hair. Eating was a similar hassle, and occasionally a tongue would poke out from the hair to snatch something off a plate or suck the drippings from his hair if a stray potato or something like that got caught tangled up *en route*.

I once caught sight of a moustache and beard under the hair, which I thought were a touch excessive in the circumstances, but then it must have been a task for him to shave.

He also kept large bowls of grease in the kitchen, presumably for cooking, but they took up every available work surface, and gave off the most awful pong.

The place was unbearable. I had two years of it. There was nothing left of the house at the end of it, and I lost my deposit, as burka hair man had managed to trash the place by falling into everything.

So, my incredibly well-laid plans to avoid nutter house mates had been foiled again.

Apart from that, bugger all happened at Law School. Absolutely nothing. Apart from studying law. There are years of our lives when nothing seems to happen, and we are condemned to tedium. These were such years.

I was grateful, after two years of nothing memorable, that I was about to be off and away again. Fortunately, I had secured a training contract with a City of London firm of solicitors.

I was about to start my training contract, in September, 1994.

London beckoned – that beacon of Middle-Classness.

And an amazing Middle-Class influence was about to come into my life…

The Amazing Adventures of the Old Lady

The hideousness of Middle-Class work is something I will cover in a future chapter, and it is probably the most hideous part of this book, as indeed it is in life generally.

But first, let's step forward in time a little. Let's assume that I already have a job. More than that: I'm already leaving it.

We have now moved forward from 1994, some five years, to 1999. I will fill in the missing bits later. But let's assume that I'm now a qualified lawyer, and I'm in the process of moving jobs from one law firm to another. And at that time, I meet the Old Lady.

And she is to be pivotal to *everything*. That's why she is coming in now.

My new firm had organised drinks for me, so that I could meet the new people I would be working with.

I got drinking away, and seemed to be getting along with this other chap from the firm, chatting away merrily.

He was in his late forties/early fifties at that point, gay, very funny and charismatic, with a very dry turn of phrase, and a self-deprecating, deadpan manner. He never looked like he was making an effort, and, indeed, seemed to regard working and living as something to be endured, so he put as little effort as possible into both. He turned up, but he never gave the impression that he wanted or needed to be there.

I could give a further and deeper description of him; but suffice it to say that he just looks like, moves and, in fact, is a mildly irritable Womble.

We carried on drinking, but weren't too drunk, and we lost track of time until we suddenly discovered it was closing time.

We left the pub, and tried to hail a cab so that this chap could get home.

A typical London black cab chugged up beside us, after he had gaily waved it in our direction with a silk handkerchief, and maybe a long white glove, and I opened the door to let him in.

He couldn't get in.

I'm not sure how, but it seemed beyond him to push or squeeze himself through the cab door.

He started to fuss, "Oh dear, oh no, oh how does this work again?" He tried to lift his leg up, "Oh dear, I can't get this thing to rise in the air...' As he tried to lift his leg over the cab threshold, it simply refused to go in. He would also turn his body one way, fail to get it through the door, and then turn the other way, and be equally incompetent at trying to get into the cab.

This went on for several minutes, as did the, "oh ahhhhssss," and, "no, oh I can't possibly, oh now what, oh how am I supposed to do this, oh my, well I never, ooh this is a bit of a struggle, isn't it... how do I get this in... how did I do this last time? Now how long ago was that? Oh dear, what a tangle."

I realised he wasn't drunk.

He was simply incapable.

Beneath that bumbling exterior was more bumbling.

He stood back, exasperated. "Oh, this is all too much for an old lady of my age!"

"How old are you, dear?" I asked.

"157" snapped back the reply, and I never questioned its accuracy for a moment, as the Old Lady once again resumed her hapless attempts to get her legs off the pavement and into the cab.

"I'm an Old Lady, don't you see? I could break a hip if I get this wrong," she snapped, matter-of-factly.

There was no artifice to any of this.

He/she genuinely was an old lady of one hundred and fifty-seven.

I tried a bit of pushing and shoving at the Old Lady's carcass; this too failed to get anywhere. I managed to raise her leg with my hands, at the same time as pushing her head down to lever her through the gap, but that, too, was met with wails of protest, "No, no, it just isn't going to happen... mind that, dear, it might snap at my age. In fact, it just has..."

Sweat was pouring off her now, as we tried to bundle her through the cab door yet again, the silk hanky now wet, limp and tragic-looking.

There was only one thing for it. With much swearing and general irritation from its driver, I managed to get the taxi to inch forward until the door was next to a lamp-post. I leaned against the lamp-post, raised my legs off the ground, placed my feet firmly onto the Old Lady's immense fat arse, and gave an almighty shove.

She careered headlong into the back of the cab with effeminate incompetence, on to her back; her legs went into the air, before finally smashing back down to the ground, and she lay on the floor of the cab, crumpled and dishevelled.

"Aren't you going to get off the floor and use the seat, dear?" I enquired.

"No, too much effort, dear," she said, "I'll just stay on the floor."

Then she raised her head up, and nonchalantly waved her hand in the air, like the Queen, "Oh, by the way, dear, I'm a Partner in this firm of solicitors you are joining."

And then the cab sped off, with her still on the floor.

This was, technically, in a way, my new boss.

Partners in City law firms tended to be terrifying, aggressive beasts, demanding to be feared, who breathed nothing but fire and testosterone, especially the ladies.

The Old Lady seemed a bit different from the usual Partnership model, though, to be fair, I had just joined a particularly crap firm.

It was going to be very hard to act professionally every day in the office, with the Old Lady.

But I needn't have worried too much about my professionalism.

The firm was so bad that there was simply no point in making an effort, and over the next two years for which the Old Lady and I worked there, guess how much work we actually did?

Nothing.

As the Old Lady said to me, from the dizzy heights of Partnership, "It's all too much effort, dear."

She did residential conveyancing.

You always knew when she had exchanged contracts, as she did a little "exchange of contracts" dance around the office, which wasn't bad for an Old Lady of her age.

But that was all she actually did. No one quite knew how they had actually got to exchange of contracts, as she seemed to do nothing.

But the Old Lady became a beacon of the Middle-Class lifestyle. She was a shining example on a hill top.

She used to take us impressionable, young, aspiring, but broke assistant solicitors out to her "Club". This was the rather grand-looking "National Liberal Club" on the Embankment, close to the Houses of Parliament. We called it "the Club".

And there she would regale us with the joys of the Middle-Class lifestyle, once we had "made it", like her.

It was dizzying – tales of home ownership, coming back to cats every night, and the joys of ordering a new kitchen with granite work surfaces, and flip-top bins.

This was to be aspired to. This was "it". The peak of the Middle-Class lifestyle. My whole reason for being was now clear, in the form of this mad Old Lady, who was, in fact, a man.

This kept us going for hours, as she would wax lyrical about the slate floor tiles in her new kitchen, and how the granite work surface had reflective chips in it that gleamed when the lights were turned on.

She would wave her hands, and her aura expanded all around the room, as she could barely contain her happiness at the prospect of buying a pair of John Lewis tongs, or a floor mop, at the weekend.

And she had her own club of course. The Club.

Oh, how we all wanted to be her! How we all wanted to "arrive", and to be like this Middle-Class Old Lady, with a Middle-Class-Old-Lady lifestyle, and her Old-Lady-Middle-Class utensils.

She squealed every time she went into John Lewis, as John Lewis is the height of Middle-Classness. The dizzy old moo was so taken by the place that she fell asleep in there overnight once, and probably had the only orgasm she'd had in a century at the realisation she'd been in there for such a long period of time, until the doors were flung open in the morning and they let her out. But then she lamented, "At my age, I can't remember any of it."

At the age of about twenty-five, I had found my role model!

But even so, the layers gradually started to peel even from this state of Middle-Class perfection.

The Old Lady's Club, whilst amazing to look at, hid a ton of defects behind the perfect façade.

The first was that the Old Lady didn't even want to be a member.

"I tried to get into the Carlton Club, dear, but they wouldn't have me," she said, wistfully. A tear glistened in her eye, as she was clearly hurt at the social affront.

Evidently, she had been forced to accept second-best in membership of the Club.

"I'm not even a Liberal," she blubbed, "I'm a High Tory, for God's sake." Whatever that was.

And then there was the service in the Club. Having been to other clubs, where the staff know your name, and know your favourite drink – where, in fact they just know everything you could possibly want – the experience in the Club was somewhat different.

The head barman didn't know who you were, because he didn't even know who he was himself. Or where he was.

He existed in a fog of confusion, and stood behind the bar most of the time, looking bewildered. When he made a round of drinks, he had no idea what the prices were. He'd scratch his head, having made two gin and tonics, desperate to remember the prices, and would then announce, with a flash of remembrance, "That'll be £67.47, madam," and, to the next person, with exactly the same order, "That'll be £3.51, sir."

There was another bar tender there as well, who, when faced with one customer and an otherwise empty bar, would exclaim with utter indignation, "Look at what I've got to put up with." The customer would order a glass of water. "Just look at the pressure I'm under," he would bark, the gentle customer jumping out of her skin and running off, as he growled yet again at the sheer exertion required of him to turn on a tap, and turn it off again.

The members of the Club, of which I am now one, were also a curious bunch. There didn't seem to be any under two hundred years of age, apart from the Old Lady and me. The Old Lady looked sprightly in comparison. So all one could hear, when the sound of all conversation stopped, was the creak of hip replacements across the Smoking Room, as one of them foolishly went to the bar again.

On election night in 2010, I expected some excitement at the prospect of the Liberals' getting back into Government, for the first time in a hundred years.

I looked around the room, expecting to see excited faces at the prospect of the Liberals yet again being masters of the nation, their cherished goal of coalition government finally come true.

But they'd all fallen asleep. It was the equivalent of Brexit's being met in UKIP HQ with an all-round gentle "zzzzzzz."

It was such a curious place. The Liberal Party, as a real force of government, had died in the 1920s. It became near-extinct in the 1950s. And yet here was this club that simply refused either to function properly, or to die. It had survived the First World War, the collapse of the Liberal Party in the 1920s, the 1930s depression, the Second World War, the even more shambolic state of the Liberal Party from the fifties onwards, the great crash of 2008, until nearly a century had passed, and the most enthusiasm that the Party could rouse by getting into Government, after a hundred years in opposition, was the practical suspension of consciousness on election night.

But the key point is this: as one ascends to the Middle-Class, especially in London, one needs to acquire a proper olde-worlde club, of course. And the one that the Old Lady had got, and didn't even want to be a member of, was something that shambled on long after the main event had ceased to be.

I do love the place, really, but it has its comic idiosyncrasies, such as the fact that it shouldn't be there, but it is, with its seemingly indestructible quality. And, as the Liberal Party sinks even further, it has, inversely, upped its game and become rather good of late. No one can explain it.

The Old Lady leaned over once and said something in revered, hushed tones, "Well dear, my friend at one club made a fortune, as the place went under after it got into financial trouble. They did a sale and leaseback on the building, and had to distribute the proceeds of sale to the members. She made a fortune, dear. Look at this place," she waved her arm around the Club, "it's empty, and everyone is older than me, which isn't possible. It's got to go under dear, got to, and then…"

She gazed into the distance, dreaming. "And then, once I am rich beyond the dreams of avarice from the sale proceeds, I will buy a bigger flat with… a *second bedroom!*" She tailed off. That seemed a bit of an anti-climax. And that summed it up generally.

In seeing the defects of the Club, and the Old Lady's limited desire for a second bedroom, which was dependent on this ancient institution's going bust, a sudden realisation dawned – was this Middle-Class lark all it was cracked up to be?

The fog began to clear; the curtain began to lift... you pay a fortune for crap service, a fortune for a flat the size of a shoe box, and everything seems just a bit of a struggle to get anything vaguely decent. You have to join London clubs in the hope that they go under, just in order to fund a second bedroom.

It didn't seem to be this way in earlier decades. Service seemed to be impeccable, polite, and things affordable.

When I was a trainee solicitor in the late 1990s, a Partner at the first law firm for which I worked said to me, "Well, as trainees in the 1960s, we all lived in Kensington, we started work at ten a.m., had a long lunch, finished work at about four thirty, then, after two years of qualification, got a Partnership, and then we did nothing; we just got the work in from long lunches, and pushed it all downwards."

As I look around the profession now, newly qualified solicitors can't afford a flat in even the cheapest of areas, and Partnership is a horrendous struggle.

It shows, in microcosm, what has happened at so many income bands, careers, and professions in society.

Everything has just got harder.

We all know that this has happened. But that was the first glimmer I got of it: that things were getting tougher, not easier.

For everyone.

What did a Middle-Class lifestyle look like in the nineteenth and early twentieth centuries?

The evidence is there all around us, in big, swooping Victorian houses. They were proper houses then, not broken up into flats.

As someone said (probably the Old Lady), a Middle-Class lifestyle now is like a Working-Class lifestyle thirty years ago;

and equally large sections of the Working Classes have slipped back beyond that.

I wandered into the Club one day. I'd taken the day off, and arrived at four thirty in the afternoon, to find the Old Lady (on a work day for her) asleep under a copy of the *Daily Telegraph* (her act of defiance against the Liberal Establishment), and an empty bottle of Club claret next to her on the table in the Smoking Room (where you now can't smoke).

I woke her up. "Hard day at the office, dear?"

"Purgatory," she hiccupped. It took her about thirty minutes to wake up. She tried stretching, but her limbs refused to move. She decided that being hunched in the chair was far less effort than stretching, and so she just slobbed there in a leather arm chair, like an ergonomic health and safety disaster. This was followed by: "I was rushed off my feet, for five whole minutes. Who do they think I am?"

Then the Old Lady snorted. "I've had enough of this," she fumed.

"This bloody firm doesn't pay anything, even at Partner level. And this bloody Club I'm in? It's shambolic, it fails to go bust, it just *survives* against all the odds, a bit like me. I don't earn enough. I've made a decision. I need to earn more, and go up the ladder of life. So… I'm going to have to get a lodger in. I live in a one-bedroom flat so he can go on the sofa."

"Have you ever thought of doing any work?" I asked.

"NEVER!" she roared, outraged. Her hair, normally immovable, shook visibly in indignation. But the rage subsided very quickly, as she slumped back into uselessness, and was unable to complete the sentence which she was about to mutter, as her languid ineptitude gripped her once more.

I did warn her just what lodgers could be like, "You might end up with a religious fundamentalist for years on end. Or people who run off unexpectedly. Or someone with Burka hair, who can't see where they are going, who might crash into your flower displays from sheer giddiness..." I paused. "Oh, hang on; they're all you."

"No, dear," she said, "I think I've found someone completely suitable." She flushed with that triumphant look that Granny used to have when she had found a brand of panty-girdle that no one else in the Hartlepool area had.

She'd found this nineteen year old Essex lad hanging round the office, who had all the appearance of being a stray. Nothing sexual was going on; the fit between them just seemed to be comic. This chap was exactly the Essex lad cliché you would expect, and came to be known as "Stud", because of his hard womanising. It's hard to imagine this beer-swilling laddish thing getting on with the Middle-Class gentility, and senility, of the Old Lady. But on to the sofa he moved. And, once he'd moved on to it, eighteen years ago, and counting, he never moved off it.

The chemistry was seismic in its clash. But strangely, it felt as if he'd always been there, and always would be there, until the Old Lady finally expired.

He once moved out, to get married, but, within months, came back, as fast as his legs would carry him, back to the rigid certainty of the Old Lady's iron bosom, and Radio Three on a Saturday.

Like a leaking, spraying, rutting, feral tomcat, Stud isn't on the title deeds, but owns the home, and the Old Lady exists simply to service the tomcat.

The Old Lady once recounted her hopes for Stud. When the Old Lady had reached "an age", about two and a half years from that date, Stud would be her care-giver. The Old Lady would have her own mobility scooter, with Stud in the basket on the front. Or she would have her own wheelchair, with tartan rug, pushed around by Stud, whacking people out of the way with her walking stick, on the way to John Lewis.

This seemed a vain hope.

More likely, Stud could get something pregnant (it really could be anything). The Old Lady, at the grand old age of one hundred and seventy-two, raddled, shaking, gin and piss soaked, would become a Granny to the first of Stud's copious off-spring and drippings. And, after decades of procreation, and the Old Lady maintaining Stud's brood of work-house size proportions, with all of his kids going badly off-the-rails and delinquent, Stud would finally collapse, and be pushed around and attended to by the Old Lady instead, now well over two hundred. The Old Lady would be the care-giver to the lodger.

But whatever the scenario, the lodger will always be there!

Middle-Class Hell… The incompatible lodger who never leaves, and who actually takes over the house, despite being a complete liability. She hasn't made a penny from him in nearly two decades and counting, and the whole money-making scheme has descended into pointless disaster, as Stud ended up costing far more than he paid in rent, as a result of the damage caused by his "habits".

The revelation of the Old Lady's fate at the hands of Stud came to us one day on an Old-Lady-Middle-Class trip out to "the country". We discussed in detail how the remains of her life would pan out, and, now that she had the Stud the lodger, how she would never get rid of him.

We would organise an Old-Lady-Middle-Class trip out every year. It really is worth trying one.

Old-Lady-Middle-Class days out simply had to involve all three of: (a) travelling by train, *but first class only, not standard in any circumstances*; (b) having afternoon tea, either at the best tea shop at our destination, or at the most prestigious hotel; and then (c) getting bored, and leaving after about thirty minutes of our arrival. You simply have to do it.

On this occasion, we decided to visit Oxford, so that I could show the Old Lady the priest holes that had remained hidden since the seventeenth century, that I had used when escaping from the religious fundamentalists. We also decided to take Old-Lady-Middle-Class tea at the Randolph Hotel, in the traditional fashion.

When the Old-Lady-Middle-Class day out arrived, we tipped up at Paddington station, to catch the train to our exciting destination.

We shelled out a fortune for first-class day returns.

We did reflect on the wisdom of this.

"Dear," I said, "first class isn't like it used to be on these short-range services. It's changed since you were a girl in the 1870s." So had everything else.

"Back then, first class used to be sealed off from second and third class, so that the stinkies couldn't get in. Now, it's utterly pointless. You don't even get a partition any more. Not even a curtain, like on a plane, to divide you from the mingin' masses."

"Not even a curtain?" she enquired, aghast.

"Not even a curtain, dear."

"But I have curtains at home! From John Lewis."

"I know, dear, you keep telling everyone. You never stop telling everyone."

Dear reader, do please go and check out first-class seats on commuter services now. The seats are the same, but you get absolutely nothing extra for the hard cash you fork out. Nothing. Apart from a velcro doily on the back of the chair announcing "First Class", but that's it. Otherwise it's the same tat as the rest of the train, except that it requires a lot more cash to go in there.

As we typically arrived three hours early at Paddington, we hooked up to the internet, and looked at pictures of first-class carriages that used to operate on these routes. They seemed to contain seating that was large, plush and comfy, with beautiful detail in the carriages, including wood panels, leather straps to open the windows, and dainty reading lamps – and curtains at the window! On seeing pictures of the curtains the Old Lady then set off on yet another unending ramble about her John Lewis curtains, about which everyone had heard a hundred times before. Then we looked at pictures of the Brighton Belle train interior – though that was at the top of the chain, admittedly – but still, only an hour's journey from Brighton to London, came with a proper breakfast, at a table with ironed tableware.

Even standard looked roomy and comfortable then.

The Old Lady fumed, and then became quite incandescent.

"This is typical! Everything is being dumbed down dear, everything."

It's like chocolate bars and tins of chocolates in the 1970s. They were HUGE, and they came in proper wrappers and proper enormous, bulky tins – which were made out of tin. Now, they are getting smaller and smaller, and are dumbed down in cheap plastic containers. But we are supposedly getting fatter, when our chocolate is getting smaller. Now explain that one... You can't, except through the prism of Middle-Class Hell.

So, imagine our surprise when we flopped on to the platform. We expected disappointment.

But going to and terminating at Oxford, non-stop (bar Reading), was a whole 125 train. Excluding the engine cars, it was about eight carriages in total.

It was a non-peak service, so, in addition to the Old Lady and me, about one other person got on. There is a tragic fact: when the Old Lady and I travel first class, there are always more people getting into first class than standard, so we are crowded in first class, and the rest of the train is empty. Middle-Class Hell again.

But still, there was a whole train for about three of us. So we whooped as we got on board, as we had a whole carriage all to ourselves. The other first-class customer made sure that he got his own carriage.

Bliss! This was what it was supposed to be about.

As we luxuriated back into large leather seats, with a coffee and a copy of the *Daily Telegraph* each, it seemed as though Middle-Class Bliss had finally come. We had a proper train with a proper first class. The train was not one of those short-distance commuter trains that you have to pull backwards repeatedly for about three days to get the spring wound up, before finally releasing it in a wound-up frenzy, for the thing to only move about three feet. It was a proper big-ass train, with comfy leather seats.

There are some who say that, when you are bad, karma pays you back quickly, and big time. But when you are good, it seems like a lifetime for karma to pay back something nice; and just possibly, just possibly, when you are in your eighties, after a life of good works, the bus might turn up on time. The injustice of good and bad karma.

But it felt as though we had had our good karma day.

We got to the Randolph Hotel in Oxford, had tea, then the Old Lady dozed off (again), and we decided to come back home.

Amazingly, we got the same train back, just as empty.

"That was a lovely day out, dear, how long were we there for, wherever we were?" she slurred.

"About half an hour, dear," I answered.

"Oh that's about right for us, I think, dear. At our age." I was about thirty.

"We must do another one, dear."

"We must, dear, yes."

"Where...?"

"Edinburgh."

"First class, on the train? In July?"

"Yeah."

"How long shall we stay, dear?"

"About half an hour, dear. Then back again. That's the practice."

"Won't it be freezing in July?"

"Stay about fifteen minutes, then? I don't want to be there too long and catch a chill. Then come back?"

"Yeah."

Work Hell

Work is surely the pinnacle of Middle-Class Hell.

Well, it's probably just Hell, actually.

As noted, in previous decades, like the 1950s and 1960s, work seemed easy.

Our ancestors glided out of educational establishments with no debt, and into jobs, and did practically nothing all day. When they did do any work, it was at a snail's pace, with no pressure. They had job security and fantastic pensions, and, after doing about a week's work in a career spanning thirty years, retired on a healthy income, their mortgage debts, etc., finally eroded by a nice dose of inflation and rampant pay rises.

The Old Lady has made it her mission to continue this; but she is fighting a losing battle.

Compared to how things were, it's all gone horribly wrong.

The rot started with Harold Wilson's "White Heat of Technology" speech in 1963, and seemed to accelerate at a vast pace under Mrs Thatcher. Whilst I admire both prime ministers, they made the fatal mistake of requiring us to make an effort, and thus it's all become harder.

Things were far better when we didn't bother, or didn't get into a flap.

As Harold Macmillan, Prime Minister in the late 1950s and early 1960s, put it, "When things got a little rough, I just used to read a couple of chapters of Jane Austen, and then things didn't seem so bad… zzzzz."

Quite. He's right, you know.

At the first sign of work-related pressure, just read Jane Austen, and then doze off. The problem usually goes away, as, in today's breakneck speed, people simply change their minds before you actually get round to doing anything, if you wait long enough.

Need I start listing the work-related problems now? (i) massive student debt before you even get started; (ii) crushing competition for jobs, and salaries which make home ownership or rent a struggle; (iii) pension and job security gone; (iv) immense pressure and long hours (but not for the Old Lady); and (v) a working culture that seems distinctly less polite than it used to be. By the time you get to your thirties, in some professions, you are a burnt-out wreck.

After all those years in "service", just look at the addled wreck that is the Old Lady; and she's never done anything.

The Old Lady once received a handwritten letter in 2014 from a solicitor on the other side of a transaction, and she squealed in delight at its politeness and courtesy. Handwritten! She couldn't do a stroke of work for the rest of the day due to the shock, but, for her, it was a memory of a working culture long dead, a bit like her.

The state of things amounts to the beginnings of a political manifesto. A new movement… with the Old Lady at its head. A return to the old ways, with Old Lady values… [1]

---

[1] See my second book "The Pong of Power" in which the Old Lady becomes Prime Minister, and makes a complete mess of it.

But, as I've noted, I first got wind of this decline when I started my first job as a trainee solicitor in a law firm in the City.

There were one or two duffers around who remembered the early days, when law was a profession, but the new cut and thrusting generation were coming through, who knew it was a hard business. But to be fair to them, it's like everything else that's had to change.

I started my first seat in my training contract doing residential conveyancing, in 1996, just after I finished Law School in York.

I was young, keen, eager, and also utterly incompetent.

One of my first jobs was to sell a house which had recently been vacated when the owner died.

The house was empty, but, unfortunately for me, and the sellers, buyers and everyone else, it exploded two days before exchange of contracts.

An issue with the gas, or some barbecue gas canisters, or an exploding Granny was the cause, but, by one account, it went up in a spectacular fire, and the shattered remnants burnt down very quickly. It was all gone in a matter of minutes.

It was a lovely house. I would have been delighted to live there. But it was gone. A bit like the Old Lady's control of "down below".

The buyers were enraged, and the seller's estate wasn't too happy either.

The Partner who had referred the client to me wandered into the office and shook his head at me in dismay, with barely suppressed rage, "You should have spotted that on the enquiries," he barked, in terrible accusation.

He specialised in employment law, so knew nothing of conveyancing, and was deaf to my protests that there was nothing on the Seller's Property Information Form requiring disclosure of an imminent explosion (caused by incendiary Grannies or otherwise), and, therefore, I had no reason to believe it was about to go up with a bang.

Astonishingly, some of the real estate Partners seemed to take the view that I should have spotted this too.

I thought the whole world was going mad. There is simply no way that a lawyer can spot this.

And thus the injustices of the office environment became clear to me. The Middle-Class Hell of turning up and getting paid, not to work, but to get caught up in office politics, and to deal with people who, often in senior positions, are also quite, quite bonkers.

Fortunately, someone in authority eventually came to the view that "domestic pyrotechnics were probably outwith the range of your reasonable foreseeability". Those exact words. It was as though my gravy-covered Oxford tutor had suddenly re-surfaced.

As soon as I had got out of that one, without a pause in the legal calendar, I was in hot judge's wigs and tights again.

I was sent into the deeds room, which was a vast room with thick concrete walls and a huge, heavy metal door. Deeds going back centuries were in this dusty room, rows and rows of them, and they required thick walls and a thick door to protect them from fire.

I was collecting some deeds one day for my boss on an extremely complex property deal. Everything depended on the information in these deeds packets, for a meeting the following morning, and it was needed urgently. Though menial, my trip to the basement to get the deeds was rather important.

We had a keeper of the deeds room, who was a delightful old duffer, whom we called Mr Deeds. He was aptly named, as, over the years, he had gone a curious wrinkly yellow colour, and from a side angle, he seemed to be flat, with no visible protuberances, apart from his nose. To all intents and purposes, he actually did look like an old yellow crinkly deeds envelope.

Normally, he retrieved all deeds packets from the deeds room, but, as he was notoriously slow and stopped off on every floor for a coffee, he usually delivered the wrong packets to the wrong people, and he wasn't sure which firm he even worked for, after fifty years in the same place. So it was usually safer to send a trainee down for them if you wanted them in the same month.

So I was tasked with getting them, and I set off down to the basement, with a key to the deeds room. I opened the enormous metal door and crossed over the musty threshold of the room.

There was a table in the corner of the room, and Mr Deeds was standing at it, pottering about aimlessly.

As was usual, he started a conversation, and all thoughts of work went out of the window.

He rambled on for a grand total of about twenty minutes, then, leaving his work half done on the table, started to leave the room.

I had no idea about what he was on about, but all I could make out were the following words: "Pastry... Dettol... bathroom... cleaner... baking powder... in the oven... since last Wednesday." I decided never to eat any cakes he brought in. He continued, "So I said to her, never leave a teapot in a kebab shop, no good will come of it..."

As he was rambling away, he asked me how I was.

"Fine," I answered, suddenly taking notice. "I've almost found what I was looking for. I will be here just a minute longer."

"Good, good," he said. "Well, it's home time for me. I'll lock up and see you tomorrow."

"See you, Mr Deeds. Have a good evening."

And with that, still rambling on, he swung the enormous steel door shut, with me still in the room. I heard his key rattling into the lock, and he switched off the lights from the outside. Through the door he was still chuntering away. "If you put them in on a Tuesday, very low light, they should be done to a turn a week on Thursday... You'll be as high as a kite on those, Mrs Humpeldypop, put them down... it's sheep dip, not Assam..." He was off home, with the fairies.

"The silly sod," I thought, "he's locked me in."

I felt in my pocket, and found the key that I'd used to unlock the door and get into the room in the first place.

I'm fine, I thought. Though it was pitch black, I should be able to make my way over to the door. After several visits there, I knew that there was no light switch on the inside, and the lights had to be turned on from the outside. But no matter, I would soon reach the door, unlock it and get outside, turn the lights on, and finish my search.

I stumbled around in the gloom, falling once or twice over boxes of deeds on the floor, getting my suit, face and hair covered in dust. I looked a state. Finally, I reached the door, felt in my pocket for the key, and, finding it, scrambled around on the door for the lock.

My hand caught the handle. The key hole couldn't be far away, and I felt the area around the handle.

But it was smooth, completely smooth.

There was no keyhole on the inside. Only on the outside.

No way out. No lights. No internal phone to call for help. This was before mobile phones, so forget calling someone.

I was, genuinely, trapped in a very large fireproof safe. But what if it was airtight? There was no sign of a gap around the door seal; no light came through. I had to assume it was airtight, and that the oxygen would soon run out.

Death beckoned.

As I sat on the floor, I reflected on the long journey from Hartlepool. As one faces death, life does indeed flash before one's eyes.

My journey to Oxford, Law School, and a brilliant career in the City (exploding houses aside) would be cut short, after being locked in the basement by a geriatric who looked like a deeds packet.

But then I had a brain wave.

We had been assigned a career mentor, who was also a Partner in the firm. I remembered that he had health and safety training in the basement that afternoon.

The deeds room was not far away from the training room he would be in. If I shouted loud enough, he might hear me.

So I lost all my pride, and shouted and banged my fists on the door.

I paused for a moment and I heard a slamming door in the distance. Then... nothing... silence, and the prospect of death returned.

As the hours passed, I felt myself drift off.

I had no idea how many hours I slept.

But I awoke when I heard what could only be the rattling of a tea trolley, passing slowly by.

I banged on the door.

Moments later, I was met by someone with a key, and the grumpy, imposing figure of the firm's frosty tea lady appeared. She'd opened the door from the outside, looked startled at my presence in the deeds room, and hacked at me, "What the 'ell are you doin' in there? Wanna cup o' tea and a bun?" She proffered a wobbling, shaking tea cup and saucer at me – the china rattling, and a dusty, dirty old bun.

It was Granny all over again. Was there no escape?

But I had to be gracious, "Thank you for rescuing me. I thought it might be airtight and was worried I might not make it out alive."

The light was turned back on, and I rushed back in to retrieve the deeds packet.

I had been there some considerable time.

I walked proudly into my boss's office, forgetting the dust-covered dishevelled wreck I was, and handed him the deeds triumphantly.

"Sorry these are a bit late but..." I was cut off before I could explain.

He was livid, "How dare you come into the office looking like that! Look at the state of you. And what time do you call this for the delivery of those deeds."

Finally I got the story out in front of a group of Partners, and, the day after, Mr Deeds was dragged in to give an account of why he had locked me in the deeds room.

"Well I didn't know he was in there," he turned to me, "but there's a cemetery next to it. Why didn't you dig your way out?"

There was much nodding among the Partners. There was indeed a small cemetery next to the deeds room but I wasn't sure about getting through a concrete wall... or what I might find on the other side.

"I did cry for help," was my more practical suggestion.

My mentor had now joined the group of deliberating Partners. "Oh, yes, I was in the basement, having health and safety training. Our door was open. We heard this awful din, which must have been you crying for help, and suffocating. We just closed the door on it. Sorry."

So that was the slamming door I had heard.

But I was glad to finish my first seat, and move on to the next. As a result of exploding houses and near suffocation, there had been far too much excitement in residential conveyancing... My next destination was the Tax and Trusts Department... wills, probate tax... after all the excitement, this sedate area of law was surely welcome, as six months into my 'career' and in my mid-twenties, I was already slowing down fast.

When I arrived, everything seemed fine. I was to share an office with my supervising Partner, who was known throughout the firm for just being thoroughly nice.

He was a typical Probate Partner in a City firm. He had a wonderful list of very rich clients, all of them fruitcake, and about to die.

Despite being a very nice and charming guy to talk to, he had his macabre side. Whenever a rich and batty client died, he would be on the phone to the relatives, all reassurance and soothing words. As soon as he put down the phone, there would be a large war-whoop from his office, and a loud exclamation that would echo down the corridor, "There's another one dead! Thank you, God! I thought the batty old cow would never die. Thank you, God! The fees on this one will be enormous."

And they were. Because they were so loaded and nutty, they were constantly squirreling money away in bank accounts and trust funds about which they had completely forgotten about, so the fees just shot up for administering the mess. Just when you closed an estate down, another load of bank accounts would suddenly crop up.

These estates made the estate administration in Charles Dickens's *Bleak House* look like a picnic. The court case in *Bleak House* went on for a hundred and fifty years, I recall. Not a patch on these.

On the whole, my Partner was very laid back and languid, like my Neville Chamberlain tutor at Oxford. He was a lawyer of the old school, urbane, charming, and always drunk from a long lunch, where he'd charm another bunch of rich batty old ladies.

He lived in Kensington, naturally, but had occasional lapses of memory, because the red brick mansion block he lived in was prone to falling plant pots from the higher floors. They were usually owned by his mad clients. A plant pot would smash onto the cobbles next to him, frightening him out of his skin, to be followed by a geranium, which had fallen out of the plant pot on its way down, landing on his head. He'd walk into the office, dazed, with bits of geranium still on his head, covered in soil, and mumble, "Sorry I'm late, another plant pot fell on me."

So he was never quite with it, usually as a result of hard drinking, long lunches and concussion.

But he was nice to work for.

Then he left the firm, suddenly, overnight. He was leaving for another firm, and was put on immediate gardening leave, no doubt tending to the plant pots that regularly rained down on him.

Also, that weekend, the Tax Department was split from the Trusts Department, and was sent five floors up.

As the department had split, most of the staff had been moved upstairs, and my old boss had been kicked out overnight on gardening leave; I now had space. Not just an office to myself, but a whole corridor to myself.

I felt, in one sense, tremendously important. Not just an office all to me. I had a vast echoing corridor. In another sense, I wondered what on earth I was doing there, as I echoed around the place.

Looking back, I now reflect that it was the most space I've ever had in my working career!

Enclosed offices have gone out of fashion, and open plan has become the norm, especially in London working environments.

Well, frankly, open-plan offices are just another form of Middle-Class Hell. The space that we used to have in working environments years ago has been whittled back to a tiny desk in an over-crowded, noisy office, where it is often impossible to concentrate.

As the Old Lady put it, "However hard one flagellates oneself, one is still only a battery hen, dear."

She is one of the only people in the City of London I know who still has an office, but even that's not enough for her. "Dear, I need a chaise longue to doze off on after my eleven o'clock victuals," she says. "Where on earth am I supposed to start my siesta? I work much better when I'm asleep anyway, I'm far more productive."

Many years after we had both left the firm where we met, I did once get through the door of her new organization, and into her actual office, where she purported to do some work. Her office seemed a vast affair, compared to the tiny desks from which everyone else has to work.

I looked at her desk. There was nothing on it, apart from a computer and a phone, but no paper or work. I looked at her in-tray. It was empty. There was one piece of paper in her out-tray, which a secretary hurriedly came in and removed, but not before popping a grape into the Old Lady's mouth, and wiping away some dribble from the Old Lady's numerous chins. Her in-tray and out-tray were now completely empty. As was her desk.

"Having a busy day, are we, dear?" I enquired.

She mopped her brow, "Rushed off my feet, dear. I've delegated everything. I've got nothing to do for the rest of the week, and it's Monday lunchtime already. I've worked ten minutes this morning, that's quite enough. Now let's go off to lunch. I need to get out of this tiny office and all this clutter of work," as her voice echoed in its vast empty cavern.

I left after a longish lunch, to go back to my work. She then went to the Club. Every day she left her office for lunch; her parting words to her colleagues were, "See you tomorrow, then."

But at least she didn't work in open plan! Whilst middle management might have had an office in times gone by, that seems to have changed. I've noticed that, in a number of cases, open plan has come in for middle management and everyone else, yet senior management have increased the size of their office space. Hmm.

Again, it's worth reflecting on the size of office space from, say, the 1950s onwards. The space we have to work in has got progressively smaller. We spend more time at work, and it's more pressured, but we have less space, and less comfort. Open plan has been justified as breaking down barriers and encouraging team working, but let's be honest about this: it's just being plain cheap.

If only I'd known what was coming, I could have enjoyed the only period in my working life when I had my own office, indeed a whole corridor.

I've had to reflect that the more senior I have become in my career, the less space I have. Even when open plan came in, the desks, in a horseshoe shape, were spacious and manageable.

They seem like a luxury now, and the desks are no bigger than a coffee cup tray.

It is, indeed, Middle-Class Hell!

Another aspect of the Hell at that time was covering up the extra-marital affairs of a senior member of the firm who decided to waltz into my corridor from time to time.

This one was a decomposing, chain-smoking Victorian-looking gentleman. He had large, scruffy hair and immense sideburns that were too huge and bushy even for a Dickens novel, and would almost certainly have been rejected back in the day by Dickens himself, on the grounds of literary improbability. His nose also grew vast amounts of hair. Not nostril hair, but hair that protruded from all over the outer casing of his nose, and that ended in a vast forestation on the bobble at the end. The nose hair was a huge Donald Trump bouffant, which blew around in the wind. He held an absolute hatred for humanity, one of several people I'd met like that up to now, but, most of all, he had a very loud booming voice.

He boomed into my corridor one day; his voice was clipped like an army sergeant's, but barrack loud. "Now," my office shook as he continued, "I'm just off for a week's holiday with my mistress. If my wife calls, tell her I'm not coming back to Buckinghamshire this week; I will be staying in the flat in Belgravia. But don't tell her that I'm really in the Caribbean, with my mistress."

He wore this double-breasted suit that seemed to be physically decomposing, and had few buttons. A damp smell pervaded from him. His hair was lank, and he always seemed greasy, but of course he seemed irresistible to a large number of women, though I struggled with the concept myself as he had BO, and his suit arms once peeled off in protest.

What on earth could I do?

This put me in an awful position, if his wife called.

Fortunately, in that regard, the phone never rang.

He came back from holiday, and he walked into my corridor.

"Now, how has everything gone in my absence?" he bellowed. Somewhere, in deepest darkest Africa, there is a tribe that do willy dances every day. Their big doodahs protrude from grass skirts as they jump around all day, exposing their willies to each other, in this centuries-old tribal ritual. The booming sound wave from his larynx caused a minor earthquake, as it reached this tribe in Africa, and, as the ground shook, they all fell over, a pile of disorganised willies in a big heap, without a clue as to what was going on hundreds of miles away in London. "Not again!" they said.

He leaned close to me, giving off an awful whiff, and whispered. His whisper was a strange sound, but still loud enough to cause a rupture, "Did I get away with it? Did my wife call? I'm seeing her tonight for dinner."

He had gone on holiday in November in an absolutely howling cold snap, and come back from the Caribbean with this glorious suntan. He was golden, and, for once, looked vaguely healthy, and his hair was a little bleached through the grease.

"No calls," I said. "I don't think she will ever guess you've not been in London all last week," I said slightly sarcastically, as I surveyed his tan.

He stood up, beaming proudly, as another button flew off his suit in protest at his stench.

Later that day, he entered the restaurant with his golden "November" tan that he had somehow failed to explain away. She divorced him soon afterwards. She hadn't called that week, because she already knew. Ahh, office affairs!

As I left that department, I needed to consider proper qualification as a solicitor, and whether I would stay with the firm with which I had trained.

I'd had some knocks – the exploding house, the basement incident, and doing nothing except sitting in my own corridor for six months, might make it a bit of a challenge. The department had also fallen apart while I was in it, with the separation of Tax from Trusts.

Then, about six months before qualification, news came of a merger between the firm I was in and another firm. All hiring was frozen until merger discussions were concluded, or broke down.

Then the department I wanted to qualify into split as well. One of the Partners decided to join another firm, and the department broke in two. That was the second time that that had happened.

So I eventually decided that I had to move to another firm. This was another law firm in the City, and was probably a little more cut-and-thrust than the one I'd trained in, which, looking back, had been quite laid back.

This new place was monstrous!

They were at each other's throats.

I shared an office (the dumbing down had now started) with this absolutely mad associate solicitor, who would regularly pull her hair out, and had no self-control.

I walked in one day, and she screamed, "Don't talk to me today… I don't want to talk to anyone, I'm in no fit state. I'm pre-menstrual. It's a particularly bad one." She went bright red and pulled at more hair.

I replied, very gently, so as not to cause offence, "By my reckoning, you've been pre-menstrual every day for the last six weeks. Shouldn't you go and talk to someone about this?"

By my, and everyone else's, calculations in the office – and we plotted it on a calendar – her PMT went on for six months in total without a day of interruption. I only stayed there for six months so her PMT probably went on for as long as my employment contract did. I asked the Old Lady if it was possible to be pre-menstrual for six months. The Old Lady looked aghast. "I have vague recollections of the menopause dear, but when you have a problem in that department, just work the mangle a bit harder and keep your mouth shut. I may remember a pre-menstrual tremor when I was on the Stockton to Darlington railway when it opened in 1825, but all that bouncing at the back of a third-class carriage wrecked my lady bits for good, dear." After that, I never asked her again.

Mrs PMT was medically fine; she just needed an excuse to be unpleasant, and persistent PMT gave her legitimate cover.

But she was nothing compared to the head of the department.

This guy was twisted. A real nasty piece of work. He used to hide other people's files in the ceiling, then blame them for losing them.

But hey, office politics and Middle-Class Hell.

The place became intolerable, so I decided to leave after just six months. I learned a valuable lesson. If you spend most of your life somewhere at work, make sure the place is happy and civil. We're not supposed to be miserable! As I was leaving, to move on to my next job, a file fell out of the ceiling one day, and so "Ceilinggate" was out in the open, causing relationships in the department to rupture, and the department to split apart.

"Oh dear," I thought, as I ran out of the building on my last day, "another departmental split... is this becoming a pattern...?"

As I was about to join another law firm, it was that very night, when I went to drinks with my future colleagues, that I met the Old Lady.

Working for the Old Lady's firm was a very happy time in my career. The firm was a small boutique firm, and, though happy, was also comically bad as a law firm.

A client once came into the firm, looked around our client reception area and remarked, "My God, this looks like a social security office."

It did.

We didn't have an IT department. We just had one Partner who knew the odd thing or two about IT, who would regularly fling things and kick the server every time it went down. This was daily.

The fax machine once broke down, and one of the assistant solicitors, out of sheer frustration, left the office, went shopping, and returned later with a screw-driver. Fuming, he clattered away at the fax machine, and gradually took it apart to fix it. As he knew nothing about fax machines, and as he therefore, understandably, couldn't find the fault, he just left the fax machine in pieces in the corner, and resigned the day after, in protest at the general shambles of the firm.

The fax machine was never fixed, and remained there, a wreck, until the day I left too.

We also had a cheap and knackered old hat stand that used to fall on people, but the Senior Partner refused to spend any money on replacing it. With a loud creak, it would fall on someone every day, and a shout and a scream would emerge from the person underneath it. The Senior Partner would stop work and put the hat stand back together again, and, ostensibly, it was repaired every day. There would be a loud and defiant declaration from the Senior Partner (because he had nothing better to do than mend the hat stand) that, "Now that's finally sorted out, we don't need to spend any money and buy a new one!" The firm held its breath, knowing that, the morning after, it would all fall apart all over again; some poor unfortunate usually had to scramble out from underneath its huge pile of coats, after it had toppled over on them.

The Senior Partner seemed oblivious to this. The firm was doing extremely well, and, in his view, that was down to tight cost control, especially when it came to not buying new hat stands.

He fitted the firm perfectly, and revelled in off-the-wall eccentricity. He would fall about in howls of genuine laughter as the hat stand fell over again, or the fax machine exploded, or the IT system went down yet again. He loved the slapstick comedy of his firm's falling apart in front of his eyes every day.

He turned up every day in an ill-fitting suit that was the cheapest he could find, and he was proud of it. Other lawyers, from more prestigious firms, would come into our offices in made-to-measure Savile Row suits and freshly shined, expensive shoes. And he'd fly into the room, in a whirlwind, with a cheap suit and a plastic carrier bag. He never carried important papers around in a leather briefcase or a smart leather hold-all. A plastic ASDA carrier bag was good enough.

Anything sent out of the firm, even to clients, was always a mess. Incomplete sentences, typos everywhere: usually a stream of consciousness was just dictated, was haplessly typed up by the cheapest secretary they could find, and was flung out to clients, unchecked, on faxes that rarely went and e-mails that barely got out of the firm's server.

"Clients love it," the Senior Partner would say, "It looks commercial and not over-lawyerly."

No, it looked a bloody state, that was if it ever got out of the door.

He also had this "endearing" habit of shoving his hands down his trousers and fondling himself as he spoke to you, oblivious to his own self-groping. Then, after fondling himself, he'd grab a piece of fruit, getting his hands covered in sticky fruit juice as he ate it. Then he'd wipe his hands, covered in his genital drippings and fruit juice, all over your face, rub you enthusiastically, and declare, "I think you're wonderful, sweetie."

He was very endearing, in his way, and always hated the thought of going to another firm because he'd have to "grow up". He was a brilliant lawyer, very sharp and fun to work with, but maddening at the same time.

Sadly, all things come to an end, and after years of doing nothing, the Old Lady got fed up with this firm and left to pursue an even more sedate career elsewhere in the City.

Her departure from the firm was typically half asleep. Conversations with other Partners would typically end with, "I don't care, I'm leaving." She wasn't aggressive. She'd just wave a hanky in the air, languidly.

It was the perfect way to leave that place, actually. Not drama-filled or shouty, just half-dead.

At that point, also, the firm got bought out by the Americans. Well, half of it, anyway.

The even more ramshackle bit was rejected by the Americans, but the profitable bit we were in got snapped up.

So the whole firm fell apart.

I had seen three departmental splits. Now the whole firm I worked for had fallen apart. I was getting better at this.

I ended up working for an American law firm in the City. Sounds posh. Suddenly, we were in very nice premises, close to

Bank station, and everything seemed fine, except that I now had to call the Senior Partner, "Mr..." and the billable hours target was crucifying.

All the fun had gone out of it.

A lot of money was being paid to Partners at this point. This was about the year 2000, and the big boom was just starting.

But something didn't feel right. A sixth sense kept nagging me.

I was right to be on my guard, as word came through that the firm, which had expanded across the world in recent years, had taken on too much debt. The firm went bust, worldwide, from the U.S.

I looked at the notches on my career bedpost. A whole firm had now gone bust, to add to the rest of my career disasters.

I had only been working for four years. I still had about forty years of working life to go. What else could happen? What else could I wreck, simply as a result of turning up?

Given the scale of the boom at that point, it was almost impossible to go bust at that time in the legal world. If you got in at eight a.m., and had your day planned, forget it, another instruction would come in at eight fifteen a.m., and bang would go your plans for the day. There was just too much work around for a firm to fail.

But it did.

I got blamed for that, too. But now I was starting to think that maybe there was something in this; maybe I was the jinxing factor.

Sensing something wrong in that firm, I left before it went bust, for a legal job in-house in a construction company. It proved to be a good reminder to trust my instincts.

The Partners I worked with, who moved across to the American firm, were hit hard when it went bust. The firm was liable to creditors for a multi-million dollar sum, and, as Partners in the business, they all shared in the liability.

I had lots of sympathy for them. I saw what it did to them on a personal level, as they were completely financially wiped out. They went to another firm, and the same thing happened again.

But they carried on, and, finally, they ended up at another firm, and did very well.

They got all their losses back, eventually... but it was Middle-Class Hell for them in the intervening period.

At this point, I was glad that I was out of private practice law firms, and in the relative security of an almost hundred-year-old construction and engineering company.

As I sat in this rock-solid, almost century-old company, nothing could possibly go wrong, I thought. This was safe as houses, especially as law firms are very volatile. Everything I surveyed before me was absolutely clear, as far as the eye could see, and there seemed to be nothing but calm ahead.

In that job, I caught a flight from London to Glasgow one day. I was on the plane, going up to Scotland for a meeting.

It was April 2007, and amazing weather had gone on, it seemed, for weeks on end. We enjoyed hot summer temperatures, and amazing clear days, though it was only early spring. As we progressed in the plane, the pilot came over the intercom, marvelling at the weather. What he said I will never forget, "I have never seen it this clear," he crooned. "Normally, even on the clearest day, you can see a cloud bank ahead, in the distance. But today, everything looks so clear. There is nothing but calm ahead."

"There is nothing but calm ahead." Then, an atrocious summer followed. And then, in the autumn, the financial crash.

I was in that job for a long time. It took an age for the curse of "me" to catch up with my employer, but it did. Gradually, one profit warning turned into seven profit warnings, and the whole place became infected with vitriolic madness, as all such organisations do when they go into decline, break up, or die.

They were too dependent on public-sector contracts, and as cuts started to bite, so the flaws in their business model became painfully apparent.

As my career started to draw to a close here, I had a particularly mad boss towards the end. This one was madder than anyone else I had ever worked with. And let's face it, most had been pretty mad so far.

But this Mad Boss was the worst of the lot.

I went to see a fortune teller one day in "Mysteries", a psychic shop in Covent Garden. The fortune teller sat there, ancient and wizened, high as a kite on incense, picking at her own warts.

"I've seen everything, darling, everything in the sixty years I've been doing this," she husked, clearly on Granny's Players Full Strength fags by the sound of her voice. "Nothing surprises me now. I'm un-shockable," she exclaimed proudly, her head held high. "So I'll handle anything this reading throws up, anything. I've read for the worst murderers and abusers in the land, no problem."

Then she shuffled a set of ancient tarot cards, and went into a trance, as she pulled out cards covering my work situation.

"Dear God," she exclaimed. The shock revived her from her half-dead state, though she still went white as death, and what remained of her jaw dropped.

"Who the hell is this you're working with?" I knew immediately who she meant: The Mad Boss.

"I've never seen anyone like this in the working environment before," she boggled. "Dear God, how do you survive it?"

The tarot cards were also mixed with other cards, and she said, "Let's see if there is any hope here, and draw another card from a different deck."

She drew another card from the pack, and turned it over on the table in front of us.

The card had no picture on it. It was black on its face, totally black.

She squeaked.

"What in the name of Beelzebub's Balls? This is the worst card you can get."

She leaned forward and gripped me, her eyes staring in terror.

"This card represents evil. Pure evil. This person, your boss, is just pure evil! You need protection, dear boy, protection."

Part of her nose fell off with the shock. Not all of it, just the nobbly, warty and overhanging pointy bit at the end. But that was big enough.

And with that, she creaked herself up out of her chair, and shuffled, stooped, across the room, but with obvious urgency in what can be described as the remains of her gait.

She flung open a jewellery box, and pulled out what looked like a couple of crystals.

"You need protection from this person," she said, with wide eyes and a shaking pointy finger. Strangely, though, her warty old nose had just grown back, moments after falling off.

That still puzzles me to this day, and I think about it regularly. Just how did her nose grow back, so soon after falling off?

With a wheezing, groaning noise, she handed me a large black stone. "That's tourmaline. It provides protection against negative energy of all kinds. You'll need this. There's evil from this person. Go and get it attached to a chain and wear it round your neck," she implored.

Then she handed me another one. It was a large, red crystal. "This is fire agate. This creates a powerful shield around you." She waved a vague outline around my aura. "You'll be almost invisible, so people don't give you their negative energy. Confers psychic protection, it does."

She nodded, and kept nodding, like a gothic headbanger.

"Thank you," I blushed. "It can't be all that bad."

She got flustered again, and shrieked hysterically, "Oh dear me, it will be, it's going to be terrible, absolutely awful."

She ushered me out, "Now peace be with you, which it won't, but off you go; you'll live, but only just. Please rate your experience with me at reception. I need a lie down after that. Make an 'orse sick, that reading would… ohhh," she puffed, and collapsed into a chair, drained.

She died the day after that reading.

I went and got the stones made into a necklace, and put them around my neck. There was a scene in a "Superman" film where Superman had a large chunk of Kryponite put around his neck. It was a large, green unsightly rock, and he could barely walk under the strain.

This was the same. The crystals bulged out of my shirt, ostensibly giving off their protective rays.

The first day I used them, on the way to work, they worked. I did not experience a push, a rude shove, a filthy look, or any negative energy from anyone around me, even on packed trains full of angry, red-faced commuters.

They got angry with everyone else, even with each other, but just seemed to avoid me, not quite noticing I was there.

There was a bonkers bloke outside the station, screaming, with a shaking fist at everyone that went past, "I hate you, I hate you all... damn you... burn in hell, all of you!"

But as I walked past, he doffed his cap at me. "Lovely morning," he beamed, only for his UKIP rant to start again at others, just as I was getting out of earshot.

"This just might work," I thought, as I made it to the office on Monday morning, carrying half a ton of Kryptonite around my neck.

The Mad Boss was there, banging the headset of the phone against the desk in yet another rage, screaming, "Our relationship is toast," down the phone at a cleaner or a nanny.

But when I walked in, for a moment The Mad Boss brow un-furrowed, and calm came across The Mad Boss face as the phone was finally put to rest, its electronics hanging out after yet another bashing. A fresh phone was placed out daily, and the remains of the previous one, bashed to pieces, was removed each day, in a black cloth.

"Good morning," the Mad Boss said, and we were both surprised with the sweetness of the greeting. The Mad Boss brow then furrowed again. The Mad Boss couldn't understand such niceness sent in my direction. The crystals were clearly working.

Then the Mad Boss paused. Something was not right. A gulp. Does not compute. Something building. Then, after the blockage was removed, another rage erupted, and exploded in my direction: "Rrrrrroaaaaaaaaaarghhhhhhhhhhh!" began the sentence, and off the Mad Boss went.

Oh well, the crystals worked with everyone else, and worked even with the Mad Boss, but only for about a minute. Ultimately, The Mad Boss was impervious to the power of the crystals. And that meant, sadly, that the fortune teller was going to be right in her predictions. Things really did get worse with The Mad Boss, who went even madder.

I had some sympathy for The Mad Boss, as The Mad Boss had bitten off more than any Mad Boss could chew, and the Mad Boss was under more pressure than any Mad Boss could handle. But my sympathy could not extend to the Mad Boss' treating everyone else as a doormat, as a Mad Boss coping mechanism.

And then I left, just as the place of my employment crashed into ruins. Again.

These are, of course, the edited highlights of twenty years of Middle-Class Hell working life.

We each have our own definition of Work Hell. Just add yours here [ ], and carry on for another thousand pages. You've got the idea.

Just to give some further observations of the horror of some other aspects of work.

1. Interviews. You get asked questions like, "Silence is golden – discuss." What has this got to do with anything? I went through one potty interview on Skype with two people in Spain over a dodgy internet connection for a legal job in London, as Spanish HR had to do the interview first and they were in Barcelona. Why? Couldn't someone have seen me in London, someone who actually understood the line of work I did? The link kept failing, they couldn't understand English, and my cat kept leaping onto the laptop and shoving its face into the camera, just to add its opinion. "That went well," I thought... I never heard back. Oh, and qualifications: you now need a

degree and tens of thousands of pounds of student debt for the same job that you didn't need any serious qualifications for thirty years ago, and which probably paid comparatively better than it does now.

2. Commuting. Going through Hell to get to somewhere unbearable. When it works. When it doesn't, the Hell is compounded. Strikes, leaves on the line, things breaking down, over-crowding, congestion, and the list of horrors goes on. For years, Beelzebub has governed commuting. By the time you get there, your sanity is freaked-out. That's before your day has started.

3. Teamwork bonding days, Christmas parties, management conferences, and all that stuff. I worked at one place where they were in the process of devising a company song, which included the words, "[insert organization name] you are the only thing that matters to me", which we had to sing at every management conference. No, just no. Or the words from a Senior Partner in one law firm I worked for, "You are my family." No, you're not. You are as mad as members of my family, you'd fit in, but you are not a member of it. Bugger off.

4. Appraisals. The forms go on and on and on and take ages to complete. They contain things like marks out of ten for, "teamwork, making a contribution, empathy, going the extra mile, being helpful, appreciating diversity". Nowhere is the question, "Can this person actually *do* the job?" Nowhere. HR Hell. If you take on more tasks and new lines of work, you get marked *down* whilst you are going up the learning curve, as you learn the new job, whilst still doing your old one. So you get marked *down* for actually doing more work. Hmm.

5. Salary reviews and bonuses. Here is a common one, "We have increased revenue and profit by thirteen per cent this year, but your pay increase is one per cent". Thanks. Bonuses

are often linked to completing certain objectives, so, if you complete them you get more bonus. So if you are rushed off your feet and don't complete them, you get less bonus. This makes no sense, except to HR. And the Old Lady, because she never does anything, gets her huge bonus regardless.

6. IT never works, anywhere. You are expected to perform to the highest standards, but when the IT system goes down, everyone just shrugs their shoulders, and no one in the IT department ever gets told off because everyone just expects IT to be crap.

7. Promotion. You are expected to jump through hoops and sweat blood to get a promotion. No point. If you threaten to resign, and they want to keep you, you get a promotion for which others are made to sweat blood. If you find another job, you automatically get a promotion to tempt you to go there. It's so easy. So why do organizations insist staff kill themselves to get promoted? This makes no sense, except to HR.

8. Work culture generally. It's all-pervasive that we have to flog ourselves to death to be judged successes. I once boarded a Continental Airlines flight with the Old Lady. She caused some degree of consternation when she saw the company logo and strapline on a doily on the back of her seat which read "*Work Hard. Fly Right®*". There was a hiss of steam as she exploded, and she waved her finger vigorously until a stewardess came over, and then off she ranted. "My dear," she warbled, her voice reaching a high-pitched shrill, as she reached boiling point, "Don't you lot tell me in your corporate logo to 'work hard'. I've barely lifted a finger in over a century! I don't intend to start working now just because some airline tells me to." She had a point. It's none of their business. The only time I ever saw the Old Lady move at anything more than a five-mile-a-fortnight shuffling lurch was when someone

at a party, who worked for a magic circle law firm, said, "I love my job". She actually *ran* out of the room. No one has ever seen that before, or since. In fact, it's not possible. Yet it happened.

9. Mad people and mad bosses.

10. Then, after putting you through all that, they just get sick of you one day, and throw you out.

On the subject of The Mad Boss, it's worth reflecting that The Mad Boss was normal once. But work had transformed this once mild-mannered individual into a screaming, vengeful wreck.

I asked the Old Lady about it.

"You always seem to maintain a certain poise at work when under pressure – how do you do that?" I enquired.

"Best thing is to do nothing dear, like me. Old Ladies survive in the world of work by doing nothing for forty years, whilst those career people who take it seriously, go potty. It's best to be an Old Lady, of an age, who does nothing. That's why I am still sane," she said.

One day in 2012 she turned to me, puzzled, "What's an e-mail?" she enquired. She waved a contraption around, "Because my work phone says I have five million of them, unread. I don't suppose any of them are important, do you, dear? I'll just ignore them and carry on regardless. If it's important, they'll send a telegram."

I leaned over and ventured, "It might be a good idea if you delete them…"

I took the rattling contraption from her withered hands and pressed "select all" for every e-mail. I handed it back to her. The "delete" button was large, red, inviting and wanted to be pressed.

"Just press the delete button, dear," I said gently, "and those five million e-mails will all be gone. They are clogging up your system anyway. Better out than in. Just press the delete button, dear…"

The Old Lady looked aghast, "Can I?" She went ashen. Her finger hovered over the "delete" button, as if it were a great moral decision, or the nuclear button, and then she went hysterical and frothy. "Oh dear, oh my word, how do I cope with this, how can I press that, what a decision, oh can I really do this… it's too much!"

"You just press one button, and they are all gone…"

She stiffened and looked horrified, "One button… ONE BUTTON… I don't press buttons dear… not at my age… press just one button… oh no, I'll get repetitive strain injury doing that. NEVER!" she yelled, almost manly. It echoed with volume and intensity.

And so it stayed.

Then, a year or two later, she turned up at the Club, and the same contraption fell out of her pocket and on to the floor. She looked at it in complete disgust. She clearly wasn't going to make the effort to pick that up. It just stayed on the floor for the whole evening.

After several hours, I nodded at the device on the floor. "How many work e-mails now, dear?"

"Fifteen million," she paused, then continued, "unread."

"Oh, better not start now then, dear. You'll injure yourself."

"Quite, dear," she said. "I've told work I'm due to have a seizure any day now, so I'm easing off in my responsibilities."

A man who thinks he is an Old Lady of one hundred and fifty-seven, who takes this kind of view about work, simply cannot be wrong about these things.

Domestics

One of the "joys" of being Middle-Class is employing other people.

It's basically one of the reasons for working (or not, in the case of the Old Lady), and spending your hard-earned cash just getting other people to… do things.

It's almost a status symbol in some circles, to boast how many more people you can employ than other Middle-Class people: employing people to do things that you can't, such as cleaning, and personal training at the gym.

I had high hopes for both, getting a cleaner and a personal trainer. Both would save hours in my life, literally hours in my time-starved life, as I worried about yet another place of employment I had joined crashing into ruins just after I got there.

After finally becoming a mortgage slave and buying my own place, I decided I needed a cleaner.

Now having a cleaner is one of those things the Middle-Classes do. But, in my case, I had something of a guilt complex, too, worried that they would be living on the breadline in some hovel somewhere, burning with envy, cleaning my tiny flat.

I needn't have worried.

In swooped this glorious, glamorous-looking lady whom I was interviewing to be my cleaner.

"Daaaahling!" she exclaimed, in a cut-glass English accent.

She was immaculately dressed, in an extremely expensive suit, and her hair was perfectly coiffured, standing on end and more huge than even Margaret Thatcher's hair-do at its most international-summit-domineering.

"Ermmm, have you come about the cleaning job?"

"Daaaahling."

"Oh good, well this is the place."

She took a large gin bottle from her designer bag, and took a huge, heavy swig.

"Daaaahling."

"Well anyway, is this alright? The flat…"

"Daaaahling."

I worked out that this clearly meant, "Yes."

She looked round again, took another swig of gin, and finally slurred something approaching speech. "It's a bit small, Daaaahling, not as big as my place, but you can't help being poor."

What a bitch! I liked her.

"And where do you live?" I asked.

"Penthouse. Further down the dock." I knew the building she was referring to. "Made a million out of my divorce, Daaaahling. Now I clean to keep myself occupied. I gossip with the rich owners too, if they are in; get some interior design tips, if they have taste, and we have coffee; then I tidy up, but just a little. I might put the cups in the dishwasher. They are pretty tidy, anyway, so I get paid to have a coffee morning. What's not to like?" She smiled pure poison.

She took another swig of gin and staggered. She was also pissed. But she also maintained her glamour and poise somehow.

"Daaaahling, I also work on the gin palaces." There are boats that go up and down the River Thames, which serve drinks and very expensive dinners, and which are known as the gin palaces. Or that's what she called them. "There was a party on one today. Good class of customer. Invited them all back to my place, and we're carrying on the party. I fitted them all into my flat, no problem."

I needed to see her place. To see what was going on in this woman's life.

But for the moment, I showed her round mine.

She saw the kitchen.

"Daaaahling, I can't clean work surfaces like that." She held up a finger, with an amazing diamond ring on it. "The diamond will scratch the work surface; I refuse to cause any damage to your apartment, and I can't get the ring off unfortunately."

I showed her the cleaning cloths.

"Daaaahling, I can't use cloths, and no to rubber gloves." She held up her fingers again. "See these nails?" They were very, very long and razor sharp. "I can't risk breaking these, I'm sorry. I can use a long-handled duster though. Anything long that I can lightly grip with my fingertips is fine, but I can't scrub, I'm sorry. I only clean places that require no scrubbing, anyway."

I showed her the vacuum cleaner and mop.

"Daaaahling, I can't use those. Ex-husband gave me a lower back problem, I can't bend down. If you get ones that require no bending or heavy pushing I might be able to use them, but I can't promise anything."

Then she looked at me sternly, ""Daaaahling, I will not use conventional cleaning products, full of chemicals, no way. Do you know the vapours they give off? Killers."

"So what do you use? What cleaning fluids are appropriate?" I asked.

She pulled out her bottle of gin from her posh handbag.

"Gin," she said, matter-of-factly.

"It's far better than white vinegar. I supply it free of charge; it's inclusive in the hourly rate," she purred.

My God, this woman also drank her own cleaning fluid on the job.

"You're hired," I said.

She then invited me to see her flat, and, oh, it was marvellous! It was vast and palatial. Three large bedrooms, and two dock-facing balconies, and the interior design choices suited her venom perfectly.

It was wonderful. I had a glamorous millionaire gin-soaked alcoholic cleaner who looked down on me, and never cleaned. I mean, this is "it".

Having pets whilst having a cleaner does tend to make two different worlds collide though. One, in theory, does the cleaning and the other trashes the place. Most people see no contradiction between these two, and they happily have both, and expect it to work out fine. As I discovered, having a pet and having a cleaner requires massive tolerance and patience. The cleaner requires massive amounts of attention and forgiveness, is generally high-maintenance, and often smashes things, usually of considerable value. The pet generally just sits there and causes no bother. Or it just eats everything, ensuring that there is never a spillage or a mess.

Both take up vast amounts of space on the sofa; the pet usually sleeps there, and, in the case of the Gin Soaked Alcoholic Cleaner, she'd usually just pass out.

I met a number of Burmese cats, owned by two sets of friends, and thought they were delightful. So I decided to make the flat less cold, and adopted a rescue cat, to bring some warmth to the place. I picked up a British Shorthair female from a rescue centre one fine, sunny day, called "Lily".

I expected a lovely, docile and gentle companion, as befitted the British Shorthair temperament, but she was the grumpiest thing I have ever encountered. Lily seemed to hate everyone. She wasn't feral or semi-feral, or anything of that description, she just hated everyone, and had a constantly grumpy expression, like Granny when confronted with an empty teapot and a dirty pinny. She simply glowered her way through life.

Then, suddenly, one day, she just started to wee on everything. Everything. And it was continuous. You could pick her up, squeeze her gently to see if there was any wee left inside, and, satisfied she was empty, you could pop her down, knowing she wouldn't wee on anything. She'd look at you, give an evil glint of her orange eyes, and then she'd start. And the wee was never-ending. She was medically fine. I had her checked out; she showed no signs of illness or stress. She saw a behavioural expert (*so* Middle-Class Hell) who drew a blank. She just decided to wee everywhere.

Nothing was safe. Sofas, beds, carpets, everything was drenched by the Pissing Pussy.

The Old Lady came round once, and I was embarrassed that the flat was starting to smell like an old British Rail urinal from the 1870s. You know the ones I mean – the old Victorian ones in the stations, that haven't been cleaned since 1950.

I warned the Old Lady in advance, "Bring wellies; the Pissing Pussy is particularly pissy today. Nothing is safe."

The Old Lady turned up and looked around the flat, simply not noticing the smell of the Pissing Pussy and her leakages. That surprised me, as I was expecting some barbed comment.

Then, amazingly, the Pissing Pussy stopped pissing. She just sat there looking at the Old Lady, curious and uncomprehending at what had just walked in.

The relief was palpable that she'd stopped leaking.

Then, the Pissing Pussy bounced forward and leapt onto the Old Lady's lap.

This was the first sign of human affection she had ever shown. I was amazed. Maybe this would make her settle down. Maybe she'd stop leaking everywhere.

At first, the Pissing Pussy looked content and even purred when the Old Lady extended a bony finger, and stroked it gently on the head. The Old Lady had cats, but, as befitting her, one had got so old and bony that it was uncomfortable even to touch it, as the poor thing was all nobbly and simply rattled with old age.

Then the Pissing Pussy cocked her head and gave the evil look I had become accustomed to. After not leaking for about three minutes, she had filled up to a voluminous size, like a Pufferfish, and I knew what was going to happen. She was going to mark the Old Lady as territory. The Pissing Pussy then relaxed and unleashed the most enormous wee that I'd ever seen her emit, all over the Old Lady.

I reacted in terror, "Get up, get up, you're going to get soaked, dear."

But the Old Lady just carried on; she sat still, tea in hand, chuntering on about the weather or the hideous week at work she'd just had, utterly oblivious to the Pissing Pussy gushing all over her.

After the Pissing Pussy had finished, she gave another look of contempt and strutted off.

I looked at the Old Lady, aghast, "Are you alright, dear," I asked, "your lap is soaked in piss."

The Old Lady looked down at her mid-section, rather startled, "Am I really? I hadn't noticed." She squelched around. "At my age though, this is normal, I'm used to it. I do it myself about three times a day." She looked at the Pissing Pussy. "What a lovely cat, she's so like me," and she carried on with her tea and her monologue.

As you can imagine, the Gin-Soaked Alcoholic Cleaner did not take to the Pissing Pussy. They would glare at each other across the room, and it was impossible to say which had the most vicious stare.

Eventually, the Pissing Pussy was happily rehomed. She wanted to be on her own, at the end of the day, and is very happy on a farm with minimal contact with anything, pissing into the wind by all accounts.

The Gin-Soaked Alcoholic Cleaner was ecstatic. She'd won. I concluded that she was the kind of cleaner that always had to win.

The personal trainer whom I employed was an altogether more mild-mannered character, but he had his own rather different "problem".

I decided to hire a personal trainer as I had been training in the gym for five days a week, for about ten years, and had decided that now might be a good time to see whether I actually knew what I was doing, as I sustained injury after injury and creaked more than the Old Lady when I moved.

I went to my local gym, to see which of the trainers could take me on, and the girl behind reception beamed, "We have someone new, I'm sure he'd like to meet you."

"Wonderful," I thought. I was genuinely excited at the thought, but was a little put off by tales of people at the gym who had experienced the Satanic yoga teacher, and wondered whether I'd got anyone similar.

This Yoga teacher was a psycho, by all accounts. Most yoga types are quiet, gentle and serene, but this guy had jet black hair, jet black evil eyes, and a jet black character to match. Once you'd signed the exclusion of liability form, exempting the gym from liability for physical injury, he had you. Nothing could stop him inflicting as many bendy injuries as possible. He had an evil glint in his eye, and a menacing chuckle, as someone snapped something doing one of his poses, and screamed in agony. He would end every session, not with the usual, "Sat Nam," (though it has many meanings it can be translated as "I recognize the divinity within you"), but with a slight alteration: he'd mutter "Satan" under his lips. Then he'd give an evil smile, as he soaked up the groaning and screams all around, before sending your remains on their way. Then he'd spent the rest of his day in worship to Satan.

So, I was relieved when I walked into the main gym area and met my new personal trainer, who beamed at me with perfect white teeth. "Hullo, I'm Pug," he shouted across the gym floor, very friendly in his manner, not at all like the Satanic Yoga Teacher, and then he started to walk towards me.

This seems promising, I thought. But there was something curious about the way he walked. He had his head turned towards me and he was still beaming, but he was walking towards me with his back to me. It was kind of like *The*

Exorcist, where that possessed girl's head turns as she cackles madly.

I'm not sure how, but he managed to extend a hand and still have his face to me with his back turned. It was like some freaky yoga manoeuvre, but he managed it with ease.

"So it's Pug, is it?"

He honked, "Yeh". Honk honk, again.

"Short for 'Pouglas'. Meant to be 'Douglas', but my birth certificate went wrong." He snorted and honked again. He was quite endearing really.

We started to train, but he was clearly having some difficulty.

"I want you to do this special type of exercise, but I'm really sorry I can't get into the right position to show you..." He grunted uncomfortably, and I noticed that he still had his back to me.

"Are you alright?" I asked. "You don't seem to be able to face forwards."

He looked shy and uncomfortable.

And then he said, "Well I think I can trust you; you seem OK." He turned around to face me.

I looked him up and down. "Dear God!" I exclaimed.

"I know..." He looked sheepish. "Sorry about this. It hardly ever goes down."

"You've got a constant erection?"

He nodded enthusiastically.

"Basically, I'm straight," he said, "but just about anything sets me off." He honked, "Once something sets me off it's uncontrollable for ages. It goes down now and again. It's a real problem on a crowded train, it causes an obstruction in the doors, and people keep slapping me thinking I'm poking them, but I can't help it..."

He suddenly looked very vulnerable again.

I ventured a suggestion, "Would you like to go into a quiet corner and take care of it? I will wait here for you."

"Already done that," and he groped it manfully. "Five times a day usually. I've drained it four times already today."

"Its eight a.m."

"It's a particularly bad day today."

He looked crestfallen. "Plus," he continued, "I've constantly got to hide it... There was this woman in here yesterday; she caught sight of it through my gym shorts, and she screamed." He tried to shove it somewhere comfortable, but it had a mind of its own, and just protruded hugely and voluminously from somewhere else. "And, I'm sorry to say, it's hard to show customers certain exercises. I just can't get into certain positions without snapping it."

"That's not nice," I sympathised.

"Oh and one more thing..." he said. "A bit delicate, but it gets itchy. I can't scratch it myself, as people think I'm about to expose myself, so do you mind if I use you as a scratch post? Like a cat, you know, that rubs itself against its scratch post. I don't mean anything by it... just the odd rub; I won't poke your eye out or anything..."

What on earth was I agreeing to? "Well, OK, then... just the odd rub – but not too vigorously; we are in public."

"You won't notice it!" he beamed.

I looked down at it again. "I bet I will."

He wasn't a bad trainer, except for the following problems: (i) he couldn't get into any key exercise position because of his rigid genital monstrosity; (ii) he hardly ever turned up to early-morning appointments, due to either being hungover, or his erection being particularly bad that morning, rendering him immobile; and (iii) we got on like a house on fire, just chatted for our whole training session, and did virtually no exercise.

I called the Old Lady about it, and we agreed that I had unwittingly found my own version of Stud, but God help us if we ever put them in the same room together.

And so Middle-Class Hell continued. I slaved away and paid for an alcoholic cleaner who never cleaned, I had a Pissing Pussy that wrecked everything, and an erect personal trainer with whom I never did any exercise. Middle-Class Hell.

Why wouldn't my cleaner, personal trainer or pet behave like everyone else's? But that wouldn't have been any fun, would it?

Housing

One of the joys of being Middle-Class is having a better house, or flat, than poor people.

Like all of these supposed joys, it all seems to be "in theory".

On arriving in London, I had at least a decent wage to get something reasonably OK.

My first venture into the property market seemed to go well; then the curse of Oxford and York came back to haunt me, in that I ended up, yet again, with a bunch of "colourful characters".

I moved into a house share in North London, at the time when I began work as a trainee solicitor.

A married couple owned the house, and they lived in a sectioned-off lounge, bedroom and kitchen on the ground floor. The rest of the house was rented out to tenants. There were three large bedrooms on the second and third floors, all with a bathroom, and a separate lounge and kitchen for the tenants. It was all very well thought out.

They had two darling German Shepherd dogs: one male, one female, both of whom ran around in the yard.

The male was an absolutely lovely dog, with whom I really bonded, who just sat there whimpering when I used to sit in front of him on the floor, and kiss his nose.

I used to think he liked me, but, looking back he was probably whimpering in terror at the thought of another nose lick. Have you ever noticed that a dog thinks it has the right to lick you with free abandon and you are just expected to take it, but if you lick the dog, it looks at you really strangely, as if to say, "Why are you licking me?"

The female German Shepherd was an odd creature, and I was told she had "issues", as the house owners used to feed her with anti-depressants every day. She was apparently a bit barking (pun), and the only way to get her to act normal, for a female German Shepherd, was to give her a Valium or something once a day.

She was freaked out, as the male constantly tried to hump her all the time, in the yard. She started out normalish, but once they had introduced the male as a puppy, she went loopy as a result of his advances.

The Old Lady visited me for an Old Lady afternoon tea in the yard one day, to check out my new lodgings, on a lovely summer day. The yard was just a large concrete area, sadly, as the owners had decided that the dogs would trash any normal garden, so had covered the area in concrete.

But I managed to get a little table and chairs out there, and to cover them in the best floral tablecloth I could find, to keep the Old Lady happy, and make her feel at home. Just as we sat down to an Old Lady cup of tea and an Old Lady scone, she was forced to bear witness to what was the third copulation between the two canines that day. Her summer bonnet and pince nez fell off with the excitement.

Three hours later, after they'd finished, she mopped her brow, and remarked, "Now you know what I have to live with dear; that beast performs exactly like my Stud, my lodger, except that Stud is far worse. Oh yes, I've heard it! The constant rutting! I shove the eiderdown in my ears at night, and even that does no good. An Old Lady at my age, in a nylon nightie, shouldn't be subjected to that, but I am! And you try baking an Old Lady cake in the kitchen, with that going on upstairs. Impossible!" She threw the scone down in disgust at her inability to enjoy an Old Lady life without being interrupted by never-ending copulation.

I enquired about Stud's habits. "Is there anyone with him?"

"Oh no, dear. It's just him with a bottle of my lavender and camomile hand lotion, and a box of my man-size tissues. He goes through a box a week, but frankly, dear, it's all too much at my age."

The monstrous shagging between the two dogs became so frequent, and irrepressible, that the whole neighbourhood became jealous. The yard was surrounded by a lot of other houses, so it seemed that the whole street could peer in to the goings on in the concrete yard.

Once the dogs started, you could hear the whole neighbourhood flinging open windows, to gaze open-mouthed at the spectacle below.

Aged husbands and wives would peer out of the window, looking wistfully at the dogs in the yard, thinking of a bygone age. Young couples would gaze at each other amorously as they howled into the night, while singletons would grasp desperately at the lavender and camomile hand lotion, and a box of man-sized tissues.

Gradually, the dogs' humping became an issue, after they spawned so many births in the neighbourhood over the next nine months. You couldn't walk down the street without being accosted by prams and baby things, and all because of these two German Shepherds bonking away, encouraging all others to do the same. The place became its own Babylon.

Then, finally, after one performance of Romeo and Juliet too many, the curtain came down, and my landlords castrated the male. The female couldn't take any more.

I remember coming home to see him looking forlorn after this chopping, sitting in his basket, so I gave him a kiss on his nose.

That seemed to perk him up, and then, two days later, he was humping away happily as if nothing had happened, even though he was minus a few bits and bobs.

"Stud is the same," the Old Lady would huff and puff, shaking her head in incomprehension. "I've castrated him many a time, but he still keeps going."

The poor female dog was too far gone by this point though, and, even post-castration, she still needed her Valium. After that, she still seemed to pass her time quite happily, though a little sorely.

It was a perfect marriage, in the end. He was castrated, and thus incapable; and she was off her face on Valium. They lived like any normal human couple.

But that also summed up the couple who lived there, who were living in their own liberal paradise. On rent payment day you'd wander down to their floor below, and they'd be doing a dance around the living room, high on something and wearing bed sheets, flapping about to some Buddhist chant in the background, with the two German Shepherds looking quizzically on.

One of the tenants in the house, though, was to disappear into the night... suddenly, and for unexplained reasons.

He was a hairdresser, and used to do the landlady wife's hair. They did it when they were both high so she'd come away looking like a Muppet.

But the High Hairdresser had run up huge debts, and the bailiffs turned up one day, only for him to have done a runner the night before. No one heard of him ever again.

I moved out shortly after, but neither the absconding High Hairdresser, the religious fundamentalists, nor the Burka hair-do man could have prepared me for the Fat Banker.

I looked into an area called Surrey Quays, in Docklands, in 1998, for a new place, after I'd decided to leave the house of free love, castration and Valium.

I found Surrey Quays after looking at a tube map and finding this quaint tube line called the East London Line.

It seemed to be the shortest tube line on the Underground, and ran from Whitechapel to New Cross and New Cross Gate.

In other words, it ran from nowhere to nowhere, but it passed through a place called Surrey Quays, in South East London. It was a former dockyard that hadn't yet become gentrified. In fact, back then, there was only one tower in Canary Wharf; it was a long, long way from the sky-scraper metropolis that it was to become.

I arrived there just to see what it was like. Curiously, I found it rather nice. Regeneration was just happening, but, amazingly it had vast, vast docks, that hadn't been filled in, and developers were only just moving in to build flats and associated infrastructure into the place. But the docks were working, and boat houses and sailing clubs existed all around the area. And it was phenomenally cheap.

We forget the concept of London's being cheap just before the turn of the Millennium, but it was.

I found an advert for a three-bedroom flat, with a gym, a swimming pool in the basement, and a balcony with a river view. With bills included, this was £297 a month for my room. This was simply unthinkable later, as prices escalated.

The only downside was that the flat was occupied by this chap who became the Fat Banker.

At first the Fat Banker possessed charm and sophistication. He was also thin to start with.

The fat bit came later.

Everything seemed normal, in fact, perfect, on the surface, as he just seemed the embodiment of charm, wealth and class on every level... and he worked for the London office of one of the best private client banks in the world.

Until one day when he came home, rather sheepish, and said that he'd been refused access to the bank; that he had, in fact, been marched off the premises.

It turned out that he was a bit of a conman, and had been wandering around the bank proclaiming that he had the Sultan of Brunei as a client, when, in fact, he didn't. In fact, he didn't have any clients.

After he was frogmarched out of the bank, he decided as a consolation to take a long holiday in Morocco. He came back from this holiday wearing a large white muumuu that went from head to foot, and was simply vast. Then he started to eat corpulent quantities of pizza, Häagen Dazs ice cream, and full-sugar Coke, and he just expanded, and expanded, and expanded, until the muumuu was simply filled with this vast carcass.

He had a pair of elasticated fat-pants, I recall, but, as he ballooned, the fat-pant elastic snapped under the strain, until all that could contain him in the end was the enormous white muumuu. It had turned out to be a smart, forward-thinking investment. It was the only decent investment the Fat Banker ever made. Just under a decade later, he crashed the banks, simply by walking through the door.

Now it would be absolutely appropriate to sympathise with someone who has lost their job in these circumstances and, who has, in sorrow, gorged themselves into a vast fatness.

That's just therapeutic.

But the Fat Banker was slightly different.

Rather than trying to get a new job on the same money, and to acquire an honest client base, the Fat Banker decided that begging, borrowing, and stealing was the way to go. In fact, at bottom, he'd always wanted to be corrupt, a sort of cross between Richard Nixon and Gordon Gekko in a muumuu.

As the Old Lady always says, "Always listen to your winkle about someone; if you think they are up to no good, take action accordingly."

Yes, we all know that the Old Lady does absolutely nothing, but at least there is some honesty to her complete laziness. She turns up. She makes some sort of effort, after a fashion, to go in to do an honest day's work, even if she doesn't get past nine thirty a.m. And there is an odd spark of usefulness every decade, among the befuddlement.

Yet the Fat Banker really had no redeeming qualities. I saw him cheat, crook and swindle a lot of people with money, to pay his rent and fund his lifestyle after he'd been sacked for incompetence and dishonesty.

And by the end of it, the fatness was so vast that all you could see, if you peered underneath the muumuu, were a pair of castors, as he wheeled himself around. And, for some strange reason, he started packing belongings into plastic bin bags and just left them in the lounge. Quite what was going on was unclear. It was an odd sight to witness, this sea of black bin bags and the Fat Banker, beached on the sofa in his enormous white muumuu.

It was too much.

Thankfully, in 2001, I exchanged contracts on a flat, and finally, finally, moved out into my own place.

My first place was a tiny two-bedroom two-bathroom flat in Surrey Quays. It was neglected, and the day I moved in, the oven door fell off, and the boiler gave way and leaked everywhere. I had to spend a reasonable sum of money putting two new bathrooms and a new kitchen in, to make the place habitable.

I found an absolutely fantastic bathroom fitter, who I used to do two new bathrooms; but sadly, and foolishly, I didn't use him for the kitchen refit, which, for such a tiny space, turned into months of pure Middle-Class Hell.

You simply haven't lived Middle-Class Hell unless you have had a kitchen refit that goes horribly wrong.

I moved in late 2001, and started the kitchen refit in early 2002. It went on for nearly a year.

I used a firm called MFI, which gained notoriety in its day. It went bust in 2008, because everything it touched seemed to turn into disaster, including my life. But in all the commercials everything looked nice, and I heard good word of mouth about them, so I thought... why not...?

The Old Lady waxed lyrical about the Middle-Class joy of putting in a new kitchen, so I thought that this was going to be fun. She was, after all, never wrong.

This chap from MFI came along to do the fitting and give me costings, and all seemed to go OK.

But there was something about him that I didn't like... hmm, my winkle was exploding, with the same instinct I had learned in my dealings with the Fat Banker. I didn't trust him for some reason. He had the same air about him as the evil twin Nazi-Granny, many a year ago. I decided to keep an eye on him…

Plus, he also looked like a Baboon, as he hissed and spat a lot, and had a big fat red arse poking out of his shorts. He seemed generally bad tempered, and lolloped around on all fours.

The first day of the fit-out seemed to begin fine, as the Baboon brought another load of hairy friends with him, and ripped the old kitchen out.

Then the washer-dryer got delivered, but the Baboon hadn't measured the space properly, so it didn't fit. It was an integrated unit, and he'd built housing for a non-integrated unit, so the door wouldn't fit on it. Oh well, never mind, I'm not that bothered, though I could imagine the Old Lady going into meltdown at this.

When I turned the washer-dryer on, the Baboon had also forgotten to take the screws holding the drum in place out of the back of the washer-dryer. Rather like the woman with the house full of knickers in Hartlepool, the washer-dryer then went on a rampage around the kitchen as it washed (in homage to knicker lady) a particularly large load of underpants, smashing into and cracking the newly constructed units.

Oh dear. New units to replace the smashed-up ones would take three weeks to turn up, but they would at least give me a new washer-dryer in the meantime.

Arranging deliveries is always hell, have you noticed?

"We tried to deliver, but no one was in," someone at the end of the phone will say.

At this point, we all protest along the following lines. "But you came on Monday at eleven a.m. when I was at work. Most of the population is at work then. You have my phone number, you could have called to arrange delivery. You've gone to the expense of trying to deliver it, and, because no one was there, you've wasted your time, and I will have to try and have it delivered again. I'm not being unreasonable, but would it have been better all round to have arranged delivery by calling me, rather than delivering it out of the blue?"

"Well, it's policy that we just pop round and try to deliver it without telling you."

"What? You just come round unannounced at the least likely time of the week that anyone is going to be there?"

"Yes. It's industry practice."

"What about calling ahead, or delivering at weekends when people are *likely* to be there? You're meant to be making this easy for me…"

"Oh no, we can't do that! You have to fit in with us."

"So, when can you deliver?"

"I can give you a delivery slot of nine to five, Monday to Friday."

"But I'm at work!"

"That's all we have. And don't get exasperated, sir. And we need to charge you a £20 non-delivery charge for the first time you weren't there… that was most inconsiderate of you…"

"But I didn't know you were coming!"

"Well, that's no excuse… don't you have an elderly relative permanently at hand for this sort of thing? That's the only reason I keep mine alive."

"No. Because they're all dead, or insane! Which, incidentally, is what I will be if this goes on for much longer."

Finally, I give in. "Oh, I will take a day off. Deliver it next Tuesday. What hours can you give me?"

"Nine a.m. to five p.m., sir."

"What, all day? Can't you give me a rough estimate, like 'in the morning'?"

"We can't do that, sir, I'm sorry."

"What if I need to go out?"

"Feel free, but you will probably miss us."

So you stay in. All day. But, at some point during that day something inevitably emerges that requires you to go out. It's unavoidable.

For instance, you discover that everything edible has, overnight, gone off, become mould-encrusted, and looks like a dead Muppet. So you have to go out to buy something in. Or a neighbour's cat or child has got itself stuck somewhere, and you are the only one that can rescue it. Or the fire alarm goes off. Or the house itself collapses. Or, as in some horror film, you are lured out into the night, on your own, to search for something, in the darkness, with every sane member of the audience screaming at the telly, 'For God's sake, don't leave the house'. And, of course, the character is usually garrotted in some winter woodland in the night, for being stupid enough to leave the house.

And you miss your delivery. And, possibly, are also garrotted at the same time.

We all know this. You have to seal yourself in hermetically. But you just know, know, that it is going to fail, and that something will eventually succeed in luring you out of the house for two wafer-thin minutes, when some delivery van will come trundling down the street.

And when you come back, you see a little paper note: "Sorry you were out. We came to deliver. You said you would be in all day, but you lied. Please call this number to re-arrange delivery, and next time be considerate enough to take the day off work, or get an elderly relative actually to be here. You will be charged £40 for this attempted re-delivery, which was unsuccessful as a result of your thoughtlessness and inability to organise your life."

You call the helpline. If I call now, I thought, they can call the delivery man, and he might be close enough to turn round, and deliver.

You call.

First, you are greeted with, "Please visit our website..." spoken impossibly slowly.

This is then followed by an advert or some rambling apology about something not working. And screeching background music that destroys your hearing and your sanity.

Then you might get diverted to some bingo or sex chat line.

Then, when you get back, a recorded message goes on forever, "We'd like to congratulate Mrs Haemorrhoid of Hartlepool for winning our competition question on Prince Philip... your fantastic prize of a month's supply of pinnies is on its way to you now, but first please announce yourself..."

This is then followed by a list of menu options, none of which have any relevance to anyone, anywhere.

You pick the one that you think is most appropriate to you.

Which can then be followed by another recorded voice: "I'm awfully sorry, we can't help with that. Please go to our website. Goodbye."

And it hangs up. No chance of going back to the main menu. You're cut off. So you have to ring back and go through the whole dreary process again.

You are screaming in desperation, "I just want to talk to a real person... please..."

Finally, you get through to the menu options again.

As you ponder which one to choose, the line goes dead. Then, after a pause, it suddenly springs back to life again. "If you want to talk to our customer representatives, please press #." Of course, this option only comes up after an age, because they want to select the earlier menu options and cut you off, because, really, they don't want to speak to you at all.

You might be asked to enter a username and password.

Voice recognition software inevitably mangles this into a complete mess, and you get cut off again.

But back to user names and passwords.

I have lost count of the number of usernames and passwords I have.

And because some organisations insist on having different password and username requirements, you cannot have the same username or password for all your accounts. You are basically not allowed to have the usernames and passwords that you can actually remember. You are forced to come up with ones that are impossible to remember, and are invalid, unless they have the following characters in them: "* o #?!^~ $`\~".

So you end up with about fifty different passwords and usernames, none of which you have any recollection of. And, naturally, you are made to feel like a complete idiot when you can't remember some password which you were forced to dream up two years ago, for a service you probably didn't need then, and never expected to use again.

And every time you try to access your account, and fail, you have to set up another password, which you can't remember, and so the process gets even more lunatic.

You could write them all down... I know someone who did, and then they got burgled and lost the lot; but the burglars had a great time gaining access to their whole life.

Gradually, it becomes impossible to access any account you have, as a result of the sheer volume of different usernames and passwords you have.

You find yourself saying, "Can't I just have usernames and passwords I can remember for all my accounts?"

If you do get through this morass, there is then usually a message along the lines of, "Please wait fifty thousand years to be connected to one of our operatives. However, you are actually next in the queue. Calls may be recorded."

Lots of crackling. It's taking an age to route through to some call centre in the middle of nowhere.

Finally an inaudible voice comes over the phone. You can't understand a word. It could be Glasgow or India, it really doesn't matter.

"Good evening, madam," says the barely audible, unintelligible accent. They then read through this impossibly long script, because they will be fired if they don't. And it drives you up the wall, because you just want to get to the point.

"My name is mister... not madam, but that's OK. Please, no more of that script. It's late afternoon here. I can barely hear a word, where are you speaking from?"

"The North Pole, madam. Very cheap labour here. Sorry for the long wait, madam. We are understaffed today. It is very cold. All my colleagues have frozen to death. I am the only one left. I die soon too. But I help you first."

"I'm very sorry to hear about your impending death, but could you help me? I'm calling about a delivery. Here is my reference number... can you look me up and help me with the delivery, please?"

"I'm very sorry, but I can't hear reference number. Line frozen. Very bad. Are you Mrs Haemorrhoid of Hartlepool, calling about month's supplies of pinnies? Congratulations, you are very clever regarding Mr Prince Philip. Many congratulations."

"No, I'm not Mrs Haemorrhoid of Hartlepool, but I think I know her. I don't think she will be collecting the pinnies, though, she's probably dead by now. How long have you been waiting for her to call? I noticed the recorded message."

"Message running for twenty years. But good to hear from you Mrs Haemorrhoid."

"No, no, she's dead."

"You kill her? For pinnies?"

"No... no... look, I'm calling about a delivery of a washer-dryer..."

"You want to wash pinnies?"

Just say anything by now, "Yes, yes, me wash pinnies. In memory of Mrs Haemorrhoid."

"Ah good, madam."

I explained about the failed delivery of the washer-dryer.

"It's just possible that the deliveryman is still in the area. It's taken a while to get through to you, but it's just possible he is still there and could re-deliver."

"I check... oh yes, our GPS says he's round the corner from you, having tea break. No more deliveries to do. Finished early. Literally round the corner from you, in his van."

"Great, can you drop him a line and get him to deliver, please? It will be really easy, and far better than re-arranging."

"Oh no, cannot do that. Delivery failed. That's all there is to it. No exceptions; you very inconsiderate for not being in. Now we have to re-arrange... plus Baboon man never goes back."

"You know the Baboon? Even in the North Pole?"

"Everyone know Baboon man. I take all the customer complaints about his red-arsed incompetence."

"I can't arrange another delivery now, as I have to clear taking another day off at work."

"Oh... then you pay storage charge on top of failed delivery fee, and another re-delivery fee."

"Please, no... oh look, OK, let's arrange another delivery day."

We arrange a day, in the hope that I can take yet another day's leave.

And then, "We have to give pinnies to someone... I arrange delivery day with you to get pinnies... you need to wash pinnies, I send you pinnies."

"No... no... no... no... I don't even have a kitchen... I just have a pile of rubble, a load of broken cabinets and a Baboon for a kitchen fitter. I can't take organising another delivery day, just deliver the pinnies with the washer dryer..."

"Oh no, separate delivery day needed!" Then there was a crash, followed by a howling arctic blast. "I'm very sorry, madam. Roof blown off call centre. Freezing wind and snow. I die now, sir. Please rate our level of helpfulness today."

Eventually, delivery day arrived three weeks after the old washer dryer had careered around the flat in a frenzy, and with an explosive clang, had finally expired.

To make sure that everything was organised correctly, I called another call centre, to check that the proposed delivery was all in order. The call centre was somewhere in the middle of a war zone. Yet again, it was impossible to make anything out, as the sound of bullets whizzed through the building, and the sound of someone's dying scream, in all its cadences, echoed down the receiver. For my life, I stressed, at some length, "I'm three floors up with no lift. I'm taking the day off work, please please please turn up with the washer dryer, as I can't take a holiday now, as I'm using up the rest of my leave on this kitchen refurb, and I've been driven to screaming distraction!"

A shell landed with a huge CRUMMPH.

"Where is your call centre? Are you alright?" I bellowed down the line.

"Arab Spring Call Centre. Call centre opened to encourage peace initiative and democracy. All gone badly wrong. Now war zone…"

And with that, the place went up, but not before the delivery had been logged.

Then, later in the day, Baboon turned up with a lorry. Delivery arrived, and I was here to collect it.

"I've got yer new washer-dryer. Sorry about the delay. We keep losing our call centres," said Baboon.

The Gin-Soaked Alcoholic Cleaner had been doing all my washing but had apparently lost most of it, as it blew off her balcony into the dock, so I was desperate to get the washer-dryer going.

"How many of them are you? To get it to the third floor, all stairs, and no lift, remember?" I asked.

"Just me," proclaimed the Baboon, as he lifted himself off all fours and beat his chest.

"Are you sure you can carry that?"

"No."

"Then what's it doing here?"

"I was told to deliver it," said the Baboon. "And I have. I've driven it into the car park".

"But what about getting it three floors up into the flat and installing it?"

"That's the job of the bloke who looks like an orangutan… he's coming tomorrow. He installs."

"Ok, you drive it here, he installs, what about getting it up the stairs?"

"We don't have anyone to do that. All I was told to do was drive it here… and he installs." Then he produced a clip board and pen. "Will you sign for it, guv?"

I had to reject it, of course, and face the prospect of going through the call centre yet again.

And then he suddenly exclaimed, "Oh, there's another problem… I forgot to include a sink in the kitchen design."

"What? How can I have a kitchen without a sink?"

"Yeah, there's no sink, and we have a six week wait on sinks…"

"How long have you worked at MFI?"

"Two years."

"And how many kitchens have you installed, signed off and completed in two years?"

"None," he said.

Adding everything together, this meant that my kitchen, about the size of a small portable television, was going to take nearly a year to complete.

Then Baboon, defying predictions of his incompetence, said, "I can run to B&Q to get a sink for you, and you can pay me for it."

"Brilliant!" I exclaimed. Things were finally looking up.

As the new kitchen units were about to arrive (but still no washer-dryer), Baboon lolloped into the flat one day with a new sink clamped into his mouth. His jaw relaxed and it fell onto the floor, with a clang.

"Got it!" It looked awfully cheap, utterly impractical, and about the size of a dog bowl, but by that stage I was grateful for small mercies.

"Two hundred and fifty quid, mate."

"What… what… what… for that? A bit much, but if you give me a receipt I will pay you."

His face went as red as his Baboon backside, "Ah, think I lost the receipt, but it's two hundred and fifty quid…"

Hmmmm something fishy, I thought. I went to B&Q a day or so later, found the same sink for £50, and got a print-off receipt so that I could demonstrate that it was the same model.

I would happily have given Baboon far more than it cost for his trouble, but I wasn't happy about such blatant dishonesty.

As I'd caught him red-handed (and arsed), he failed to turn up for a few days. I called the store to tell them what had happened, and to ask for a new fitter as he wasn't turning up. I got a call a day or so later, and Baboon ranted down the phone that they'd sacked him. I wasn't the only customer with a problem, it seemed, and the weight of the complaints meant that they finally chucked him out of the zoo.

He refused to return the keys to my flat and said that he'd handed them over to a criminal mastermind gang who had a habit of torturing their victims in the sink. At least they'd got one, as he'd run off with the replacement sink as his parting shot.

I did at least have kitchen units in place. I had plug sockets, after a fashion, as the plug sockets were connected up but just sort of hung out of the wall, in a health and safety disaster waiting to happen. Other than that, the flat was a complete catastrophe, with boxes of stuff all over the place and dust, dust, dust everywhere.

And still no washer-dryer… Granny was becoming more incensed by the day, and advised me, all-knowing, that none of this would have happened if only I'd ordered a top loading twin tub, and mangle.

Expecting a swift resolution now that the Baboon had been fired, I had a phone call with a store manager that sent everything from bad to worse.

"Well, all our teams are booked out, so we have to treat your kitchen as a new order. That means that it's at the back of the queue. As you know, it's a three-month waiting list from order to getting anyone on site to fit. As you've gone to the back of the queue, I'm afraid you will have to wait another three months to completion. Well, four, actually, as it takes another month to cut the granite for your work top."

I just sat there, my head in my hands. This wasn't supposed to happen. This isn't like the commercials. In the commercials, all of your friends come round and laugh and giggle in the kitchen, and gape in amazement at soft close doors with lots of "ohhhs" and "ahhhs", usually followed by a marriage and perfect looking children, all because of a new kitchen.

This wasn't how it was supposed to be! But Middle-Class Hell dictates otherwise.

Then the Gin-Soaked Alcoholic Cleaner came round with a load of my washing, and to do the cleaning, and flipped her lid. "That's it," she slurred. It had been a particularly heavy morning on the gin, and whilst she couldn't string a sentence together, she looked as glamorous as ever. "I can't clean in this mess. It's too much. I can't wander into a place like this in my Escada suit, what will people think. I'm sorry, but you're not making the grade in terms of the customer I keep."

She fell like a drunken marine onto the sofa and fished around for her bottle of gin in her Prada handbag. She raised the bottle to her lips and missed completely, sending a torrent of gin over what remained of the sofa; the torrent actually, miraculously, cleared away several layers of dust, as it dribbled down the armrest. Otherwise, what was a brand-new sofa just looked like an old judge's wig from the seventeenth century, after months of devastation by kitchen refit dust. She pulled herself up and lurched out, "I will come back and clean (a) when the kitchen is finished; and (b) after someone else has first cleaned this up."

The only person who did have a whale of a time was Pug, as he could come round and shove his knob in the open electrical sockets and give himself a thrilling electric knob shock.

Finally, finally, after this had gone on for a year, the kitchen from hell was finally finished. Finally! The sink fell out of its casing in the work surface the moment I put some water in it, but hey, it was expected, and easily mended. I had of course written a nineteen-page letter of complaint to the directors of MFI plc, which I sent to their home addresses, as they were listed on Companies House in those days. You can't do this anymore, but it gave me great satisfaction at the time, and I think I got some compensation and the promise of a slot in their "Satisfied Customers" magazine, which involved a picture of me looking old and haggard after all the strain, and shoving up two fingers at my new kitchen. They didn't print it.

They went bust five years later, of course.

But, oh dear, Middle-Class home ownership wasn't going terribly well. The Old Lady was fine, but I wasn't. Why couldn't my life be more like hers?

It's not as if buying and selling the places is any easier, either.

They say that moving house is one of the most stressful things you can do. After going through the property conveyancing process in the UK, if you survive it, you long for death.

After each occasion you say, "Never again."

And then, a couple of years later, you forget the pain, decide you'd like a better place, and do the whole thing all over again. And you shout and scream at the pain and terror of it all and wonder why you bothered.

Now, as you will recall, I hadn't had a great deal of success in the conveyancing field, when, as a trainee solicitor, I tried to sell that house which exploded days before exchange of contracts.

It didn't get any better when I was the buyer.

I started looking just at the point when the London market really started to boom, in about 2000-2001. There were people who said that it was a short-lived boom, that affordability had been stretched to its limits, and that things would crash shortly thereafter. We all know how that prediction went.

The first thing to deal with is estate agents. The Old Lady had a wonderful experience there. She got this strapping twenty-odd-year-old, who wore impossibly tight trousers, and the Old Lady simply couldn't focus every time he took her to view a property, as she just got distracted by all his bulges.

She came away from one viewing wide-eyed in astonishment.

"I've just put an offer in on that place I've just looked at, dear," she said.

I asked, "What's it like?"

"I don't know!" she looked bemused. "I couldn't take my eyes off the estate agent's bulges through those tight trousers. Ever so distracting, dear. I'm afraid it made me so giddy, dear, that I've just put an offer in for three quarters of a million pounds. I don't know where I'll get that from, and I'm utterly clueless as to what the place is like, but never mind. Still, I'll find out what it's like on the day I move in. I hope I like it – if I don't, well that's just Middle-Class Hell."

She moved in eventually, and hated it.

The estate agent was definitely straight, he just seemed to take an unusual interest in this Old Lady in her mid-fifties/mid-one-hundred-and-fifties, and asked her out for a drink.

The estate agent got on like a house on fire with Stud, which used to lead to drunken naked water fights between the two on the Old Lady's patio. She'd sit on the edge of the patio in her rocking chair, watching this naked wrestling spectacle, lunging backwards and forwards in so much excitement that she'd drop her knitting.

She had no sex drive left, due to the blood pressure tablets, but she admitted that watching a spectacle like this did clear the odd blockage once in a while, and, on occasion, she even exhibited a pulse.

After the water fight had stopped, and the naked estate agent sat there dripping, she'd lean over and say, "Now young man, how are my sale and purchase proceeding? All this naked tussling with my lodger is all very well, but I might actually need to move abode at some point, dear boy."

"Dunno mate, will check on Monday, but thanks for the Sunday roast."

It was a distinctly bizarre relationship to have with one's estate agent, mid-transaction.

I never had anything like that, just the usual loutish conmen in red braces and ghastly slip-ons.

I looked at one place which simply had a bare concrete floor. The estate agent banged it with her high heel and exclaimed in delight, "This will last for ages this. So hard wearing. Don't worry about the low ceiling heights, sir. They will ride up with wear."

Or this, "The flat comes with its own injunctible right to light, sir. So, when they build the twenty-storey apartment block right outside your window, sir, blocking all your light, you will have the right to go to Court, sir, and obtain an injunction to stop it being built, thus preserving this excellent view over this Catford industrial estate. It's one of many selling points, sir."

On the subject of conveyancing solicitors, I engaged the most user-unfriendly solicitor I have ever met, on personal recommendation naturally.

She was terrifying.

Seasoned laddish estate agents refused to call her. Clients were terrified to call her. My transaction had been going on for months so I decided to call her one week, after about six months of hearing nothing.

"Hello, may I just enquire how my purchase is going? Are there any problems, and do you need anything from me? I hope you're not too stressed," I asked, in the most civil and delicate tone I could muster.

There was silence at the end of the phone. You could cut the hostility of this silence with a knife.

She gave a long sigh. "Well..." she began, her tone incredulous at the question. "If people like you just stopped calling me, then maybe I could actually get on with things. You know, if you got off the sodding phone, I could get on with it. And then maybe I would make some progress. And no, I can't update you, as the file has been on my secretary's desk for a month, waiting to have a letter typed. And I never, ever, comment on a file unless it's in front of me. I could get sued you know. My secretary is not back for another month, until her tribunal case against me is resolved, so you know, you'll just have to fucking wait, OK. Jesus Christ, who do people think I am!" And she slammed the phone down.

Oh wonderful, I thought, I have to become like her.

In a normal working environment, it would be unacceptable, but the place I was working in at the time was so dysfunctional that it proved to be an invaluable way just to survive.

I became pure steel; I listened with nothing but an unmoving, icy gaze, and a contemptuous sniff if I agreed, and a silent, poisonous glare if I didn't. I barely said a word. My boss, surprisingly, said to me, "We need a bit of that round here." My workload halved, and, for the first time in years, I achieved work/life balance because nobody bothered me. They were too terrified.

The Old Lady exclaimed, "Oh, I'm overworked too, I shall try that," but she couldn't quite make it, as she would gaze terrifyingly at someone, and then, about ten seconds later, nod off according to her usual custom at nine thirty a.m. That was it; she was done for the day.

Anyway, it kept me in a job, so I could afford the mortgage.

Which enabled me to keep on moving house, and create yet more Middle-Class Hell.

The most astonishing place I ended up in, which was a stroke of good fortune, was a two-bed riverside flat with a roof terrace overlooking the River Thames and Canary Wharf. I stumbled upon it by complete chance one January, when everyone else couldn't be bothered, and managed to pick it up on the cheap.

It did have its issues. The day after I moved in there was a torrential downpour, and the previous owner had placed plant pots in the gutters on the terrace. They overflowed, and the whole flat flooded. Then there was an ant nest in one of the plant pots, and the ants decided that now would be a great time to migrate through a hole in the wall in the second bedroom, down the hall, and into the kitchen, and take up residence in the kitchen cabinets.

I arrived home that day and sank into despair, as the carpets were soaking after the downpour, and a chain of ants, about three inches wide and never ending, trotted its way round the flat, making itself at home in the kitchen. "Shoo, shoo," I cried, which predictably had zero effect, as they just kept coming.

How could this happen, four floors up?

I got ill at that point, and discovered the joys of Traditional Chinese Medicine, as I got violent head pains that Western Medicine could not diagnose. The strain of Middle-Class Hell was starting to take its toll. So I wandered past this Chinese herbalist, and noticed this ancient looking man in a doctor's white coat, standing on one leg in the window, unmoving, eyes closed in meditation.

I went about my business, and came back later to notice him in the same position; he obviously hadn't moved. "He looks peaceful," I thought, so I popped in.

It turned out that he was doing Qi-Gong, but he seemed so unruffled and serene that I thought I needed whatever he was on, even if it did involve standing on one leg in the window in front of a packed street all day long.

He diagnosed the problem straight away – excess liver energy – and I was put right in about twenty-four hours. Wonderful.

When I decided to sell the place, I thought it would be nice to sell to a first-time buyer, to give someone a chance to get on the ladder in a rampant market. This chap in his twenties came round with his girlfriend, took one look at the roof terrace, and I could see straight away what he was thinking… "I'm gonna turn this place into a shag palace!"

And so he tried. The chap who ran the management company lived in the flat immediately below the roof terrace.

All manner of requests were made before exchange of contracts. Could a massive Shag Jacuzzi please be installed on the roof terrace, which sat immediately above the flat of the guy who ran the block management company?

Put yourself in the block manager's shoes. This twenty-year-old thing is moving in and wants to build an enormous Shag Jacuzzi on top of your roof. Not only is the weight of the thing probably going to cause the roof to collapse, but, until that happens, there is also the issue of the noise of the engine motor pumping the water around, which is likely to cause the most enormous din, added to the noise of shagging, plus water cascading over the edge of the Shag Jacuzzi, and flooding the rest of the building.

Understandably, "No," was the answer.

I used the same Terrifying Solicitor, just in case there was any nonsense.

My buyer was simply undeterred. He wouldn't take no for an answer, and he was the only person not to be remotely phased by the Terrifying Solicitor, which narked her beyond words.

She called me one day, more incensed than usual.

"You idiot!" she screamed at me, her client. "Why did you accept an offer from this guy? After a solid Shag Jacuzzi has been refused by the management company, he has now written to ask if an inflatable Shag Jacuzzi can now be installed instead. He's now said that an inflatable Shag Jacuzzi won't bring the roof in, but, if it bursts, it will be more erotic. Who the hell are you selling to?"

"A City banker," I replied.

Then, on the day of exchange, I called my Terrifying Solicitor, to instruct her to exchange contracts.

"Oh, she's just been sacked," said a PA. "She was in so many industrial tribunals for being an appalling manager. They had to send her on a course on how to work with people more effectively. Well, she came back worse than ever, even more unbearable, so the Partners have just thrown her out of the building. She's screaming outside in the street right now, if you want speak to her, but she has no authority in the firm any longer, so I'm afraid you can't exchange contracts. I've no idea when we will have someone around who can exchange contracts for you, sir."

Dear Lord, would this exchange ever happen? There were only three people in the chain, and it went on for months... months. I remembered the Old Lady's dances in the office whenever she exchanged contracts, and now I longed so much for it.

Finally, it went through, but I was a wreck, a complete wreck, at the end of it.

"Oh, never again," I said. "Never, ever again will I move house... the ultimate Middle-Class Hell..."

That is, until the next time I decide to move house.

But of course, we can only afford to live somewhere decent if we have a job; and this is the source of the last, and worst Middle-Class Hell there is – recession and redundancy...

Work is Middle-Class Hell. Until you lose it; then you panic...

Economic Crash and the Great Recession

Not just any old recession, of course.

No, only the worst economic crash in about a hundred years (though measuring recorded data is tricky). And in many respects, the 2008 crash was worse even than the 1930s.

Output in the UK fell by approximately six per cent after 2008; in the 1930s it fell by around eight per cent (though economists are bound to disagree), but it took longer for the economy to return to its pre-recession level of output than it took in the 1930s. This contraction was almost as steep, but it went on for far longer. Though unemployment was far lower, as people kept their jobs, the pay-off was a collapse in wage growth, whilst the cost of assets like housing rocketed. Plus, the level of personal and government debt was higher than in the 1930s, making any Keynesian deficit expansionary policies and stimulating consumer demand, in theory, much harder to do.

Typical.

Bloody typical.

The Old Lady and I had a phone conversation about it, as the markets went into meltdown one day in October 2008. We had known for about a year that bad things were coming, after seeing all those Grannies queuing outside Northern Rock (or

Northern Wreck) as it became the first British Bank to experience a bank run since the 1920s.

Like migrating birds, before an earthquake or a tsunami, Grannies are always the first to spot looming disaster.

If you want an open window on any situation, just watch the Grannies, and see what they are doing. It's usually foolproof. The Grannies of Great Britain knew full well that a bank run was coming, even if those in Government did not. While others, supposedly "in the know", scorned these queues of Grannies, in pinnies, cardigans, with tartan-covered four-wheeled personal shoppers, and immaculately permed hair, and knitting tucked away under an armpit, the Governor of the Bank of England got it right, by declaring that the amassed queue of Grannies waiting to draw their money out of a broke bank were behaving perfectly sensibly. Well, of course, that's what Grannies do.

Although the Old Lady had a slightly different take on it. "Queue? Queue? I don't do queuing! I'm not used to queuing. I don't think I could cope with being in a queue."

It was in the afternoon, and she took my call. "She's actually awake at this time," I thought. "This must be serious." It wasn't the usual, "How dare you wake me up in ze middle of the day!" when I called her after lunch, if she was there.

It was the Friday before the Government went into a panicked huddle with the banks, to ensure that the banking system did not collapse, and that the cashpoints opened on Monday morning, thus ensuring that things did not tip into anarchy. Yes, that really was how close it got.

Can you imagine the Old Lady's not being able to shop at John Lewis, whilst she slipped out in her lunch hour (all afternoon), not able to buy a matching occasional table and lavender poufs, due to the collapse of the banking system? The social consequences of that are incalculable.

"Well, dear, I think we are doomed." I could imagine her blinking furiously as she said those words. "I don't think I can possibly work the rest of the afternoon, it's so shocking. I don't know how we get out of this one, dear..."

"We need a plan, dear," I said. "Let's think on it overnight and come up with a plan. We simply can't have this. I'll come round to yours tomorrow with a bottle of Pol Roger champagne. Best stock up before it's looted."

"Good idea," she said. "I'm off for a nap," and she put down the receiver on her busy Friday afternoon at the office.

So I tipped up at the Old Lady's place the next day, the calm on the streets not reflecting the potential catastrophe about to engulf us. Only the Grannies looked worried, as they were seen stocking up on tins of spam in their four-wheeled tartan personal shoppers. I decided that I needed a four-wheeled tartan personal shopper too, in the disasters looming ahead.

There is this story of a banker's having moved out that weekend to his farm in Sussex, and having counted his sheep just in case he needed to eat them, if all went bonkers on Monday morning and the cash machines didn't work. He talked to a chap in the Treasury that weekend who, on hearing the number of sheep he had, remarked coldly, "That's not enough. You'll need far more than that if the bank rescue goes wrong. Have you got a bunker to hide in?"

When I arrived at the Old Lady's house, she invited me in; gentle classical music was playing in the background, and her place had been newly scented with lavender fragrance. Stud was there in the lounge, in his trackie bottoms, watching footie, clearly becalmed and sated for ten minutes, after a vigorous night with some "lady" the evening before, or the lavender hand lotion.

We sat in the Old Lady's Middle-Class kitchen and cracked open a bottle of Pol Roger, ready to discuss our solution to the unfolding crisis.

"I hear the Duke of Buckinghamshire has cut back on his foie gras orders," I said. "There is all this talk of a coming 'age of austerity'."

"I was there during the last one, dear, during the late 1940s, when I was about a hundred years old," the Old Lady said. "Stockings were rationed, and I kept losing mine, after they were torn off by squaddies when I got my high heels stuck in the tram lines down at the docks. The humiliation of a ration book, dear, and vast oversized elasticated knickers, when no stockings could be found."

"We're going back to that," I warned.

"We are, dear." She shuddered.

"We've worked ourselves into the grave trying to get this far," I said. "You only do thirty minutes a day, but I bet it's pure uranium!"

She nodded as vigorously as I'd ever seen, "It is, dear... if only I could remember any of it."

I was slightly startled, "Can you remember anything you've done at work for the last ten years?"

"No," she said, matter of fact.

"Well, anyway, we have to get out of this." I got the laptop out. "I've got a plan," I said. "Let's look on the internet."

"What's that interweb thing?" she asked. "Is that the thing Stud uses to watch porn on? Does it have any other uses?"

"No, it doesn't. But we can look at properties."

"Why?" she asked.

"Well, dear," I said, about to launch into a Granny-style monologue, "We're bound to get made redundant with lousy pay-offs. No way will we be able to pay our mortgages, so we are going to be repossessed. Property values are going to plummet, by about twenty per cent, I reckon, so the amount of equity we have left after the mortgages are paid off, on repossession, will be this…"

She looked in horror at the total.

"We need to buy somewhere outright, no mortgage. We will never get work again. You can barely lift a finger, and I destroy every place I end up in. In the coming calamity, you and I are simply unemployable dear. Not even in B&Q."

"What's B&Q?" she asked.

I carried on. "It comes down to this… and it's going to be rough."

She squealed.

"We can only afford a one-bedroom former crystal meth den in Catford, South East London… it's a bit rough and stabby there, I'm afraid," I told her, as I pulled up a newspaper article on stabbings at the old Catford Bridge Tavern.

"As other areas have gentrified, Catford hasn't. Right now, it's so us."

I am convinced that the Old Lady will never die. She's far too evil to ever leave us. But at that moment, I thought she just might.

She emitted this terrible gargling, guttural sound of pure terror, the sort my Granny used to emit when she realised the teapot was empty.

The irony of all of this is that I have recently moved to Catford, quite voluntarily. Despite the chaotic, dilapidated wreckage of the town centre, and the fact that all of South East England's tradesmen seem to use Catford's streets for fly tipping, it does have some very nice houses and a large fibreglass black cat hanging off a building at the entrance to the shopping centre. As we know from the introduction to this work…

"Are there any Middle-Class people there?" she trembled.

"No, dear. Just us, but we're finished anyway, so what does it matter?"

She choked again, and then emitted some high-pitched whine of agony, like an old whistling steam kettle being tortured by the Gestapo.

Later that afternoon, she finally calmed down. "This really is it…" She gazed wistfully at the well-stocked wine cooler, the basin sink with extendable washing-jet thingy that seemed to be encased in a spring for no obvious reason, and granite work surfaces, gleaming after being smeared in something from John Lewis and shined with a special cloth. "I had expected to retire, in a few decades, to a cottage in Cornwall with a modest Middle-Class retirement income, sea flowers and beaches, floral dresses, and an antique bamboo wheelchair, with a wheel on the front and a plaid rug on my lap, with a complimentary ear trumpet, with Stud married off, and finally out of my life…"

I stopped her. "Forget it. We're in a one-bed crack den in Catford. We're unemployable. There's no point in making an effort any more. We're going to eat lard; we can't afford anything else. It's time to just let ourselves go and accept defeat. The Fat Banker is our precedent, our inspiration here. We're going to become enormously fat, sit outside in cheap deckchairs in all weathers, our vast blubber encased in the biggest muumuus or maternity dresses we can find, and we're going to shout abuse at everyone who walks past us, and cackle madly. It's the only way to go in a deep recession when you're Middle Class and you've lost everything."

"I quite like the sound of that," she suddenly said, perking up. "You know..." She paused in thought, her mind drifting. "Sometimes, it's good to just get off the rat wheel, to just let yourself go and become a vast mound of blubber in a muumuu, outside a South East London drug den flat in a deck chair in January – no work to do, no office politics, no stress, no keeping up appearances. No expectations. No striving, just wallowing in your own blubber and muumuu, just eating lard, shouting 'bugger off' to passers-by, without a care in the world..."

I could see her point. There were upsides.

That was exactly the point at which my Granny had arrived, and she seemed perfectly happy. Were things coming, as they say, full circle? Was I about to become a South East London version of Granny?

Our flow was interrupted by Stud's coming into the kitchen, and then moping out again back to watch his footie on the telly, seemingly oblivious to the life-changing events taking place in the face of impending disaster.

"What about him?" I asked. "There is only a lounge and a bedroom in the old meth den. I thought that you could have the lounge and I would have the bedroom. Nothing too glamorous. This is an age of austerity, so I thought we could get two of those old 1940s NHS metal single beds that creak every time two fat old gits like us come near them, and we can hang medical records on the end. We are eating lard, after all, so we're finished health-wise; so the medical records are there simply to record how fat we are. But what about Stud?"

The Old Lady disappeared into the room next door for a conversation with the over-sexed lodger.

She came back, moments later, slightly distressed.

"I've updated him on the macro-economic situation," she sighed, her tits sagging further than usual. "He didn't understand a word on the finer points of economic theory, Keynesian and Monetarist principles, and just kept groping himself through his trackie bottoms. But he did get enough of it to understand that the situation is serious and, despite the fact that his intellect is ruled purely at penis level, he does grasp that, to put it gently, we're fucked."

She sat down and sighed. "I accepted a long time ago that I'd never get rid of him. It really is death until us do part. I've been dead for centuries," she said, "but this carcass encasing my remnants still keeps going and, though now dead, I am still conscious to a small extent... and I'm afraid that Stud and I are now bound together until the first of us expires..." She waved her hand grandly and regally.

"You mean he knows it's desperate, and it's in his self-interest to stick with the Old Lady rather than be on the streets?" I ventured.

She shrugged. "That's about it, dear, yes. He's coming with us."

The Old Lady continued making plans. "You and I have single NHS 1940s metal beds, with only a small wardrobe for our fat garments, like our muumuus, and elasticated Primark fat-pants. As times are tight, Stud has agreed to sleep in a dog basket in the kitchen. He's agreed to sell himself for odd jobs, and we can use a collection tin if anyone wants to hire him out. Even though the mortgage is paid off, we can use him to generate an income to keep us topped up with lard..."

"Well, that's it then, that's the plan."

"I think this is the only way through this."

"Hurrah!" we both chanted, as we clinked what we thought were our last ever glasses of champagne.

I can assure you this conversation did happen in exactly these terms, as Government Ministers and officials beavered away that weekend trying to stave off disaster; but we'd already come up with a plan to survive the crash of all crashes.

But it still felt like the end of an era.

Albinoni's "Adagio in G Minor" came on in the background, as it always does in moments of pathos and sad reflection.

"Well, this is it, dear." I sighed.

"It is, dear," she whimpered, "we're at the end. All that striving to be Middle-Class, and now we are completely brought down by the worst economic crash there has almost ever been. What a cliffhanger!"

"This feels like a season finale episode in a DVD box set. How will we ever get out of this? Will we survive the end of season cliffhanger and survive until the next season?" I was genuinely puzzled at this conundrum.

"It really does feel like a season finale, dear," she agreed, "and the darkness feels like it's coming... can't you feel it? The darkness is coming..."

I looked around, apprehensively. "You are right, dear; the tension is building to a tumultuous climax."

"No, that was Stud last night with my hand lotion, dear," she wagged her finger. "But this does have the feeling of a season finale but, like all bad season finales, it feels like a completely artificial build-up just for the sake of having a bloody finale."

I hit upon something, "Yeah, but if this is the season finale, shouldn't we get all the cast together? We can't leave Pug or the Gin-Soaked Alcoholic Cleaner, or any of the others out of this. What about the Pissing Pussy? She'll fit our crack den perfectly; no one will come around if she leaks all over the place. Or the

Booming Victorian? Or the Terrifying Solicitor? Even The Mad Boss ... The Mad Boss is mad, but is just about driven enough to get us out of this. And we need to know that they are coming back next season. And what about Granny, and Mrs Haemorrhoid? We have to bring them back, somehow... what about getting us all back together in the Club? We can get everyone in the Club and blow it up. It will be a mystery who survives the explosion. You've always wanted that extra bedroom – we have to blow the Club up and you get an extra bedroom out of the sale proceeds money! What a season finale!"

The Old Lady stiffened and then shook her head vigorously, so vigorously that she went red, and sounded like a horse snorting as her mouth flaps slapped around. "There is no extra bedroom. The whole dynamics have changed. It's a crack den in Catford. Or nothing. Because we are done for! Both of us. DONE FOR!" she snapped, dramatically.

As for the suggestion to bring back the other cast members for the grand finale, "It's just us dear, on our own in our NHS beds and muumuus, with Stud in his dog basket, in our crack den. The others, they've got to fend for themselves in this impending catastrophe."

And she continued. "And you've got to be careful about season finales..." the Old Lady said, wisely, as she pulled her cardigan around her in the rapidly advancing gloom. "You never know which cast members will come back. They always get rid of those who die, go insane, or ask for too much money. If you turn up on time, stay sober, and say your lines in the right order, you stand a chance."

"Lord!" I exclaimed. "We're ruled out on every count."

"I know, dear... we really are finished."

And so things started to fade to black. The darkness really was coming. As the darkness closed around, so the Middle-Class dream ended, fading into the distance. A fantasy born of hubris that was never to be.

With that crashing, hopeless realisation, Granny zoomed into view, a reminder of what had passed and what was to come. As she zoomed closer, her features grew triumphant, terrifying and mocking, and with these words she portentously pronounced: "Hartlepool... Mrs Haemorrhoid... Prince Philip... pinnies... panty-girdle... twin-tub washing machine... mangle... impitent bugger." And with a final, soul-wrenching bellow, she screamed one final word – "TEAPOT!"

And then I knew no more. Everything went black.

It had all ended.

I woke up at my desk in the office.

It was no dream or death; this was reality, as the office was as chaotic and dysfunctional as usual. The Mad Boss was head-butting the phone, and the department PA was off her face after the night before. No fake reality could create this monstrosity. It was real all right.

I picked up the phone to the Old Lady, "What's going on? I haven't been made redundant. I'm still bloody here."

"Oh there you are, dear!" she exclaimed. "You've been wandering around for weeks in a daze, did anyone notice?"

I shook my head. "I don't think so, but I think I'm back in this conscious reality. And looking at my inbox, I've got tons of work to do. What about you?"

She sighed, "Me too, more's the pity. I still have a job too. Everyone I know is really rushed off their feet. More work than ever, just fewer people to do it. Some recession. And pay rises look lousy for the foreseeable future. We're just doing more work now, but for less. And I was looking forward to giving it all up, and our Catford crack den."

So that conversation had really happened. We had made those plans to survive the coming calamity.

"We might need it yet, we never know," I counselled.

I continued. "So what happened was a really crap season finale. The tension was ramped up except that, at the start of the following episode, the re-set button was pressed and everything is back as it was before. Bloody typical! I feel really ripped off. Typically crap season finale. After the over-blown cliffhanger, nothing actually changes."

I pondered further. "After all that build-up and drama, the impending economic doom, growing fat in a meth den, Stud in a dog basket, we're back in the same Middle-Class Hell as before, aren't we, dear?"

"Yes, dear," she said.

The Old Lady is always right, "Except that now we're just bloody poorer, dear," she said.

I asked her, "You've been around for ever. In your vast experience, does everything just suck? Is it all just Middle-Class Hell?"

"Yes, it all just sucks," she answered, and she slammed the phone down in disgust at everything that ever was, and everything that ever will be.

Part Three
And How to Cure It

Introduction

"Do what you love, and if you can't yet do what you love, love what you do."

Buddhist monk, in conversation with the author, Wat Prah That Doi Suthep Temple, Chiang Mai, Thailand, January 2016.

I might be guilty of a certain amount of misdirection.

The events you have read about so far, in all material respects, happened. Well, mostly.

But the slant I have put on them has been, to some extent, misdirection. Deliberate of course. Not an illusion of the truth, but an illusion of perspective.

To classify my life as either Working-Class or Middle-Class "Hell" is the misdirection.

The reality is, I have had a wonderful life, absolutely wonderful as some of you, reading about my journey, might conclude. Absolutely mad, but also wonderful. And, as we shall see, gratitude is critically important to what we bring into our lives.

The perspective I've offered has been to amuse in the first two parts of this book, nothing more, and for that reason the darker episodes (and there have been many) haven't been included for the honest reason that I see no reason to spoil your fun, or mine. If I've put a "negative" spin on anything, it doesn't represent my outlook at all, except that I'm having fun playing with it.

Whether the experiences are classified as "Heaven" or "Hell" is also something of a misdirection too. Whatever has manifested in my life, I am solely responsible for it. It hasn't been the product of fate, or anything else. It's all down to me. And in your life, it's all down to you.

The things that have come into my life that I have created, manifested or actualised, have happened as a result, not of physical actions on my part, but of my own thoughts and emotions. I didn't realise, at the time, the extent to which I was creating my own reality; but I do now.

In essence, what you think and feel, and give your attention to, so you create.

I didn't realise that that's what I was doing, of course, but I was conscious of wanting a better lifestyle than many experienced in Hartlepool in the nineteen-seventies and eighties, when de-industrialisation and recession gripped.

And that is what I created. Circumstances were later reflected back to me in answer to my thoughts and to what I wanted emotionally.

Granny, she created her reality. The Old Lady created her reality. She even got a promotion. She got it because she created it. Oh, and she got the second bedroom... she got a whole house in fact. The characters in this book, as real people, created their own reality.

The reason for this is that the Universe is one big, great mirror. What we put out there comes back. The point here is simple – if you look into a mirror, a reflection has to come back. This is how the Universe works, this is how life works, and it took me the better part of forty years to get it, even though the evidence of it was all around me; but I didn't get it for a long time. There was no element of fate or pre-destination to events. No element of karma. I will go into the concepts of fate and karma later. But what is important to understand here is that events were created by me, not by an outside force.

I look back, and I was asking the Universe to deliver an improvement in my material circumstances. It did. I also asked it to deliver comedy into my life. It did. And for both I am immeasurably grateful. The delivery of both required far more trust in the Universe than I had at the time. Now I simply trust it; and what I don't like, I work to change not complain about. If the Universe is a mirror, and we don't like the reflection, what is being reflected back is always, always, giving us the capacity to change it.

Let us get to the nub here. If any of you are living your own Working-Class, or Middle-Class "Hell", or any other kind of "Hell", you can change it by simply… asking.

But most of us never actually ask. And if we ask and receive, we don't know how to accept.

The Universe is a mirror. It is here to reflect back at you what you think and feel. Want a better life? It can give it to you. But if you focus on your negatives, your "Hell", it will give you more of that too.

You can't stop thinking and feeling. So you might as well focus on what you want, because whatever you think and feel, it's going to get reflected back *in any event*. That reflection can't be stopped, but it can consciously be altered.

At a very basic level, we choose to come in and have an experience of life, and have fun.

The Universe reflects our experiences back at us as the product of what we have thought and felt. But it doesn't have the ability to distinguish whether that is good, bad, moral, immoral, serious, funny, or the quality of what we are thinking.

It accepts our free will to create our own reality. It's why we are the author of our own good or bad fortune, to a very large extent.

That's incredibly liberating. To answer the philosopher's question, free will does exist, and fate does not, and the extent to which fate exists is that it is simply an event, or set of events, coming back at us, reflecting our own free will or as guidance. People might say a chance event is "destiny". It isn't. It's what you created.

You choose what comes in. Light or dark, success or failure.

But here is a key point – you are not dependent on fate, or anyone else, to improve your circumstances. You are dependent on one thing – the ability to alter your thoughts and feelings to focus on bringing into existence what you want, and not more of what you don't want.

The Universe is designed to help us. It's not meant to be unkind or cruel, but it exists to facilitate the experience which we have chosen to have. Once we put our choices – positive or negative – into our consciousness, then the Universe, in its helpful way, facilitates their reflection on the physical plane of our lives, because it thinks that that is the experience we have chosen to have.

Many of you who have seen the film *The Secret*, or have read the book of the same name, know where I am going with all this – into "law of attraction" territory.

It's a fantastic film, and book, and I urge all of you to give it a go. The reason why it's so wonderful is that it takes ideas in both the scientific and spiritual fields, and makes them accessible to all. It takes the kind of ideas that you will find in some amazing books in the spirituality and scientific sections of book shops. But most people don't wander into those sections of book shops. In consequence, they are not seeing or experiencing these amazing, life-changing ideas. Further, even if people get there, some of those books, despite having some amazing life-changing ideas in them, are so hard to get into. Some are written in off-putting spiritual-speak that frighten off the casual reader. Some are way, way over-long. But they still contain ideas that should be out there, and more accessible.

I am attempting to do several things here, and let me be candid about it: (i) write a comedy about the frustrations of everyday life – the kind of book which someone will pick up at an airport and breeze through in a couple of hours just to be amused; and then (ii) actually offer some genuine answers about how to create the life you want under the cover of a comedy on modern life.

I'm -trying to get across a combination of madcap and spiritual, but also getting across some ideas that are life-changing but which, bar *The Secret*, simply haven't got out there. As wonderful as *The Secret* is, there are also other ideas I'd like to add here. On top of the basic *law of attraction* idea – that what we think and feel comes back to us – there is so much more I'd like to discuss about how the Universe – and our lives – really work.

So, there have been two elements of misdirection here: (i) that certain aspects of my life have been "Hell" when in fact they haven't been that at all, but they are presented as such for fun; and (ii) if you have been thinking that this book is a comedy, it isn't. The comedy is ruse, a cover, a misdirection, to get another subject across that needs much wider exposure. *The Secret* got these ideas out there to an extent, but not widely enough or deeply enough because it's still in the "self-help" category in a book or DVD shop that most people won't go near. But what if these ideas could be got across and "into the mainstream", under the cover of a comedy? I had fun thinking of the idea, so decided to try it. Anything really to get this stuff further out there.

But if I have been guilty of misdirection, please stay with me for the simple reason that – I hope – what's coming is worth it. And life-changing.

Most of the observations that are about to follow are those that have just flowed as I have sat down to write this. Occasionally, I add ideas from specific books or works, but I actually wrote much of this before reading them in depth. There are some wonderful books on this subject though, which are listed in the "Recommended Reading" Section.

None of this, I hasten to add, is a religion or anything like it.

Quite the reverse, it puts you in the driving seat and asks *you to accept the power of you.*

Even if some people don't like what I'm about to describe, or agree with it, for many I hope it will still be life-changing, or at least make you think.

I cannot pose "And How to Cure It" in the title to this book, without offering an answer, even if this section of the book takes a suddenly different swerve in tone and content than what you might have been expecting.

Those of you who know the *law of attraction* from *The Secret* or other sources will have an idea of what is coming, but there will also be new things to pick up here as well. For those of you who have little experience of the *law of attraction*, sit back and enjoy the ride.

The key to this is knowing that things in your life *can* be changed. And the main thing that you have to do is this – *ask in the right way and allow yourself to receive.*

"Forty-Two"

In Douglas Adams's *Hitchhikers Guide to the Galaxy*, a bunch of characters ask a super-computer the answer to the question, "What is the meaning of life, the universe and everything?"

Seven and a half million years passed before the computer gave its answer.

And its answer to the question, "What is the meaning of life, the universe and everything?" was all of the following: odd, confusing, an anti-climax, bonkers, frustrating, boring, inspirational, perfectly simple but, above all, still inexplicable.

So, in answer to the question: "What is the meaning of life, the universe and everything?" the super computer, after eons of consideration, eventually simply droned, semi-apologetically, its answer: "Forty-two."

Quite. If that's the answer, why bother asking the question, and waiting seven and a half million years?

But I'm afraid we must ask that question. Because if we want to define what a happy and successful life is like, then we simply cannot avoid the question: "What is the meaning of life, the universe and everything?"

No, I'm not going to go all religious. But I do delve a little deeper than our surface physical existence to unlock the door to allow things in. Some of you might not even want to think about these questions. Others might disagree with the answers. But we can't avoid these questions if we want to make things better – ever.

I've partially answered the question already in the last chapter with just a little bit more than the answer of "Forty-two." And, to recap, the part of the answer that I gave was that the Universe is a mirror, and it responds with practical and physical manifestation in the present in response to what we have put in our minds, the thoughts we chose, and the emotions we felt in the past.

In short, what we give our attention to is reflected back at us.

But let us start to get to grips with the substance of this.

Three Theories of Life

There are three ways of looking at life (though there might be variations on these):

1. We have a physical existence. There is nothing else, nothing before or after our physical existence. Our existence is purely physical; once we die, that's it. There is no God or other divine being. Therefore "fate", to the extent that it exists, cannot be explained because there is nothing to guide or create it. There is the physical world, and nothing else. This theory does acknowledge our right to choose, but cannot explain how events turn out as they do. And then you die… and that's it. Physical existence, then oblivion. A bit like afternoon tea with Granny… Or:

2. There is a divine being or presence and this "guides" us. We might have choice in reality or perception, but our lives *in the main* are restricted by "something" because there is a set of rules, and punishment for breaking the rules. Choice plays a

less important role because of the prominence of fate or destiny or rules. This theory operates on a sliding scale – at the extreme end, we have no choice as everything is pre-determined and we are subject to "fate" or "divine whim". At the other end, as many religions acknowledge, we have choice but there can be divine intervention, and there are still rules limiting our choice.

There are variations on this and I'm being simplistic, of course, but let us take them as a general starting point, especially as they are the polar opposites in a spectrum here. In one, there is no divine only a physical existence and no afterlife. In the other there is a guiding presence and an afterlife.

We will come on to the third theory in a moment, but I want to explore Theories 1 and 2 in a bit more detail first.

Because there are many problems with both of these theories. The main problem is that they are both extremely negative in outlook.

One ends in oblivion and a sense that nothing means much, and the other deprives us of real choice.

Both theories might recognise that some people have it lucky, but they can't explain *why*.

But they do resonate with us because the "default mode" in human thinking is "negative".

Of all the thoughts we think in a day, it has been estimated that eighty per cent of our thoughts are negative. That's an incredible amount. In reality, we are negative thinkers so negative and restrictive philosophies of life are going to gain traction and acceptance.

But don't get depressed, really! Don't. Stick with this, because here comes the third theory.

Ok, are you ready? It's a head-boggler at first, but it's really very simple:

3.   We are infinite beings. We are eternal, and reincarnate. We come into a physical body each time we reincarnate, to experience and learn. We choose our physical destiny to experience and learn. The Universe gives us that learning experience by reflecting back our thoughts and emotions as physical events in our lives – that could be happiness and abundance, or lack and limitation. Our thoughts and emotions are the "request" for the learning experience we want reflected back. The Universe is energy and matter. So are we. Thought and emotion are just forms of energy. For all forms of energy in the Universe, there must be a "Source". It's the mirror that we talked about. All energy is connected to it, and returns from it. Our thoughts and emotions, as energy, are transmitted to it. That reflection, the thing that comes back into our life, is the physical reflection in our lives of the thought and emotion we sent out in the first place. Because we have given our attention to it, that is what we have chosen to experience. The Universe is infinite. So are we. In that infinity, we have an infinite number of choices about what we want our lives to be, and the Universe has the capacity to deliver an infinite number of reflections back at us.

OK? I know I risk losing you here but please stick with it, it will all come together.

"Source"? What's he on about?

If that's a bit much, let's take it apart bit by bit. At first glance it might look complicated, yet the design of the Universe is very simple, and so is this.

There are a few key things which were raised in Theory 3 which I want to go into: (i) that we are eternal, and reincarnate, and the concept of infinity; (ii) the concept of "Source"; (iii) the power of thought and emotion; and (iv) can we prove the existence of "Source?"

(i) We are eternal, and reincarnate; and the concept of infinity

What we are talking about is very simple – that we have an existence outside of our physical body. We choose to incarnate into a physical body; when that physical body dies, our non-physical self returns to where it came from – its "Source". And after reuniting with "Source", we then come back again into physical existence, if we choose to. We keep coming and going, from "Source" to physical existence, back to "Source" again, then back to physical existence again, and so on. This is the eternal aspect of our nature.

I am not a student of religion, simply because there are so many of them to study. I think it's been estimated that if you were to count the number of "Gods" in existence, the number is in the millions. Most "Gods" will profess themselves to be "true" and the others "false". For this reason, I've never known where to start.

Except that many religions seem to start and end in the same place. The same "Source", if you like. The deity in a religion and "Source" here are the same thing. Therefore I see little distinction between them, except that the "man-made" rules which people have imposed in a religion seem to take it further away from its "Source". I'm happy to debate it. But I come from the point of view that every religion is "one", and all are talking the same language unless people have themselves perverted it. Which, of course, they have.

But whatever religion we are dealing with, "God" or whatever deity you believe in, is referred to as "Source" in spiritual circles.

At its root, it's all the same thing.

I said this wasn't a religious philosophy. It isn't.

Because I define a religion as imposing "man-made" rules to explain "Source". And these man-made rules and rituals inhibit our choice because they imply judgment. The arguments here do not represent judgment; they represent choice, which is why I say that this isn't a religious philosophy. Religious philosophies give us two choices – to obey the rules or break them. Rather, we have infinite choices.

I will talk soon about a science-based approach to "Source", just in case some of you are getting concerned that this is getting too much into "spiritual speak". In reality, there are many sides to this – the spiritual and scientific – and both will get an airing as we go on.

But to take the spiritual side first, when we talk about "Source", I will talk of its infinity and its abundance, and the extensions of these into our everyday lives. The rules of many religions in our physical world are restrictive in telling people what codes to live their lives by. Most religions do not talk about our infinite capacity to create any life you want, because certain choices are prohibited. Yet our infinite capacity to create is the centrepiece here.

Further, as the spiritual concept of "Source" is based on infinity and abundance, it does not recognise the concept of "lack" and "restriction" (unless we consciously choose them in our lives) that apply to so many of the religious philosophies that are meant to govern us.

The Universe, or "Source", is always trying to explain itself to us, and it does so through religions. All religions are trying to say that there is a "Source", but we interpret it wrongly after that base start point. We add man-made rules and restrictions when a religion is simply trying to say, "Hey, there is a 'Source' to our existence".

One of the key misinterpretations in many religions is that our physical existence is full of difficulty, hardship, and sacrifice, because of the promise of a better tomorrow in an afterlife.

What if this whole philosophy, in many religions, is simply a man-made philosophy that many just accept without hesitation? It begs the fundamental, key question – is our *physical existence* here meant to be wonderful, or miserable? What if we are meant to experience that wonderful "afterlife" now in "life"?

May I take a step back for a moment? The words "physical existence" are simply shorthand for "life".

The word "life" does not sound like a word which we would associate with misery and lack.

To look at the abundance of nature tells us that the concept of "life" is not limited. It will end, it will start again. But there is plenty of it always going on. Life always continues and it continues in abundance, if only we will look at it with an open mind. It keeps being reborn, and reborn, and reborn, and continuing, in defiance of our own limiting thoughts. And it's happening on the "physical" level, if there is any doubt that we can create that level of physical abundance in our lives. Nature is never truly lacking. In short, it's eternal and reincarnates itself all the time just like us, and its force shows little signs of abating, even after eons.

Are "life" and "Source" the same thing? The answer is "yes", "life" is an extension of "Source" by definition. They are the same thing.

If "life" is eternal, and it just keeps continuing, are we eternal too? The concept of reincarnation is familiar to many of us. If there is a "soul" after we die, we "incarnate" into another existence. Many religions acknowledge this. In spiritual terms, we do the same thing at the point of physical death, we re-join "Source".

Death is a difficult subject, but is it an end? No, it's a transition and I find it holds no fear for me, nor does fear of losing someone, because if we are infinite we never die. That "spark" always exists, and we will be reunited with it.

As we have said, this also means that we can come back again into this physical existence after we have died and gone back to our "Source". The purpose of coming into physical existence is to experience. And as Part Three of this book will go on to say, it is we ourselves who define that experience by what we give our attention to with our minds and emotions.

It's very simple: we decide to come into physical existence each time to experience more and more, and we grow in that experience. Then we go back to "Source". Physical life is a playground and a canvas at one and the same time, on which we paint our experience and play. How much fun is that? That's a whole lot of fun, if fun is what you choose to have.

Can we prove this? There are those who offer past life regression so that we can see the lives we had before this one. It's up to you to see whether you want to try it, and test the evidence. But, fundamentally, our purpose in coming into physical existence is to experience it. And we do it more than once. Because just as "Source" and "life" are eternal and infinite, as extensions of that so are we.

But if we are eternal and the Universe is also eternal, then, by definition, the scope of what it is possible for us to achieve is so much greater than we perceive it to be. If we are part, and extensions of, this vast infinite "Source", then what we are capable of is so much greater than our own negativity often imposes on us. Our negativity and limited thinking is so small and limiting compared to the eternity of the existence of which we are part, and of which we are an extension.

(ii) The concept of "Source"

Some people might find the concept of "Source" to be the difficult bit, but it's not.

We have to consider for a moment what the Universe is. When I talk of "Source" and the "Universe" here, the terms are interchangeable. They really are the same thing.

The "Universe", in essence, is two things: energy and matter.

Everything is energy or matter.

"We" are all energy. Everything that you look at is molecules existing at a different rate of vibration.

Consider a glass of water. It's a clear glass of liquid. Apply heat to it, in time it will turn to steam. The steam will turn to gas or ether.

Yet it's all the same molecules; they are just vibrating at a different frequency. They may have changed their state as a result of heat being applied, but the molecules are the same.

We are also energy vibrating at a different frequency. We are energy vibrating at a frequency that might make us appear solid matter, but physics might disagree that we are solid at all. We are simply energy in motion.

All energy in the Universe must, logically, have a "Source". It's got to come from and go to "somewhere".

But where?

Stick a proton in a particle accelerator and some physicists might say that, once "accelerated", it vibrates at such a speed as to be incapable of measurement. But they know that a form of energy exists at that maximum acceleration point. It has to. But it's reached a stage where they can't measure or define it.

Let's be clear about the experiment they are running with that particle accelerator. They are going to the nth degree. To find the Universe's base code, if you like.

What's the answer of physicists? That there is an energy form that exists, vibrating at such a high frequency that they can't measure it. But they know it exists.

A hippy or spiritualist might say, "Hey, man, I've got such a high rate of vibration," meaning they are spiritually advanced.

It's the same position in both cases. The hippy and the physicist are talking the same language, the language of "vibration", and both being at a particularly advanced state of vibration, whether it's energy or spiritual awareness.

Both are trying to define existence in relation to a form of energy that they can't define or prove, other than in theoretical or imaginative terms. Some argue that physics and spirituality are running in parallel, that physics can "prove" that the *law of attraction*, that we attract by what we think and feel, exists.

The explanation in physics for the *law of attraction* goes along these lines: everything in the Universe is energy and matter. Everything in the Universe, even if we think it is physical in form and substance, is vibrating energy. Our human form is energy moving at a particular speed of vibration. So we are energy in physical form. If there is a "Source", we are extensions of it because we are the same energy.

Among these forms of energy, there is thought and emotion.

Thought and emotion, or their frequencies, are a form of energy.

They are limitless. Other forms of energy, such as sound or light, travel at a speed. Thought is faster than that, because its speed is instantaneous.

As a form of energy or frequency, thoughts can be transmitted. Theoretically, as energetic frequencies, they are everywhere. When we think or feel them, we are radiating them out to the Universe as well.

The power to invent anything was always there. The ideas always existed out there, but it was only at a certain point in history that we accessed the information that was always there to invent what we needed. It's the same with everything we decide to invent or create. Everything we want in life is there, just out there, waiting to come in, when we ask for it.

That's an astonishing concept, but it also demonstrates that there is so much out there that we haven't even thought of, let alone decided, to create. This applies in your own life too.

When we refer to the Universe or "Source" as a reflective mirror, what we are referring to is the transmission of thought or emotional energy to its "Source", like any other form of energy, and back again.

If "Source" is energy, and if thoughts and emotions are also energy sent to an energetic "Source" and back again, can they become any more than just thoughts and energy?

Crucially, can thought and emotion be transformed into "circumstance", "events", into tangible and physical results, like money in our bank accounts? Remember that the "tangible" and "physical" is just energy vibrating at a different rate. It looks solid but it's not. Just as the problems and obstacles in your life look solid and maybe immovable, but they are not – they are energy in motion, like everything else.

We've discussed "Source" here from two perspectives.

The first is a spiritual one: that, as eternal beings, it's where we come from, and return to. We are extensions of it, leaving it to experience a physical life and then returning to it. If you want to think of it as "Heaven", where we reside in between our physical lifetimes, that's fine. Especially as the way it reflects back at us, and the way it works in our lives, takes on the appearance of the "divine" and the "conscious".

The second is a scientific concept of "Source", which I said I'd explore to give balance. In this case, the Universe is energy; it is a form of energy that we know, scientifically, exists. We can't measure it, but we are part of it because we are also energy.

Of course, there really isn't any distinction between these two perspectives; they are one and the same. Just as the language of the hippy and the physicist when talking about "vibration" is the same. But the unifying principle of the power of thought and emotion applies to both perspectives. Thought and emotion are the basis of our spiritual existence but also, in our scientific existence, they are also a phenomenally powerful form of energy. The human body and brain are a vast battery, capable of massive transmission of thought and emotion. It has to go somewhere.

It goes to "Source" and is reflected back. "Source" is our mirror. It's home to us as spiritual and energetic beings. And it reflects our lives back at us, both spiritually and energetically.

If thoughts and emotions are so powerful, can a person influence their life, circumstances, or even history, by the power of their thoughts and emotions?

(iii) The power of thought and emotion.

Let's bring this right down to earth, and use a person as an example.

Winston Churchill is a great example of the *law of attraction*. Or, frankly, any other great leader you care to think about is just as good an example.

Let us examine Churchill's career for a moment.

Churchill was thrown out of Government in 1929. Despite whatever else happened, including an economic crash, depression, and coalition governments, Churchill remained out of office, in "the wilderness" until War broke out.

That's a decade in the wilderness.

Let's examine what Churchill wanted from a *law of attraction* perspective.

He hadn't exactly had a glittering career. Though he was a rising star before the First World War, he was then associated with the failed Dardanelles military campaign in the First World War. After a period of disgrace, he came back in the 1920s, but even that was not plain sailing. After 1929, he was sacked and out in the cold. He feared the political irrelevance of his father and, by the 1930s, he seemed to have achieved it, being both a dangerously radical but reactionary figure at one and the same time.

But two things were going on inside his head:

1. A desire for "office", and
2. A desire for "glory".

We can see both of these desires in his statements and writing. Had he focussed on just the first, like most politicians, he would have got what he wanted then disappeared into history without trace not long after.

It is the combination of the two desires *together* that is interesting. He wanted both of these things *together*: office and glory.

The *law of attraction* had to scratch its head on that one, and the Great Man had to wait a decade before something came up that fulfilled both.

Hang on, isn't this *law of attraction* thing supposed to manifest my results, quickly and easily?

No, is the answer. Let me repeat that. No! You *might* manifest them quickly, but you also might have to wait. Some works on the *law of attraction* imply that the result comes quickly. It doesn't always do that. We will come on to this later. But let's look at Churchill again for now.

Churchill waited in the wilderness for ten years in the 1930s, with mental depression and ridicule, thinking that he was a failure.

But the Universe had heard him. There were a number of things going on here. Churchill was asking for something big, because that fitted his personality. But the Universe needed to move the pieces into place. It also needed to test his faith, commitment, and resolve, to see if he was up to, and capable of, what he was asking for. He wanted office and glory, fine, but could he cope with the hardships that went with both of these? He was tested for a decade in the 1930s to see if he was up to it when the real test came later in the early 1940s.

So when he eventually got to be Prime Minister at the start of the Second World War, he got "office", with the potential for "glory". But to get through it, he faced a situation where the country stood on its own. The 1930s had taught him to survive in isolation, where failure seemed to greet his every initiative. He had only his willpower and self-belief carrying him through every failure. We can see how the 1930s was his apprenticeship for what came later when the country faced a situation in which it, too, was on its own, with incredible odds stacked before it.

His experience in the 1930s delivered all the lessons he now needed to apply.

Everything, everything, clicked into place when it was needed.

What is astonishing about this manifestation was how tough it was to bring it into physical existence. Yet the man and the moment clicked together. You have one man's amazing willpower and "Source", or the Universe, responding to it.

There are numerous points here that are worth examining:

1. Churchill wanted glory and this usually meant military glory, in his case, as war fascinated him. People died, and would die as a result of his need for glory. He understood this. It's easy for us from our perspective now to criticize this glory-seeking, but it made him what we needed when the time arose. It's a tough one, which also requires us to drop some judgments, especially some moral ones. More on morality later.

2. Churchill is a bit of an exception. He was asking for something huge. It took some time for the Universe to respond because of the events that had to go into motion and the need to test him, to see if he could cope. Most of us aren't asking for this. Most of us ask for something much smaller. Things for an average person are a little easier for the Universe to manifest.

3. Force of will. He suffered political defeat, after defeat, after defeat in the 1930s. He refused to give up. It's astonishing to look back at how Churchill coped with a decade of failure. But the answer is simple. He refused to acknowledge it. There will be times when the *law of attraction* seems to fail us. We will come on to this later, but we need to consider the rewards that come from persistence and force of will. He refused to give up, despite all the temporary defeats. Because, in fact, they were opportunities to learn what he needed to learn, to be ready for the job he was asking for.

4. We've referred to the pieces being moved into place for Churchill. This is going on, every day, for billions of people on the planet. Very often, what is moving history is the colossal battle of wills between people, few in number, and the Universe, responding to the strength of their will. These people are not always at the top. Sometimes they are from below. The

stronger the individual will, the stronger the chance of prevailing. But if the Universe, or "Source", is able to respond on such a scale to the wills of billions of people, just consider, for a second, the size of the force we are dealing with. This isn't a force constrained by lack or limitation. We come back to our discussion on the eternal and the limitless. Yet so many of us ask so little of it. And even if we ask, our will-power to stay the course, waiting for it to be manifested, is so limited because we so often give up. An important point to bear in mind is that you really can ask for more from such a power that operates on this scale. There is no great figure in history who thought small when they decided to change the world. There just isn't. That's no accident. They became great figures because they believed it of themselves. But you don't need to be a Churchill to define your life. As someone eternal and limitless, you are a great figure regardless. Now ask away for what you want to experience from that perspective – large or small.

Would Churchill have agreed with all of this? We can only quote him when he said, "You create your own universe as you go along." He created his reality with these thoughts, emotions and willpower and, in his case, he affected the reality of millions of others too. Our thoughts and emotions are very, very powerful when we direct them to a specific end.

Plus, what we have just talked about also demonstrates the role of "Source" here, which some of you might still be puzzled about. Your role is to have the thoughts and emotions and to define what you want to create. But the role of "Source", or the "Universe", is the organising force that moves the pieces into place to allow it to happen. It's dealing with that for billions of people, all of whom are thinking, feeling and creating a life experience. That's a vast power. And it's why, in any analysis of this subject matter, it cannot be ignored even if, as a concept, it's a bit "out there" for some.

(iv) Proof of "Source"

Can we prove that "Source" exists?

We can witness it in our everyday experiences and, perhaps, measure it scientifically too.

When we talk of "Source" we are not talking of a religious God. Though "Source" can be seen in such terms if a person wishes, because those having a divine experience from whatever religious perspective they hold, are experiencing the same "Source" as their God, just in a different form. To those of a particular religious faith who might have an issue with the "Source" concept, what is being argued here is closer to your position at its root than you might appreciate. If "Source" is like "Heaven" because we come from and return to it, and it's reflected in our lives, there is no problem in equating its presence in our lives with divinity. "Source", in this philosophy, takes on the qualities of "Heaven"; it's the source of all love and abundance, a wonderful place to be, but we leave it to come into the physical when we choose to. I will come on to "Source" as "conscious" and "divine" later in this section. To those who are of no religious faith, but who do believe in a "force" out there, it offers some rationale for that from a non-religious perspective. At the end of the day, we are all "one" anyway; but the concept of "Source" has room for both the theist and the atheist, for the scientist and the spiritualist.

The key distinction between "Source" and a God, is that, in many instances, a God can imply events being organised around us to a divine "plan", and rules which explain our physical results and the things that manifest in our lives.

What we are arguing here is that what we think and emote is the "plan" and the Universe, or "Source", organises itself around billions of thoughts and emotions happening on this planet at any one time, and manifests them into physical reality.

The "gift" of our physical existence, when we incarnate physically from "Source", is our ability to define that physical existence.

But some of you still might be having trouble with the "Source" concept, and with the idea that thoughts and emotions can actually affect, and define, our physical reality.

The physics bit is the challenging bit.

But like economists and historians disagreeing about their subject, physicists disagree amongst themselves on the *law of attraction* and the power of thought as an energy force that has physical consequences.

Einstein seemed to agree with it, though, when he said, "Imagination is everything. It is the preview of life's coming attractions."

And there are plenty of physicists who are spiritual or religious in their beliefs, both of whom define this "Source" energy as the source of the divinity they believe in.

But what is our relationship, as physical beings, to this "Source"? Can we definitely say, "Yes, this is tangible; it exists"?

When we come into our physical existence, our focus is mainly tied to our physical experience. Our physical experience is what matters, and counts. We remember "Source" but only vaguely and there is always some religion knocking around to remind us that something happens after physical death. But reconnecting to "Source" at a physical level does happen. In fact, it happens when we "get it", when we understand what our physical and non-physical lives mean.

We "get it" when we understand that "Source" responds to our thoughts and emotions, and that we request it to manifest the things that we need to make us feel good in life. And it wants us to feel good in life. This is key. It's benevolent, and it wants us to be happy and successful. The "Heaven" analogy for this wonderful energy really is apt. The better we feel, the closer our connection to "Source" as we hook up to its wonderful, creative energy. The worse we feel, the further we are from it.

Once you know of the infinite power at the root of this, and its benevolence, the life you seek to create will be of a very different order to the life which many others are creating on the planet right now. A considerable number of people are manifesting terrible lives. Yet through this, something very different can be created.

Those in closer alignment with "Source" are said to be of a "higher vibration", and those out of alignment with it of a lower vibration.

We've touched on the alignment between physics and spirituality when we talked about vibrations earlier. On our earthly physical plane, we exist in a low level of vibration, as we are concerned with physical "stuff" like money and survival. The higher planes beyond our physical existence are on a higher vibration. As we become "better people" on the physical plane, our vibration rises because we match the higher vibration of the non-physical plane, or "Source" energy. If "Source" energy is love, abundance, universal energy, life, a wonderful place to be, then its force is benevolent, and the closer we are to it, the better people we are, the higher our "vibration".

What does a person in a higher state of vibration, connected to "Source", look like?

1. They recognize their power as creators of their own success, and they know that "Source" provides everything they might ask for.

2. They don't get hung-up second-guessing worst case scenarios, they just focus on creating and trust "Source" to provide.

3. Their lives are synchronistic; the break they need, in the form of a person or something else, appears at the right moment.

4. They won't try to persuade you of their point of view, they aren't concerned with being "right", they just create rather than bringing ego and argument into their lives. You won't find these people in internet forums trying to persuade everyone they are "right", and by consequence others are "wrong". They aren't bothered about being "right". They are too focused on creating.

5. They are always in a state of gratitude, and even thank the obstacles that show up for bringing them awareness. They honour everything, and don't give power to what is currently lacking in their lives. Instead, they focus on creating.

6. They don't have the concept of enemies because they see everything as one, and so are adept at attracting co-operation and assistance from others, rather than conflict with enemies.

7. They uplift other people with positive energy and gratitude. They convince with their energy, not their argument.

8. They are exceptionally kind and generous, and take pleasure in giving, knowing that the more they give, the more they receive.

9. They are peaceful, but are often seen as aloof and distant because they don't engage in small talk and gossip.

10. They avoid low-energy situations like crowds or negative people, but send compassion and blessing their way.

11. They aren't offended, because they have little ego invested in their opinions. They recognize that taking offence is

limiting their ability to create. They'd rather laugh than waste time focusing on a negative emotion like taking offence.

12. They have an idea about what's coming, because they have created it.

A person of lower vibration can be defined as the opposite in all cases.

Our human experience can tell us that "Source" energy exists because these types of people get the lucky breaks, because they "get" their connection to "Source" and their ability to create.

On the scientific side, many people claim to experience their God, but have had trouble finding scientific verification for it. That's fine. Science is simply another way of explaining what we already know to be, and if the verification isn't there, it's because science might not yet have found a way to measure, record or define it. Science is always catching up with and trying to explain what we already "know".

I've been looking for a way to prove that "Source" physically exists for some time, other than simply observing what I create in my life.

Without "Source", the *law of attraction* and the mirror cannot exist.

To answer this, let's talk about something called Reiki.

Reiki was 're-discovered' by a Japanese monk called Mikao Usui in 1922. Usui was meditating on the creation of a spiritual system that was not an organised religion.

And, in a classic *law of attraction* response, the Universe answered, simply because he asked.

He was attuned to what we now call Reiki, and he then attuned others.

The word "Reiki" is made of two Japanese words – "Rei" which means "God's Wisdom", or the "Higher Power", and

"Ki" which is "life force energy". So Reiki is actually "spiritually guided life-force energy".

Though Reiki is referred to as a "hands-on" healing technique, it is actually a form of energetic healing, and hands don't actually need to be laid on the physical body; the energy can be placed in a person's aura.

What will be obvious at this stage is that we are dealing with "energy" or "spiritual energy", so we are right on topic.

Those attracted to practice Reiki just feel a calling to do it.

One day I felt compelled to experience it, so I went for a treatment. I'd been thinking about it for some time and then one day, on railings outside my flat, there was an advert for a Reiki practitioner in the hotel next door. It felt as if I was being guided to do it.

It was fantastic. Remember how we have said that "Source" acts synchronistically.

Phenomenal heat came from the practitioner's hands. If she was that hot, surely she should be dead, as her body temperature would be in excess of the human body temperature range to support that level of heat? I opened my eyes to see whether the heat from her hands could be explained by wires connected to her hands. No, she was wearing a short-sleeved shirt and her arms were bare. Yet still I couldn't explain the heat from her hands. I could also *feel* an energy flow from her hands along with the heat. Clearly the heat was therefore an energetic transmission. Within minutes, I felt like I was floating, and incredible images were coming into mind, but nothing alarming. I drifted in and out of sleep and consciousness, but never once felt uneasy. The feeling was relaxing, enlightening, yet also safe and secure. I practice Reiki now, and when clients describe the effects to me, I always say to them, "This is how you are *supposed* to feel *all the time*." Relaxed, yet connected.

Reiki is used predominantly for healing. But we also feel incredibly relaxed and clear after a treatment because it is also healing the mind, which conditions so much of our thinking, which in turn affects our physical bodies.

I wanted to be attuned to this energy as it felt incredible, and I found a Reiki Master close to me to carry out the attunement.

The process of attunement involves three stages. Level I provides you with thirty-three per cent of the energy, level II with sixty-six per cent of the energy, and level III with the final wallop.

You are basically being opened up in stages to receive and transmit, for want of a better expression, the Reiki energy.

To receive and accept this, you have to be a clear channel. The attunement process can be difficult, depending on your level of spiritual development. And everyone's reaction is different. There are so many testimonials to attunements online. Please look them up if you are sceptical. The reaction is universally positive. If it's not, it's usually because a person is sadly blocking the energy, or isn't ready to deal with some of the issues that come up.

But at some level, after an attunement, a person goes through two things:

1. A physical and emotional detox. The body detoxes physically, and old emotional wounds come up for healing. This is the rough part, as every major hurt or slight comes up and, if the situation was traumatic, this can take a lot of healing and clearing away. Just acknowledge it, and be kind to yourself.

2. Spiritual enlightenment. In my own case, I experienced a massive, massive acceleration that it simply would have taken years to reach on my own, but it happened at that stage because I was ready for it. Remember how we describe how a person

looks when they are in connection with "Source" energy. You get an automatic leg up *if* you accept the physical and emotional detox in 1. If you resist, it's harder.

If you are dealing with a very spiritual form of energy, it's going to flow much better if all your mess is cleared up. You are being healed, and everyone at some level requires healing. Ego might tell you otherwise, "I am fine, sorted, nothing needs healing," but everyone has something that needs some work. And the cloak of scepticism is usually not a strength, as it often masks nothing but fear. But by letting go, life becomes bigger. And we are not meant to hold on to things in the past. They happen: learn from them, and then let go. We're not meant to be miserable, but a key thing being taught in a Reiki attunement is to let go of everything that's inconsistent with this wonderful energy.

The spiritual side for me was mind-blowingly sweet. I suddenly understood the concept of "higher vibration" because I *felt* it. I suddenly had that connection to "Source" energy as described earlier. Once out of the detox, there is an incredible feeling of being *alive*, with the possession of so much energy. You can't be around negative people, because your mood is so good.

What happens?

1. Your life changes and your ability to manifest speeds up. We deal with the blocks to manifesting in a later chapter. The process of the detox removes some of the blockages to bringing this in. I had been in the same flat for eight years, and in the same job for fourteen years. Within months, both had changed and I got a new job and a new home, better than I previously thought I could achieve.

2. Some people, but not all, meet their spiritual guides. I remember, one night, being awoken by a definite presence. I

looked and two vortexes were swirling in the air. I thought they were a trick of the light, until I looked at the Pissing Pussy on the bed. She was bolt upright, looking at them. She looked at me, she looked at them, and back again. Later, I got a name – Carl. This was my guide. It happens because your vibration is raised. Suddenly the gap between this physical world and the next is narrower, and guides can come through. Oh, and expect it between three and four a.m. in the morning. The gap between both worlds is narrower then.

3. You reach a natural state of ecstasy. No drugs are involved in the attunement process. This is a spiritual initiation. Nothing is ingested; this is an opening up of pathways to the energy. As you hit that higher level, there is a feeling of unconditional love. This can be hard. Because synchronistic relationships can happen. "Soul mates" just show up. Attractions can become very powerful. I found the answer to this later on, it's not that this means that a relationship is pending with someone. This is opening up our channels for unconditional love, and this requires that we show unconditional love to ourselves first. So, while soul-mate experiences happen, the Universe is telling us to develop a new relationship with ourselves first, before giving our energy away. This bit is important, as you can be vulnerable at this stage and miss that the lesson is unconditional love towards yourself first, rather than towards some random individual whom you have just met, with whom there – seems to be – an incredible connection.

The spiritual explosion might sound too much for some. It isn't. You are establishing your connection to "Source". Just remain grounded. This is a wonderful process, and it does not feel overwhelming, or as though it is the product of excess. You are just establishing a connection with *how you are supposed to feel*, free of the negativity that we absorb from others or condition ourselves to believe. Once you have mastered the energies you will be fine, but go easy with yourself if you make a mistake. And you will, because these are just the first steps of a new journey.

We come to the central issue here. And my ears always prick up and I beam whenever a client asks me, "So, where did that energy come from? It wasn't you. You would be drained, and yet you look great. So where are you channelling this energy *from*?"

Bingo. That's the key question. Most people react to the sensation of the Reiki experience without asking the fundamental and obvious question – what was that?

When we are attuned to Reiki, we are told this energy is benevolent, but above all it is *intelligent and conscious.*

The words in italics are crucial here.

Reiki is fundamentally a healing system. There doesn't even have to be a dialogue between patient and healer, but after the healing session, the patient often says something along the lines of, "My ankle hurts. I had an accident years ago and never got it seen to, and now it's going off like crazy."

The Reiki energy is healing this *because it knows where to go, because it's conscious.*

I had a conversation with an ex-neighbour of mine and she wanted to try Reiki out. I still see her now. She is a cancer doctor, and she sat up afterwards and she said, "I'm a scientist, and I can't explain the experience I've just had."

But the pieces were falling into place for me.

We have a benevolent healing energy that is intelligent and conscious. The more I read into "Source" energy or the concepts of divinity, the more I can't escape the obvious conclusion.

Reiki is a direct plug, or tap, into "Source" or divine energy, which, as I said earlier, is divine and conscious. That's why it's so great to be connected to it. And where else could this energy conceivably come from?

This is different from any other form of energy that we know of, because I am not aware that physics recognises any form of energy that possesses the qualities of benevolence and consciousness.

I've heard scientific figures question Reiki, figures who, at the same time, freely admit to not having experienced it. That's not a scientific analysis.

Religious figures have condemned it, without comprehending Christ's healing miracles were energetic healings.

Mikao Usui got an attunement to that energy because he asked for it. It's that simple.

Was Christ a Reiki healer? We know from documented accounts that energetic healing was more commonplace centuries ago, but was then lost to us.

In addition to Mikao Usui, Patrick Ziegler was attuned to Seichem energy after spending a night in the Great Pyramid in Egypt in 1980.

The form of Reiki that my Reiki Master and I practice is actually a combination of Reiki and Seichem energies.

There are different forms of energetic healing around the world. We cannot say which one Christ, or other similar healers, used, but we can say that he was an energetic healer, as were plenty of others at the time, and then the knowledge was lost. And now it's coming back!

And that energy, whether Reiki, Seichem, or other form of energetic healing system, is consciousness and benevolent because it comes from the same "Source".

But if Reiki or other energetic forms of healing can provide some evidence at the level of our physical experience that "Source" energy exists, because we feel it during a treatment, how do we know it reflects our thoughts back at us as a physical reality?

The answer is easy.

Because when I ask for the Reiki energy to flow, "Source" hears the request, and it sends the flow of it right back to me. I then channel this into the patient. Just like any other thought or emotion I put out there, I ask for the energy to flow, the energy I described earlier - the hot hands and the physical flow. And it comes. The link between asking and receiving is there, right in the present.

I have talked about Reiki a lot. Not because I'm trying to advertise it, but because it's been key in my journey of understanding the concepts I'm talking about. It's the missing link. It clinches the analysis for me.

To me, it proves the existence of a divine and conscious energy that responds to the request for it to flow. This is the law of attraction, in a nutshell. In energetic terms, it's "ask and receive".

It can be proved at a physical level, if you will allow yourself to experience it. So, if you want to experience it, go and find yourself a Reiki or other energetic healer. One that is properly attuned, of course. And then explain what you have experienced. You can block it with a closed mind. But with an open mind you will experience what I have talked about.

The Reiki energy enters the crown of the healer and is transmitted through the hands. We see it and experience it as gold or white in colour. Can we film or record this? Can we capture it "scientifically"?

There are recordings of healings done with the kind of cameras which capture our energetic aura, and they do show the Reiki energy flowing. These recordings do appear to be in their infancy. Whilst they exist, there is a lot more to be done, because it could be demonstrated more clearly, but the flow of energy can be seen on the recording.

But you can experience Reiki for yourself, and assess it for yourself. You can certainly prove it to yourself. Some work has been done physically to record it, but much more could be done.

I would love to work with a quantum physicist to see if we can more clearly record the energy than we have thus far. As we have said, physicists are continually trying to record things which they theorise exist but can't yet measure. To see it clearly, all we have to do is ask. Every discovery or invention started with nothing more than an idea, a request to the Universe to show us how. Reiki wanted to reveal itself to us, when Mikao Usui asked. Ultimately, it won't hide if we ask it to reveal itself a little bit more...

So, "What is the meaning of life, the universe and everything?"

Answer - we are infinite and eternal, we come here for a physical experience, we create that through what we think and feel. The Universe or "Source" is our mirror, giving back to us the life we are choosing as a result of our thoughts and emotions. "Source" is benevolent and conscious, so if we ask for a nice life as our experience this time round, it will respond. And you can actually experience that energy if you choose to, just in case you're not sure.

Hopefully, that's a slightly better answer than "Forty-two" to universal questions about life and existence.

What We Give Our Attention To

I don't wish to sound like a broken record, but once again, please, with feeling: the Universe reflects back what you give your attention to!

"Source", or the Universe, hears it, and sends it back as the experience you have requested to have.

This principle doesn't work just on a conscious level, meaning the thoughts which we *consciously* choose all the time.

It also works on what is in our heads that we might not be consciously aware of, in our *subconscious* mind.

It's not just our thoughts that are key here. It's our thoughts and our emotions as well.

Below are examples of what we might consciously think every day, but, just as importantly, of what we might be *feeling* too, emotionally and at a subconscious level:

1. *"I'm always too busy, stressed, and exhausted."* You then will keep receiving events which confirm that. Conversely, if you give attention to your boredom, more of the same will come right back at you.

2. *"Aren't people rude?"* ...You will end up getting more rude people.

3. *"The trains or roads are a disaster"* ...You'll get more of that.

4. *"I hate my job"* …It will keep giving you reasons to hate it.

5. *"My relationship sucks"* …It will keep sucking, and not in a good way.

6. *"I'm always single"* …The Universe will keep sending you unsuitable types because you have focused on your "single" status. You might have a great time in the short term with flings, but they will never be "right" or "the one".

7. *"I'm always ill"* …We can now guess the answer to that one.

We have conscious thoughts. We also have emotions in our subconscious.

Both of them make us give our attention to something. One is conscious, the other isn't. But even if you are subconsciously giving your attention to something, you are still giving it your attention. And whatever you give your attention to comes back at you.

So if you focus, consciously or subconsciously, on any of these things - your business, antiques, dogs, cats, sex, flowers, illness, health, whatever, the energy of creation will flow to what you have given energy and attention to. Have you ever noticed that when you are in a hurry, everyone moves at a snail's pace all of a sudden, and gets in your way? You've given your attention to not getting there on time, so, suddenly, things arrive to block you, and make lateness a reality.

We don't have to think a negative thought consciously on a subject. "I feel anger" is not something we think straight away, but we might feel it before we actually acknowledge that we are consciously choosing to be angry, and that's what we are transmitting, before we are even aware of it.

And how we feel can get locked into our subconscious. If we are angry, stressed, upset, unhappy, guilty, shameful, whatever negative emotion you can think of, if this gets locked into our subconscious, and without knowing it, this is what we give our attention to. And more of the same comes back, because that's what we have sent out to the mirror, to be reflected back.

Arguably, the Universe responds much more to our emotions than to our thoughts, because our emotions are stronger. As we have said, the Universe is energy, and the power of a negative emotion is a particularly strong wave of energy.

Added to which, negative emotions, such as anger, guilt, shame, loneliness, etc., usually achieve absolutely nothing, except to make us feel lousy. They rarely resolve a situation positively, so we just feel lousy without solving anything, sending impulses out for more of the same.

And all this negativity affects our physical results in life, and, it is also worth saying, our physical bodies.

There are also spiritual explanations for illnesses which, whilst doctors should always be consulted, can provide insights. Doctors, of all medical philosophies, acknowledge the power of the mind to heal, though often they can't explain this scientifically. Just as we can think ourselves well, so we can think ourselves ill, and again become what we think and feel.

Yet there is one important point to make here. Some would say this requires us to be judgemental that someone is responsible for their illness, as opposed to simply being ill as a result of misfortune. I will come onto this later, but it's worth saying now, it doesn't matter what the cause of an illness was, the obligation is to help the healing process with compassion and not judgement.

If *negative* thoughts and emotions can set up a loop, encouraging more of the same, what about *positive* thoughts and emotions?

Positive thoughts and emotions will set up a loop for more of the same to come back.

Now I know what a lot of people will say. They have very difficult lives, full of problems. Just dealing with what they have got takes everything they have, that there is no way of avoiding the negative stuff they have to deal with – not enough money, nightmare job, difficult family members, children, Grannies. Everyone has their own list.

But your subconscious mind will function from a negative position unless you control it. Those eighty per cent of negative thoughts which we think every day will plant themselves there automatically.

We have got to control the negative impulses that we automatically put there, and substitute them with positive thoughts. Whatever is going on, you've got to control your thoughts. You can't stop yourself thinking, it will happen anyway; so you might as well put something in there that's worthwhile.

Let's look at the causes of the negative thoughts or emotions which someone might have.

Causes of negativity – other people

Very simply, a considerable amount of the negativity we feel is put there by others. The points of view of others are given to us at various stages in our lives, and are now stuck there.

The negative thoughts that other people can give us run along these lines: (i) my life has been this way, so will yours, this is what we do, and so the same with you as well – in other words, the pressure to conform; (ii) you don't deserve that, you are not worth it, etc. There are other examples here, of course, but what these people are always afraid of is of your having a better life than they have; so they try to keep you down. This is about their low self-esteem; yet you have the right to be who you are meant to be.

The issue is this: these are *their ideas about their life, not yours*. But so often, we allow the views of other people to shape us, and we allow them to implant their life and views, often negative, onto us.

Are you thinking your thoughts? Or someone else's? Are you growing? Or are you living someone else's contraction, not just temporarily, but through your whole life? That's a scary thought. But it exists every day and everywhere, especially the pressure to conform to low achievement and low expectations, where this is ingrained into the consciousness of a group of people, or a place.

You can just choose to ignore or return these thoughts to their sender, and focus on what you want. It's actually quite simple. When you recognise that a thought belongs to someone else, ignore it, or send it back to them, and then get busy with your thoughts and with what you want to create.

You are an infinite being, with infinite choices, and your own light. Your thoughts and emotions, and your life, are your own natural monopoly, they belong to no one else.

You didn't choose to come here from "Source" to allow other people to implant their views into you, unless of course that is what you choose to do because it makes sense to you. But what is right for someone else, probably isn't right for you.

Every person has their own truth and being, which is not the same as someone else's. There are billions of people on the planet right now. Each has their own separate truth, and what is right for them. That's billions of alternatives. There is simply no reason to accept someone else's truth when you have your own, because there really is a lot of room for the Universe to incorporate billions of choices. And that's only billions on earth right now. What of the billions before, and the billions yet to come? This is massive. And our capacity to choose among that lot is truly awesome.

So often, we accept the views of others as true for us, when they aren't. Plus, those views are often judgemental.

Others might not agree with our choices, because we go against their flow, or the flow of society, and we are meant to feel strange or inferior. But what if being "you", as you are, is actually "right"?

How often do you genuinely choose for "you"? It can be a difficult question to ask, and the answers, when we are being honest, can be a shock.

Only we know what's right for us, because our instinct will tell us.

But if there is something that is right for "us", it's no wonder that our lives don't work when we try to live someone else's choices.

Causes of negativity – our past

To take the subject of past experience and events, and their influence on our thinking, it is sometimes said that, "A person is the sum of their memories". In other words, that a person is defined by their past. If that's negative, they might define their present and future in the same way. In fact, that is often what happens. If their past has been positive, with wonderful experiences and success, great, but there is another potential downside here – if they define themselves by past success, they may be limiting themselves now and in the future, because their concept of "success" might actually be too small.

Though the words "a person is the sum of their memories" might be an accurate description of a person's current state of mind and expectations, the reality is that it doesn't have to offer any guide as to the future whatsoever.

Because if we can change our outcomes by what we think and feel, the past is irrelevant.

Irrelevant.

That's quite hard for some people to grasp, as the past is all they have to live their life by. But in all likelihood, it will only limit us, even if that past has been positive.

But it doesn't matter how much limitation and lack we have experienced because of past events. They have no bearing on the future, because you can always change it. We hear of plenty of people who have difficult early lives who go on to become phenomenal successes later. Usually this is because they ask for something better. They refuse to be limited by their past, and in doing so, they become who they want to be. They become a different person. If we listen only to our past, we will always be that person in the past.

"But you only get one chance; and I blew it, years ago," is a common point of view. No, you have as many chances as you ask for. Let's say that sentence again – you have as many chances as you ask for. That's wonderfully liberating. In an infinite Universe there is no such thing as only "one chance". Think about that for a moment. There is simply no rational reason why there is only "one chance", unless that's what we have decided from our own self-limiting perspective.

So, there are the thoughts and emotions that other people place there.

But there is a further category!

Causes of negativity – our choice

There are also the thoughts and emotions we put there, through choice. We might get up in a bad mood, and sometimes nothing has happened to cause that. But today, we decide, I'm just going to be grumpy. And unpleasant. Because... I can.

But the reality is this. All thoughts and emotions, whether put there by someone else, or those which come from our past experience, or those which we put there ourselves today, are all there as result of our own choice. We choose and allow it to be there. Really we do; because we could just ignore it, and focus on what we want to create instead.

But what if we didn't allow those thoughts or feelings to be there?

The first steps can be quite easy.

Make one small shift of thinking now, just one. Such as, "There isn't only one chance. There are infinite chances, and I can begin to take them right now." That small shift in thinking might transform everything.

The "allowing" bit, of what we choose to think and feel, is quite important.

Sometimes, someone acts rudely towards us, or cuts us up in traffic, and we don't care. Other times, we see red and get angry at that person's behaviour.

We choose to get angry about it. We "allow" that other person to make us angry. They could do the same thing one day, and we don't react, and the same thing another day, and we go nuclear. But because it's the same act, we are totally in control of our response if we don't care one day, and hit the roof the next.

That other person might do a terrible thing. But we are in control of our reaction to it.

If we have left the house in a great frame of mind, and then someone comes along and upsets us, we have "allowed" them to do it. With our anger, we have empowered them. That's why I said that all thoughts and emotions are there as a result of our own choice. We empower ourselves, however, if we ignore them, and continue with our own positive thoughts about what we want to create. Our own positive thoughts and emotions really are one of the most powerful forces we have, crucial to our wellness and state of being. The expression "don't let it/them get to you" is worth a pot of gold. If someone enjoys pressing our buttons to get a reaction, they will soon stop when they realise it doesn't work. They will continue when they see it does.

Moving away from negativity

Our starting point for allowing should be this: other people and their views, the past, our own previous capacity to self-limit, are nothing. From now on, they don't exist. You define your reality, here and now, free of any previous limitations and misconceptions, so make it a good one. Every day, the slate is wiped clean for you to create what you want to create.

You have just taken control.

And what you will want to allow, or create, is for you to define. If you keep thinking of your problems, you will only get them reflected back.

If you don't start choosing your thoughts, you are just going to get knocked around like a small boat in a wild ocean. But you can make your life to order.

So start thinking about what you *would like* to happen.

Let's just start by changing the way we think.

Let us, for example, take our seven points above and flip them, and take them from a different perspective.

1. *"I'm in control, calm with plenty of energy. My life is easy and full of fun and stimulates me."*

2. *"People are always nice to me."*

3. *"My travel plans today will run smoothly."*

4. *"I love my job, the people I work with and it pays me £[insert here]."* This actually might lead you to changing jobs, if you are in a job you don't like, or one that is not paying enough. The Universe will respond to a positive affirmation of a job you love for that salary you have placed in your mind. Or your current role might change into what you have thought about.

5. *"My relationship is fantastic and I'm particularly grateful for [insert here] and [insert things you want to improve] is here now."*

6. If you are single, focus on the partner you want.

7. *"I'm healthy and well."*

You can add anything else of your choice. But start to notice, when you do this, how life starts to change.

It might be slow at first. The adjustment might be tough to start with. But as the new plan is implanted, over the longer term, your outcomes will reflect the permanent shift you have made.

Even if you don't agree with any of this, the positive frame of mind surely has to be a better starting point every day. It takes more effort to frown than it does to smile. The negative thought and emotional pattern uses far more energy than a positive one. You use far more energy to get angry at something than you use if you let it go over your head and focus on what you want to create instead.

And the positive frame of mind, even if it might take time to show up results in physical form, just does your body so much good. Your body really does like being in that place.

Try praising what you like about your life, or want to bring in. Because by praising it, you have given your attention to it. And by doing that, you get more of it.

Negativity constricts. Sadly, because most of our thoughts are negative, they just focus on the problem, they constrict our lives, and we don't even ask the Universe for a solution. We just focus on the problem. And get more of the problem back.

The really knotty area is that of the problems which we think we can't solve. This is when life gets really tricky. But the solution to the insoluble problem is sometimes more simple than we realise. You just ask for help, from the Universe that you are inextricably a part of. It wants to help. It wants you to be a success. And it will respond with help. It's capable of working with billions of people every moment. It really does have space for your "insoluble" problem. Your "insoluble" problem, as we discussed, is just energy anyway, and it can be manipulated. Our problems seem insoluble so often because we try to solve them ourselves, rather than "handing them over to Heaven", and asking for help, if we can't solve them. Go on! If something is too much, just hand it over to the Universe. Is this just "prayer" by another name? Yes. But people who claim to have had their prayers answered, use that as validation of a judgement based faith. But it's a bit bigger than that. It's not about validating a faith, but about acknowledging your power to create.

There are, of course, some people who just like being negative. They prefer the problem to the solution. They get off on it. That's fine, it's their choice and their life, but it doesn't have to be yours.

Very often, we don't change because we want to retain our connection to people who hold us back. The process of changing ourselves will lead to the people around us changing, either in themselves, or because they leave our life and people more suited to the person who we have now become, come into our lives.

Cutting negative ties

Sometimes it's best to cut negative people out of our life, and only ask in those people who will enhance your experience. But what if we can't cut them out, for instance if they are close family or co-workers who we have to deal with? There is a way of cutting out the negative ties in that relationship, of keeping it in place but transforming it so that it is no longer a negative drain on you. It's called cord-cutting, meaning cutting the negative cords this person has established with you. I learned this from my Reiki Master. Here is comes...

Lay down somewhere quiet where you will be undisturbed for a few minutes.

Visualise a figure eight, with yourself in one circle. The person from whom you want to untie cords is in the other circle. Visualise light flowing around the two circles in the figure eight, but there is a cord between the two people where the two circles meet.

Look at the other person. What does the cord between you look like? A thin cord, a thin rope, a huge rope, or an entangled mass? This is what is holding the negative relationship in place. We are wishing to cut these cords so that their negative influence over us goes.

What cutting instrument is appropriate? Scissors, knife, sword, or chainsaw? It depends what the cord is like.

Once you have chosen the cutting implement, breathe deeply, and say out loud, or in your head, the following: "Please help me cut the cord that lies between [you] and [the person] to the highest good of all concerned and in divine order. Thank you. So be it."

Visualise the cord being cut with the implement you have chosen.

What does the person who you are cutting cords with look like? What is their expression? Every time it's different, but gradually, quickly or slowly, they disappear. When they are gone, it's over. It takes very little time.

You might see that person again, but the nature of the relationship changes. The negativity, and the negative control over you, just goes, but the relationship with them is preserved if for various reasons you think it has to. It works for any form of negativity in a relationship. Use it for people you can't easily avoid, like family members, neighbours, or people at work. Then watch things change. If they re-establish the cord and give you their negativity, keep cutting it.

At its root here, we are recognising the role negativity plays in our lives, whether put there by others, ourselves, but always allowed by us; and we are recognising that, if we want to change things, we must deal with it.

If we may reach a landing on this subject, the power of positive thinking is awesome, as is surrounding yourself with people who celebrate when you change, and who don't hold you back. We all need more positive thinkers around us.

But the next obvious question is, "how do you know if you are asking the Universe "in the right way" to get what you want?"

You're working on changing your thinking and emotional programming. Great. It's more positive from now on. Fantastic. But how do you know if the Universe can "hear" you, and then respond?

How to Ask

In an infinite Universe, infinite possibilities exist.

One of those possibilities is the thing you are asking for.

It's out there, waiting to come in.

There are three ways of getting into this "frequency" which are discussed below.

1. Be "It"

You raise the question or desire for something to come in, and the Universe hears it, then it sends a reflection back in physical form.

But very often, that reflection back is simply a mirror image of where we were when we asked. The current projection reflects where we have been in the past in our thinking and our emotions. If we don't like that, we have to change in the present for something new to come through. The Universe reflects "back" at us, so, if we want something, it can only reflect it back if we are already, or have become, consistent with it.

If you are at a certain frequency, such as low frequency, because you are not happy, and have asked for something at a higher frequency, such as a wonderful, life-changing event, what comes back might well reflect the position you have asked from. In other words, the Universe may give you a chance to acquire what you want, an opportunity to move up and get closer to it, but it might require you to "up your game" and change who you are first.

The more you raise your vibration now, the more you get tuned in now, the quicker what you are asking for will come through. The Universe isn't going to give us the "whole works" before we are ready. It wants to know we are in the right place in ourselves to receive it. If yes, it's reflected back. If not, it reflects back the lessons we need to learn, and it tells us what we need to do to put ourselves in the right place for it – that you are a "vibrational match" to what you ask for, that you are "in alignment" with it. It's perfectly logical to think that the thing we have asked for is not going to come to us when we are not in alignment with what we are looking for. If the Universe is a mirror, it can't reflect back something which is at odds with the original image of you when you asked.

You first have to become what you want. Match the energy of the thing you want to create.

Think of it as like wanting to watch a particular TV station. You can't access it until your TV has tuned into the right frequency, but the station is out there, just waiting for you to tune in, to get into the right frequency.

If you are broke, and want to be rich, you can't be rich until you match that frequency and get comfortable with having money, and expecting it to be yours. Most people want more money, but they never think that it will happen to them, or they think about small numbers, and never get into the frame of mind of someone who is just comfortable with money, and large amounts of it.

A person seeking a fantastic relationship will never find it from a position of being closed and grumpy. You have to get into the frequency of it to receive it. Instead, become that great relationship counterparty now, as you can't attract a dream relationship if you are a nightmare yourself.

So, the tramp wants to be the lady? She must first start to think she is the lady, even when she is the tramp.

You want to be boss when you are fairly low down the pecking order? Start acting and thinking like a responsible manager now – become the part now.

You have to tune in to what you have asked for. Be "it".

2. Desire, faith and expectation

A part of being "it" is the desire for "it", and the faith and expectation that you will get "it".

We talked of thoughts and emotions. We've covered the thinking aspect of it in the last chapter, but the emotional aspect is a large part of what we want to talk about here. The emotional desire, and the faith and expectation that something will come in, is a very large part of the tuning mechanism which tunes you in to match the frequency of the thing that is out there, which you want to bring in.

It's obvious really, but if you don't desire something, if you don't have faith and don't expect it to happen, it probably won't. Having the emotional desire, and the faith and expectation, is simply one of those efforts the Universe asks of us to bring something in. The vibration matches the object in the mirror – if the object has no desire, faith and expectation, the reflection must match that.

This bit can be difficult. Sometimes what we are asking for requires us to become a very different person to whom we currently are when we ask for it.

It can take an effort, to start with, to project these emotions on to what we want. If we are sincere about wanting something, these emotions should be there anyway. If you have become comfortable with what you want to be, and you feel like you're the part already, the desire, faith and expectation part just happens naturally. For instance, if your consciousness reflects an abundance mentality, you will have a natural desire, faith and expectation that money will follow. So with every other area of life.

The practical examples of this are those people in life to whom things seem to come to with ease, who seem totally relaxed and just "expect". They are relaxed because they are already in alignment with what they are looking for. The desire for what they want, and faith and expectation are all there. But that ease is deceptive. It normally hides the fact that they have already done all the hard work to get into alignment with what they want, work that you might be just starting. It's the place where we all want to be. It can be done. So many people already do it. It is possible to do the hard work at getting into alignment and being relaxed at the same time too.

There is an important point to make about perspective here. Sometimes we have to work hard for things to get into alignment, other times we don't. It depends on the extent of the test, the hill you have set yourself and how much work you've already done to climb it.

Remember, the Universe is designed for you to be successful. It wants you to succeed, and to experience things, because that is what you have chosen to come here to do. We just have to understand what we are asking for, and ask ourselves how much work we have to do to get ourselves in alignment, if the frequency or vibration of what we are asking for is above where we are at the time of asking. You will be given tests, challenges, obstacles, only if you have a lot of work to do on yourself. But the doors will unlock, and more will come through as you pass each test, when you get into vibrational alignment. That is something of which we are in control, and the gift we already have is our ability to make those changes.

We feel great when we are connected to "Source". The "Source" of all well-being is going to have a pretty good vibration, and, when we are experiencing a positive emotion, we are in greater alignment with it, and when we are experiencing a negative emotion, we are out of alignment. Feeling good about something we want that is consistent with our well-being creates a "double whammy" of positive alignment, both with "Source" and the thing we want, which must inevitably bring it in more quickly.

There are only two emotional states here:

1. If you feel good about something, you are *allowing* it to come in; or

2. You offer thoughts or emotions which are out of connection with what you want to bring in. This is *resistance*.

You are either *allowing* or you are *resisting*.

Your emotions will tell you which; they will tell you exactly where you are.

If you just think "I want money, I want money, I want money", it's just words. It won't manifest unless you are in emotional alignment with it, and are allowing it, by practising a positive emotion about feeling great about it. If you focus on paying the bills, you are out of alignment. That's a focus on not having it, because you are focussing on the bill, not the money. Focus on receiving it and how great that will feel, then you are in alignment. You've tuned into the "frequency" we talked about.

You get much better at creating things when you listen to your emotions, and you consider whether the message you are sending out there is an allowing or resisting one, because of your emotional feeling in respect of it.

If you want to attract something different, change your thoughts, change your emotions.

3. Ask as if you already have it

You pass the desire, faith and expectation test much more easily if you speak and feel as if you already have what you are looking for. That is making it much more real.

If you can get into the emotion of already having something you want, you've sent a signal out that you are in vibrational alignment to it, and the Universe must respond by reflecting it back. Picture what you want - house, car, job, relationship. And then feel the emotion now of what you will feel like when it arrives.

To speak as if we already have something, we do not ask, "Can I have [x] please?"

Why not? Because you are already acknowledging that you don't have it! You just attract more of the "not having it." This is very important! Focusing on what you do not want is not correct.

The Universe is more likely to recognise that we are in vibrational alignment if we are thanking the Universe for already having what we are asking for, even if it hasn't come in yet. The reflection back will be of "have" and not "have not".

If the Universe is giving us something, remember the importance of gratitude. The Universe is bigger and more powerful than we are, so please be nice to it, especially if it's just given us a gift. That also applies when it sends us a hard knock, saying that we still have things to learn. Thank it for the opportunity to learn.

So when we ask for something, we can do it like this:

"Thank you for the great job/relationship/car/amount of money [whatever you want] that is now in my life." Even before we have it.

This is just an example. We will refine this more as we go along in the next chapters, so that the manner in which we ask for something gets as close to perfect as possible. But notice that we added a "thank you" at the start. Gratitude is a key part of the emotional vibration to bring something into physical existence, because it is the emotion you have when you are happy that you have received something. If the Universe is giving you something for which you have asked, it's just polite to thank it.

Gratitude is such a great energy anyway.

Retraining the subconscious mind

If you are slightly puzzled by what is happening in steps one to three, let's look at it from another perspective.

We have established the power of our thoughts and emotions, particularly those which lodge in our subconscious mind.

Controlling the subconscious mind in terms of altering our outcomes is key. Why? Because it is the bridge between us and the Universe.

It's the bridge, the negotiator, the middleman, the go-between.

As we've discussed, it will generate its own emotions and vibrations – usually negative – on its own. If that's what's in there, that's what is going to come back.

But if we convince the subconscious mind of something different, then what?

The results will be different. That's what we are doing in steps one to three.

As we have noted, the subconscious is where our emotional set points exist, such as whether we are happy or sad. When we can be "it", when we desire, have faith and expect something, and convince ourselves that we already have it, we are reconditioning our subconscious mind with those particular emotions. We are changing the whole pattern upon which we exist. In time, our subconscious will think that we are an entirely different person to the one we are, because we have convinced it that that is the case.

Are we "deceiving" our subconscious? You bet. But it's simply a means to transform our physical reality from one state to another one, because, the more often it is repeated, the more often it will become that.

It may be directed through habit, and by habit the reality will eventually be drawn in to reflect the habit.

Now we start to understand the importance of the subconscious mind, and what we put into it.

You literally have to recondition it. You choose a thought or an emotional set point with your conscious mind, and you place it in your subconscious.

We cannot totally control our subconscious. But we can try. And the way we do this is constantly to put the things in there which we want to create in our lives. It is the principle of auto-suggestion. Affirmation. Repeating the same thing over and over again. Almost self-hypnosis. You keep doing it, and keep doing it, until your subconscious positioning changes. Until you change.

Have you ever noticed how some people in life change beyond recognition? How they might go from an ugly duckling to a rare beauty? From a no-hoper to an achiever? From poor to rich? From a failure to a success? Or even, in all cases, the other way round?

They might not even have known it, but they have probably reconditioned their subconscious concerning who they are. They have become, in their own mind, the person they put into their subconscious. And then they physically became "it".

In that process, to some, they will have been a fantasist. Some people might have asked, none too kindly, "Who do you think you are? You've got ideas above your station." The answer is that they are growing, but they must first "be" in their mind before they actually become it.

Don't worry about being a fantasist or daydreamer. Nothing is ever accomplished by people who aren't. You will never achieve anything without a fantasy, a daydream, or a thought or a desire. And the chances are that others will never understand what you are thinking, but all growth must start from this point.

Whether you are changing you, or trying to bring in something you want, you must first convince your subconscious that it is "you"; that such a thing resonates with who you are. It makes perfect sense – the tramp cannot become the lady unless she believes it; the poor person cannot become rich unless they have convinced themselves that is what they are.

We are not encouraging dangerous fantasies – that if you daydream it, you will become it. This is not something for nothing. You will be expected to put the work in to make a dream a reality. Unworldly fantasists probably won't have the application.

Also, as noted, it's not instantaneous. This is probably the most difficult bit of the *law of attraction*. It's the process of starting to change your thoughts and emotions. It's hard. It's tough. Because, so often, you will fall back into the default mode, at the slightest difficulty, at the slightest intrusion of "real life", the mode from which you have been operating for years, if not for decades. But, as noted previously, we can change "real life".

Everything can change when you become "aware" or "conscious" of what you think and feel. You have probably got that awareness now. When you notice that you are in the negative, either in your thoughts or emotions, immediately focus on what you want to create, and how good that will feel.

It's tough, though. Especially at the start, as we so often look back into what we were before. It requires a lot of conscious effort, and the change from negative to positive takes time.

You can't be in a negative emotion one minute, in the depths of despair, and elevate to the heights of happiness in an instant. You can't do it. But you can change gradually, by focusing on what makes you feel good. Start off by feeling better, gradually. Usually that might mean accepting what has happened which has knocked you off balance. Then see the opportunities and choices it creates, and how good they might feel. Gradually, you swing yourself round to a better set point, but you cannot do it in one go. This might be a small matter, such as someone cutting you up in traffic, to something larger, where it really is going to take a long time to make that shift.

But go easy on yourself. Accept, first of all, that bad feelings are resistant thoughts, and that you are resisting what you want to bring in. Try to release the resistant thoughts. Switch, gradually, to things that make you feel good: a picture, a walk, some music you like. And move, gradually, into that better place.

This isn't about ignoring your results. Recognise them, but as part of recognising and acknowledging what you don't want, so that you can focus on what you do want.

As for feeling good just for the sake of it, sometimes the best part of the journey is not arriving at your destination, it's the journey itself.

We are practicing feeling good, because this is how we connect to "Source". That doesn't just allow one manifestation, it opens all sorts of doors to *constant* creation.

That's why you practice feeling good, and getting to a positive emotional state. And then the rest just flows...

Now for another tip.

<u>Be specific!</u>

This is where a lot of people fall down.

So, if someone wants both money and a new relationship, they might say something like "Thank you for £[x amount of money] in my life and my new relationship," or words to that effect.

The Universe cannot work on any more than you give it. If you put little information in, it will not fill in the blanks for you. This is where you need your wits about you.

The request above can bring us money. We might suddenly inherit exactly what we asked for in the request above, but it might come as a result of an inheritance from a death or other tragic circumstances. But we got what we asked for – purely and simply "money". In the case of the new relationship, your new other half might be a head-case, abuser, alcoholic, etc., etc. But you got what you asked for, a "new relationship".

I know of someone who asked for "a challenge". They got cancer. On the subject of "challenges", we usually ask for these when we are bored. Be careful! I've found that a "challenge" usually means that you end up being stressed and overwhelmed. That's usually not pleasant, but you've brought it in. Why not ask to be "interested", "stimulated" and "expanded" instead, and to learn new things "with ease"? You will get the same results, without losing your sanity. Growth isn't dependent on being overwhelmed by difficult experiences. You can have growth with ease.

This is where "be careful what you wish for" comes in.

How do we control this? By being very specific.

The Universe has infinite parameters from which it can respond. It can respond in an infinite number of ways. That's why you have to give it guidance, because the chances are that it might respond, from the range of all the options available to it, in the way that you didn't want because you haven't been specific about what you do want.

On the money request, thank the Universe that you and others around you are in good health when the money comes through. Or a common catch-all I always use, in any creation request, is, "Thank you for [x] in my life, *to the highest good of everyone and in divine order.*" You can't hex or jinx it with that expression.

So, in the case of the relationship request, be specific about what qualities you want this person to have. It's a really good idea to write down a list. But be careful about what is on and what is off the list! I know a woman whose relationship request turned up, down to the letter. She was amazed that everything on her list had just walked through the door. She left "good sex" off her list, so, of course, he was useless. Great relationship otherwise though. But she should have put "good sex" on the list, because that was important to her.

The Universe can't fill in the blanks in what you ask for. It can't read your mind on the specifics. So you have to be specific, and fill in all the blanks on what you want, because it's very literal. It responds to what we put out there.

What do we do when we get this wrong, and we get some, but not all, of what we want, because we missed something important off the list?

Do the list again.

Remember the bit about how we always get more than one chance in life?

This is where this idea comes in, big time.

You re-write your list, adding in the things that were missing when "it" came into existence. You don't just get one chance, you keep getting more chances. You get as many chances as you need, until you get it right.

How many of us don't do this? Most people just give up on the first go. People have one bad experience at creating something like a relationship, or money, and then assume that all similar experiences will follow the same pattern, so they give up entirely. That's the conclusion they have reached, by choice, so it's reflected back. Or they settle for less than what they want.

It sounds nuts to give up so easily, but it's what people do.

But you can go back and ask again and again, refining your list of the things you want.

This really is what so much of life is about. We start off with our list, and at first we don't quite get what we want. We blame the Universe, ourselves, other people, anything, but fundamentally we just give up because we didn't get what we wanted on the first or even second go. Ask yourself honestly, is this you?

But what we really should be doing is looking at our list and asking: (i) what worked, and thank you for that; and (ii) where have things gone wrong? Where haven't I got what I wanted? In that second area, that's where we need to realise that our list just needs some work – that we haven't been specific enough, or have just left something obvious, but crucial, off our list.

That's part of why we are here, and why we reincarnate. First to get our list wrong, learn from that, then to recreate it by adding things to our list that will improve the situation and bring in the life experience for which we are asking the Universe. That's it! Life is just a constant process of refining and redefinition of what we actually want from it. We just so often draw the wrong lesson and give up, rather than having fun playing with the list, until we get it right. That bit is important, having fun playing with your list. That's a very healthy way to view life, as you are always working upwards, and having fun. Some people think that having fun is a luxury in a miserable world. No, it's a necessity and a right.

When I think about this list thing, I find it mind-blowing. So, don't get down or depressed if things don't turn out as you wanted them to. Re-write your list. Be specific! Fix what went wrong on your list.

So our list of what we want to create is important.

And remember the list really does apply to everything: a new car, house, pet, lover, sex, romance, job, money, health, really anything you want to have fun creating. Be it big or small, in the next five minutes or the next five months. I even use it to create a parking space in a busy town centre or road.

These are just examples. The lists you can create, and the possibilities, really are limitless.

When do you want to create "it"?

This is part of being specific. When do you want your creation to show up?

Although it can take time for things to come through into physical form, depending on the work you have to do and getting into alignment, it's good to set a deadline for what you want to show up. If what you want is always "in the future", that is where it will remain, always just out of reach, which is why it's important to imagine yourself as already having it "now", and preferably subject to a deadline as to when it will turn up. I usually just ask for it "now" or by a date I know I will be ready, and thank the Universe for sending it.

Record your list in physical form

It is also a good idea to write your list down, or to record it in some way. It can be recorded in writing, or visually, or both, but there are reasons for capturing your list physically.

Some requests are better suited to being written down, placing them somewhere where you can see them regularly.

Others can better be expressed with pictures on vision boards, such as putting a picture on a board of the type of house or car you want. There is one guy who I saw on You Tube, and he put a picture of the kind of house he liked on a vision board. From recollection, he got the picture out of a magazine. Years later, he moved house. One day, he got his old vision board out of a box and realised that he had forgotten about the picture of the house on the vision board. But it was the house he had moved into. He didn't recognise the house when he went to view it because of the angles of the photographs – the picture on his vision board showed the house from the back, not the front, so he didn't recognise it when he first went through the front door. But it was the same house. That's an example of the power of visualisation. He put it on a board and gave his attention to it. Years down the line, even after he had forgotten it, it became his.

Start small, for example, asking for a parking space or seat on the train. Watch it happen. Get practice in. Then flex your muscles, and create more.

It can be great fun to get writings and vision boards out from earlier years, once you have been practicing this a while, and, like the guy noted above, have fun looking at what came in, but you forgot about. It can be astonishing how high your success rate at creating things can be.

It will only take a few minutes to write things down, or stick a picture on a board. It also allows you really to think through what you are asking for, how specific you need to be, and making sure you've captured everything you want. It's OK to go back and edit when you think of new things.

In fact, you can write your future life down as a script, novel, or film. You write the rest of your life. You really can, why not? It's a very good idea to plan out exactly where you want to be.

Then what do you do? Just spend some time with it for a few minutes or so a day, either reading the written list, or looking at your vision board. I always take a look at my list or board in the morning, and before I go to bed. Yes, I know you're busy; but it really can be stuck on the bathroom mirror or used as a screensaver. It can go anywhere where you can see it, just for that short period of time each day, just to reinforce it, and be clear to the Universe that this is what you want.

I always think it's better if your wish is said out loud too. I just think that the Universe hears us better when we verbalise it, and this includes chatting to other people about it, too. We are transmitting thousands of thoughts and emotions every day. And it's a way for the Universe to distinguish what we really want from all the other noise which is in our heads the rest of the day. Because what else are we transmitting? A lot of stuff, and most of it, frankly, is a load of old rubbish. So we need to make our request clearly audible, not just once, but every day, so that the Universe can hear and act upon it. If there is something we really want, we have to make ourselves heard.

When you first give your attention to something, the signal sent out to "Source" to bring it in is weak. As you give more attention to it, the signal to "Source" gets stronger, and, with enough attention, becomes a dominant thought. The bigger it gets, the more it becomes a part of your vibration. When you have been wanting something for a long time, your summoning power is much greater than when you first think of something. This is why the written list, the vision board, and the verbal expression are all important. And repetition, repetition, repetition, every day. And it's the way we re-programme our subconscious mind, by repeatedly ramming the idea in there, until it accepts it as truth, and as consistent with your state of being.

When you ask for something, I tend to find that three is a good number of times to make the request. It might be for a parking space on a busy day on the way to the shops. It might be in respect of the request on your list or vision board for the massive thing which you want to bring into your life, in which case, read your list, or concentrate on the image, of what you want three times a day, in the morning or the evening. Why three? The number three is said to be a very spiritual number, so I always ask three times. Plus, it's also the way the Universe answers us. More on that later…

And, on top of asking three times, the more emotion we invest in it, the better. The Universe will hear the emotional attachment to something much more clearly than something asked for without any enthusiasm or expectation of it happening.

You've established a set point. The Universe has to reflect it back. Just remember to make your set point a positive emotion, and that you are not attracting the continued lack of something. If that happens, you can recognise and change it.

Once you've got that dominant thought and emotional pattern, you start to attract things that match it, like coincidences, articles, conversations, observations - even the thing you've been asking for itself.

But it is very important to stress that we might not get what we want just by asking for it. There will in all probability be work to be done. There are plenty of examples of people who have visualised a sum of money and won it on the lottery. Whilst this happens, we don't get something for nothing. Sure, go ahead and ask for a million pounds. You might get it on a plate or with a lottery ticket; but many of those who get the easy win with no effort are miserable quickly or just blow it - the Universe is certainly teaching them a lesson. More likely, the Universe will give you signs about how to *earn* it. It's responding to what you have asked for, but it also wants something of you. And as we have said, get into alignment. Become the type of person that corresponds to what you want to be.

Ask "Source" a question

If you know what you want, hopefully the process of how to ask for what you want has become a bit clearer. We're not quite at the end of it yet, there is a little more way to go.

But what if you don't know what you want?

At a most basic level, so many of us don't even know who we are or what we want. Many people freely admit to living their lives in confusion, and just accept that they will be shaped by events. Sometimes "going with the flow" is fine; it might be your conscious choice right now. At other times, we want a direction, but don't know what we want.

We come here to experience things, but each of us also comes here with unique gifts and talents, which we have often chosen before we came here. To put this more forcefully, we each have a role and a purpose. We come here to experience, but we also decided to come in to do something, with a gift or talent to contribute: something that we are good at, that we are "meant to do". This "meant to do" can stem from an agreement which we have made on the non-physical plane, before we arrived in our physical body. It's as if we say, "OK, I'm going back again into a physical body, but this is going to be my life purpose when I get there."

We often arrive ignorant of the agreement which we have made. But as we establish truth with ourselves, we re-establish connection with "Source"; it comes back to us, and we know who we are and what we are here to do. We are all "one" and we are all extensions of "Source".

When we are disconnected from "Source", we are also disconnected from knowing what we want, what gifts and talents we have been given, or what we have agreed is our life purpose. We are adrift, and alone in confusion – or we attract others in our life who are similarly confused.

Can someone who doesn't know who they are, or what their "purpose" is in life, find out?

Yes: just as much as "Source" is here to respond to what we do want, it is also here to help us to establish who we really are. That includes answering our questions.

And how do we do that?

Like everything else, we can just ask. It's as simple as that. We can just ask.

But again, how often do we not even get to that basic first step? We carry on in confusion, and we don't even ask.

This can be big picture items like, "Who am I?" and, "What is my purpose, what am I good at?" to smaller things such as, "What shall I do today? What will give me the most fun?" If you are ill, "What is my body trying to tell me?" If we are having a hard time in life, "What is it that I need to know to improve this?"

Really, what we can ask is limitless.

"Source" always answers.

It happens at other levels we don't conceive of either. Remember the extent to which things are just pure energy. The two flats I have lived in before I moved to my current house chucked me out! They literally chucked me out. Things just started to go wrong, like doors falling off and things blowing up, as if they were conscious bodies saying, "Time to move on... I want someone else in here now. This place is right for them now, not you; you've moved on in who you are, and you shouldn't be here now."

When things go wrong, ask what "Source" is trying to tell you.

It is always trying to communicate.

We just have to get into regular dialogue with it.

So when things go wrong, we ask it to tell us what we need to know. Or we might just ask it, at a more domestic level, every day, "Thank you for telling me what I need to know today". Or, if you have a pressing situation, "Thank you for telling me what I need to know about [add situation]."

How "Source" communicates with us

So you have either asked for something specific, or you have asked "Source" for answers. Now what?

It's time to get out of the way.

This is where "Source" comes in. You have asked, now it must reflect back to you.

We deal with common mistakes in the *law of attraction* in the next chapter, but one very common mistake is trying to take control of the situation once you have asked "Source" to create something for you, or asked it a question. This involves trying to force something into being, especially "how" it will come into existence.

Leave the "how" of manifesting something to "Source"/the Universe. That's its job. It's doing this for billions of people every day. The "how" of creation, and how it comes into being, is for "Source" to arrange. It can move the pieces in a way you can't. This is why you can now relax. This isn't a struggle. You have put your intention, or question, out there, and you have to do some work getting into alignment, or doing some work when "Source" presents you with an opportunity to realise what you have asked for, but otherwise... relax. Your thoughts and emotions determine and shape events; they bring them into being. But "Source", or fate, or the Universe, call it what you like, will bring them to you, because "Source" is simply better and more able to move the pieces into place than you are.

This sounds blindingly obvious to everyone except the control freak. But there are a lot of those around.

The harder you try to manipulate the circumstances of how something should happen, the more you create resistance, and block the very thing which you are trying to bring in.

How "Source" brings in what you have given your attention to might not be obvious. You probably won't see it coming when it arrives, and how it arrives. You can ask "Source", "Is this the manifestation of what I asked for?" This is an important question. Because often we have so many pre-set expectations, we don't recognise that our desire has manifested, because it hasn't manifested in the way in which we expected it to manifest. This might be because our list of what we want isn't very good. And then we miss it and curse the Universe for not sending it, but it did send it. It was our own pre-conceptions and judgement that prevented us from recognising it when it arrived.

And this is why learning to communicate with "Source" is vitally important.

How do we do this? How do we recognise it when it comes?

Sometimes it hits you between the eyes. It's obvious. Blindingly obvious. I don't need to tell you how to communicate with "Source" when it's obvious. In the vast majority of cases, what you have given your attention to just shows up. Unmistakable.

Other times, it's an opportunity. And thinly disguised. You might see an advert in a paper, or online. It's something you need to pursue.

The thing is, be open. Go with the flow. If you see something that might be relevant to what you have asked for, try it out, but without expectation.

Your instinct will tell you when you have hit the jackpot, when what you have been asking for has just walked through the door. If, for example, you have been looking for a new job, and you get a number of offers, very often you let your instinct guide you on what is the right one. Your instinct is usually right. Whether you make the decision that feels right for you or the decision that feels wrong for you.

Let's examine how that feels. Because instinct very often isn't a thought process. It's an emotional reaction, a hunch. Listen to it. If it feels good, it's your guidance system telling you it's "right" for you, a crucial part of your development.

Care to define it a bit more?

When it feels easy, comfortable, fulfilling, promising, then it's for you. You're in tune, in vibration, you're in alignment. Your feeling matches the feeling of the energy you want to create.

It's the same as we said earlier, when we talked about how "feeling" good is our connection to "Source" and who we are.

When it feels dishonest, dark, heavy, forced, hard work, awkward, it's not for you.

Just tune yourself into the energy of any situation when you're waiting for the answer to your manifestation, or the question you've asked. I raised, earlier, the point that if you are not sure what your purpose is, you can ask "Source". You will be given things to try out. When you like them, when they feel "good", when you like it, you're getting there and establishing your connection to you, your purpose, and "Source".

This is the point at which words always take a back seat to "knowing". You cannot ignore what that inner voice tells you about a situation.

Listen to it. You will know when the inner voice is right, however hard or difficult the road ahead, and however much advice you receive from other people advising you not to do something. If you know it's right, if you know that this difficult road simply has to be travelled to get to your destination, then do it. You will also know when you need to back away because an option won't feel true for you. I find that life often sends me things that aren't true to me, so I become accustomed to how my instinctive reaction feels concerning something that isn't for me. Only by learning this and recognising it will I understand when something is true for me, as I will recognise that feeling by differentiation.

Don't know who you are, or what you are meant to do in life? Ask, and when "Source" answers and it feels "good", then it's told you. Ask. It will answer.

Of course, sometimes something is "good" but it's also tough. "Source" is testing our persistence, and whether we are up to the job. But it's hard going at first. You start to think that all the doubters were right. You start to doubt yourself and think that everyone who tried to discourage you, or thought it was a crazy idea, was, in fact, right. You have taken all sorts of risks, and they aren't paying off. But your instinct said, "Do it", and it felt good. Then – and it's happened to me several times – the bolt from the blue comes. The chance, the opportunity, the event, the coincidence, the vindication, the breakthrough, the result! The person comes along whom we need to help us, just at the right time.

People who come along just at the right time to help us are also a sign that we are in alignment. That's "Source" saying, "You've made it into the right frame of mind, you've done the work getting yourself into alignment, here comes the person that will unlock the doors to what you have asked for."

Other people's advice, discouraging you from a course of action, could simply be the result of their programming. Listen to "You".

What I cannot emphasise too much is the concept of feeling "good" when we are on the right track. Despite testing us, "Source" will try to communicate with us in all sorts of ways to tell us "yes" and "no". Signs, coincidences, feelings, circumstances, people – just start looking and listening.

Is now a good time to talk about Angels and Spirit Guides?

Well, "Source" communicates with us in different ways.

I talked about my contact with a Spirit Guide as part of my Reiki attunement.

Some people can hear or even communicate with their Spirit Guides. I had one brief clairaudience experience with mine when he/they introduced themselves.

But, for the most part, "Source" communicates by way of giving us hunches, or intuition (such as "does it feel good?"), or *signs*.

If it is communicating by way of signs, it will often send three signs over twenty-four hours. This has happened time and again to me, in the forms of images or, in the case of the street I now live in, three houses were on sale at the same time. Three was just reinforcing that it was the right place to be for me.

I just watch and listen for signs. And so your Spirit Guides will communicate with you in similar ways.

We all have Spirit Guides that act in our best interests. They will just give you signs and messages through image and circumstance. And if you don't get it, they will start to communicate louder until you do, as we usually miss the first attempts through all the noise in our day-to-day lives. Oh, and if we keep missing the message, sometimes pain can be sent, to really get our attention! Very often, pain is "Source" asking us to take notice of something in our lives that we need to change. We've usually missed all the other signs before then, so now it's shouting through pain, to get our attention to listen.

It's a good point to bring Angels in…

But hang on, didn't you say that there is no "religious stuff" in all this, just us, and our thoughts and emotions creating our lives and our reality?

Like religions trying to tell us about "Source", "Angels" are energy, like everything else. They are energetic extensions of "Source" energy. They are just another way of "Source" revealing itself with particular characteristics. So there are "Angels" for career, for love, in fact there is one for nearly everything.

Some very sane people have claimed to have seen, met, and communicated with Angels. There are plenty of nutters, but some accounts are from people we would ordinarily recognise as credible witnesses.

Very often they describe events or circumstances where they have claimed that Angels have *intervened* in some circumstance and changed an outcome.

One of the key points which those who have studied this phenomenon make, is that Angels, however they might be described, are always waiting to intervene to help, *but will only do so when asked,* except in life or death circumstances. Unless it's a life or death circumstance, our free will is respected and interventions to help us only happen when we ask.

Rarely is an intervention made without their being asked.

The key issue here is that we are going right back into the *law of attraction* territory, in terms of things appearing that we ask for.

Rather than ask "Source" for what you want, you can ask Angels to manifest things in your life, in exactly the same way.

If this is very similar to the *law of attraction* principles discussed earlier, it should be. Angels, as an energetic extension of "Source", are the same energy that is being called upon whenever we are asking "Source" to manifest something.

It's all the same thing, it's all the same energy, be it Angels, "Source", Spirit Guides, God, fate, life, the Universe. However you express it, it should be whatever works for you. But the key thing in the Angel philosophy is that help only comes when it is asked for. There is no intervention in our free will, except in exceptional circumstances. But if you are in a crisis and you want to call for help there and then, calling on an Angel is a very good and easy way to do it.

It's also worth examining the different ways of creating things in our life. The *law of attraction*, Angels, etc… all relate to "Source" energy and things will only come in *when we ask.* Once again, the Universe is designed to help us. All we have to do is ask, and then it has the permission to intervene.

Now you have asked, how to receive

This is the tough one. A real tough one.

Some people find the asking bit hard. Others find the perseverance hard, either because they have to do something or because getting into emotional alignment is hard.

But others, and this is a surprising number of people, when the thing they have wished for finally comes in... they reject it.

Yup, brilliant.

First of all, they simply might not recognise it. But more often than not, many simply say "no" to the manifestation of what they say they have always wanted.

It's like someone who tries to do you a favour and you refuse. They want to help, you need the help, but still you refuse. This is either because you don't want to put them to any trouble (even though that's not an issue), or because you feel bad about accepting something, or because accepting it takes you out of your comfort zone.

So many people have a problem accepting something. We recognise this when it's a small favour, but what if it's something bigger?

I've seen so many people say, "Oh, I don't deserve that," after the thing they have been asking for walks through the door at them.

Sometimes this is the result of fear. Because the thing that has just walked through the door represents a change in their life that takes them out of their comfort zone, so they refuse to go there and reject the thing they have asked for. Using these techniques means that you will be taken out of your comfort zone if you ask for something important to show up. Changing our lives in major ways usually means going outside our comfort zones, and when the opportunity to do this arises, sometimes people opt for what they are comfortable with and have got used to, despite having asked "Source" to change it, with all the force they could muster, just a short while ago.

But often, people don't let themselves receive, because of an inferiority or guilt complex. "I don't deserve that…", "that will never happen to me…", "oh no, I couldn't".

But if you want to improve any aspect of life, you have to allow yourself to *receive*. And you have to be comfortable with that. You have to drop the inferiority complex, or you have to drop the guilt that you can't receive something. Or accept that you might have to go outside your comfort zone.

We will deal later with money, and the guilt some people have about receiving money.

But to touch on this here, if you want a fantastic life, you can't allow yourself to feel guilty about having money or abundance. Rather, you have to allow yourself to receive, with gratitude.

Those people who are a success in life have no difficulty in receiving. They *expect* to receive.

Yes, it means that you might become much more fortunate that those around you. Refusing it probably won't help them. Refusing the abundance of the Universe simply creates more "lack". Help in other ways. But when "Source" offers you something, especially something you have asked for, it seems more churlish to reject it than to accept it. There is no nobility in poverty. It's not part of the abundant life we are supposed to have.

Remember, it's an abundant Universe; there is enough to go round. As part of your life experience, you can accept some of that abundance as yours, without guilt.

There is the expression "it's too good to be true". There is no such thing as "it's too good to be true". It really can, and should, just keep getting better and better.

I once read a book which said that there are three great things in life: (i) the hot job; (ii) the hot place to live; and (iii) the hot lover. It said that you might get one or two of these at once, but never all three at once. But in a Universe of unlimited supply, you can have all three at once. We only fail to create all three because we believe all three together are not possible, when many people in life already have all three with ease and there is no evidence to suggest that we cannot have all three at once. But we believe these things aren't possible, so we self-sabotage, and make "lack" a reality.

The Universe is unlimited; it's still growing and we are meant to *grow*. We are meant continually to do new things, to reach for new goals and to achieve new conquests.

That means that we have to get comfortable with expansion and receiving, and that it really can keep getting better and better.

There is a great difference between greed and our need to continually grow. We are meant to do the latter, and that is why the Universe has unlimited supply. This isn't an argument against conservation, quite the reverse; respecting the planet is important, and this is not a "slash and burn" philosophy. Because we live in a Universe with infinite supply, there is no need to abuse the Planet, because abuse is not part of this philosophy. Nor, in acting responsibly in terms of conservation, are we saying that we should live stunted lives, rejecting any idea of human expansion. As part of coming here, we have been given what we need to experience this physical life. The more we all ask, the bigger the pie gets, the Universe just keeps expanding.

Each new achievement leads to another in an expansive Universe. You never stop doing things. Relax into the idea that you are an eternal being, and your desires will never cease to flow. Then you begin to enjoy your journey, and receiving.

We should not be afraid to enjoy abundance, as it is a key part of our growth experience. Fret, worry and fear are based on doubting whether this supply exists, and they actually cut the supply off.

Also, greed, and the competitive struggle, are limiting emotions. They imply "lack", a fear that what is desired is in short supply, so that it has to be coveted, or obtained by cut-throat competitive methods. These merely stop the supply, and are not necessary in a Universe with unlimited supply. You don't need to beat the competition, you simply ask "Source" for more of that supply by using your abilities creatively. The creative supply is infinite. Tap into that, rather than the limited thought process of competition. Competition usually just means driving everything down to the lowest common denominator, and everyone loses.

For many businesses, the business plan is something to make, then stick in the drawer. What if many of those businesses stuck the business plan on the wall, or on screen savers, so that staff had to look at it for a short period each day? That's all it would take for the business plan to enter into the consciousness of all staff. Those new clients in the business plan, or whatever goals are set there, would materialise with much greater ease if businesses took the view that they are conscious, and that they can attract things by using the same methods as individuals.

Give to receive

But the act of giving is equally important to receiving. That's why this isn't an avaricious philosophy.

The Universe is based on balance. To give something, it has to receive something. Usually, you have to give first before you can receive. This isn't always money; it can be time, or some form of gift, or work on yourself. We discussed the work you sometimes have to do before "Source" manifests something, and this simply reinforces that. Also, the bigger you give, the bigger you get. Some of the richest people in the world are the biggest givers. There really is no accident in that, because they have just set up a good flow – they give big, so they receive big. But don't invest in giving for the sake of getting something back; do it to mean something.

It also makes us better people, which is good enough in itself.

In terms of giving, do what is right for you. Don't allow anyone to make you feel guilty or pressure you, you will know what charity, or cause, or simple act like volunteering, works for you, and the amount of money or time you want to give. I often just donate some money to charity every month, and that's that. But often, the bigger we give, the bigger we get back!

Also, you don't have to reward the person who helped you to set up a good flow. Sometimes, you will bend over backwards to help someone, and they will say "thanks for that" and then run off, taking what you have given them with no gratitude, or using it against you, or taking the credit for it. Some people can be reluctant to give ever again after that. Don't worry about that. The fact you have given means that the flow will come back. Not necessarily from that person. It might be from someone else, just when you need it. But that help might never show up unless you gave in the first place, even to someone who took advantage of it or abused it. This can happen in reverse. You might not be in a position to be able to pay back the person who helped you. Don't worry about that. They will get their reward. In this situation, you have to allow yourself to receive from them, even if you can't pay them back. You've set your own loop up here. Accept it. But it's a virtuous one. Those who only take will always find, as time goes on, that there is less to take, because they never give.

There is also the concept of sacrifice. It's similar to giving. Suffice it to say that sacrifice is not a limiting experience. Rather, something lesser has to be given up in order to obtain something higher; so making sacrifices in your life to make way for something better is not limiting, but essential to growth.

It's also true that nature abhors a vacuum. Create a space in your life, and something must, by natural law, fill it. So we make a sacrifice of things, by clearing out areas of our lives, to make way for something better. Creating this "space" in our lives for something to come into our lives is key, as it's saying, "I am serious about bringing this in so I've made space for it, now respond please." The more you demonstrate this seriousness, the more "Source" gives you a great big "Like" sign and responds.

I've seen people who want to bring a relationship into their lives literally make space in their wardrobe for someone else's clothes, or buying spare toothbrushes. It works, because it's creating the space for two people, and nature will want to fill that vacuum.

This was also demonstrated when I had the choice between another job, in the place in which I had worked for fourteen years, or voluntary redundancy. I chose voluntary redundancy, even though I had nowhere else to go, and a big mortgage. People thought I was crazy. I just had faith that something else would show up in the vacuum I was creating, because I was making a commitment to do something else. It worked; I landed an interview two days later, after I signed my redundancy papers, and got the position. But this job wouldn't have arisen had I not jumped. But I was being tested first, before being given the new position. "Source" wanted me to show commitment first before showing its hand. I wouldn't normally advise anyone to leave a job without having another one to which to go, but, on this occasion, I understood the rules, trusted my instinct, and made my commitment clear, without the promise of anything in return. As we discussed when we looked at the importance of giving, you have to show a commitment to what you want from "Source" before it will respond.

Summary

There's been a lot of information so far, so I think it's helpful at this stage to do another summary, so that you keep getting the key points.

So here are the things to bear in mind. Let's just have a recap:

1. Positive thinking is everything.

2. Be "it", desire it, have the faith and the expectation it will show up, and feel like it's already here. Don't focus on the lack of it.

3. Ask as if you already have it, now or by a deadline. Keep asking every day.

4. Be specific.

5. Have gratitude for its receipt.

6. Ask for it to be to everyone's highest good.

So, let's have some examples. This, in short form, is how to bring things in you want. Write it on your list or your vision board:

1. *"Thank you for [add x sum of money] arriving by [add date] to everyone's highest good and in divine order."* Don't just say "lots of money" – that is meaningless to "Source". Be specific about the amount.

2. *"Thank you for finding a home in [x location] by [add date] for [£x] to everyone's highest good and in divine order."*

3. *"Thank you for finding me a relationship and this person has [add qualities] who has appeared by [add date] to everyone's highest good and in divine order."* Some key things here: include all the things you want, including the boring things like "integrity", and other, less obvious ones, like living close to you and being single. Oh dear, some people miss the obvious ones and end up in an amazing tryst with someone married, three thousand miles away, but who is otherwise perfect! Their list is lacking for not specifying that this person needs to be close by and single. You can also do the same with your existing relationship, thanking "Source" for what you have, but adding in the things you want to improve as if they have already happened.

4. *"Thank you for finding [add in the job you want] in [x location] for [add salary] by [add date] to everyone's highest good and in divine order."*

5. Add in anything else you want...

That's how I do it, and I find it amazingly successful.

But what if you keep working, hoping, wishing and asking, and you apply all of the methods in this chapter, and they don't work? A lot of the *law of attraction* books don't really deal with what happens if you are not getting results, other than telling you to "get into alignment". Let me try to answer some of these problems regarding inadequate manifestation.

What if it Doesn't Work, and Other Problem Areas

There are plenty of people who got excited after *The Secret* that they could manifest or create anything they wanted in their lives.

And then they got disappointed if it didn't happen.

So, that lottery win didn't appear; they were stuck in the same annoying job, still broke, or irritating Working-Class Hell and Middle-Class Hell things kept appearing, and so they gave up on it. "This law of attraction thing is a nice idea. There are plenty of examples of its working for others. But it hasn't worked for me."

Why?

There are the obvious areas – (i) you haven't asked in the right way (e.g. it's not written down, or your list is too brief, or you've only asked once for it in the last three months, so the asking hasn't been repetitive enough); (ii) you're not changing yourself, or your thought and emotional patterns; (iii) you're being impatient; (iv) you're expecting something for nothing; (v) you're not being persistent, or are accepting defeat too early; and (vi) you're trying to control how your creation will manifest, etc. People do continue to make these mistakes without realising it, and it's just worth possessing awareness and being conscious whether we might be making an obvious mistake, but aren't seeing it. It happens to us all. Take a deep breath, and think it through. The answer might just be an obvious one concerning "method".

Or some things show up, but not everything we have asked for. We've got some of it, but not all of it.

This, of course, tends to suggest that we are doing some things right, if some things are showing up.

It's the areas where they don't that are the problem.

Let's examine below some of those problem areas.

You keep changing your mind

"Source" is going to have a hard time if you want to be a train driver, a gardener, a designer, an architect, a tree, a dog, a cat, single, in a relationship... or whatever you decide that day...

It simply cannot respond when you keep changing your mind. Or it will respond in the only obvious way it knows how – to reflect that confusion right back at you, just giving you even more reason to be confused.

If confusion is your state of being, ask "Source" to help and guide you. We all have talents, abilities and a purpose. If you are unclear as to yours, you simply have to do one very simple thing: ask for guidance. When asked in such a way, "Source" always responds.

Sometimes the thing for which we have been asking arrives at the wrong time. If you are bored and ask for excitement, don't be surprised if it shows up right when you are in the middle of something and don't have time for it. Our manifestations are always a delayed reaction. They can and will turn up right when we have moved on, or changed our minds. Don't curse it when this happens. Acknowledge with gratitude that the thing you have asked for has come up. If it's inconvenient, ask it to hang around until you have time to deal with it. If it no longer serves you, or has come in a way you didn't expect, want, or ask for, you can send it back to sender – always with gratitude – and refine your list.

"Source" is very forgiving of the fact that we mess it around. We treat it in a way that we would hate to be treated ourselves – we take it for granted, we change our mind, we constantly reject what it sends us, and yet it still remains at our service. That's why I've got into the habit of thanking it.

Still thinking and feeling negatively

The biggest problem for many people is, of course, not getting off the starting block in the first place. The hardest bit of this is changing your conscious and subconscious minds, and focusing firmly, persistently, over time, on what you want, and putting in the consistent effort to become it.

All too often, people still focus on what they don't want, what they fear, what they lack, despite having written down what they want on a bit of paper and having repeated it every day. If your emotion is negative, this is creating resistance and blocking you. It's worth acknowledging where you *really* are in your emotional set point and trying to change it, gradually, not in one leap, so that you get into alignment and feel the emotion you will feel as if it's manifested in your life.

Resistance

We've covered resistance earlier, but let's examine it a bit more.

Certain emotions we generate put us into resistance to what we want to bring in. They do this because we focus on the negative emotion and its destructive tendencies, that shift our focus away from what we want to bring in. Instead, we just bring in more negativity associated with that emotion.

Examples of these types of emotion:

- Anger, rage, fury and hate
- Blame, shame, regret and guilt
- Addictive, compulsive, obsessive behaviour
- Love, sex, jealousy
- Fear and doubt

When you are affected by a resisting emotion, you are reacting and holding yourself in a state of reaction; you are a prison of that emotion, you are stuck, rather than making a choice about what you want to create. You can't move on, and you think you have no choice in a situation.

If we live in anger (and some people consciously choose to live in anger), we are not focusing on what we can create.

Whilst this might now sound obvious, how many people are living years of their life governed by negative emotions – such as people living constantly in anger, hate, guilt, jealousy, or waiting for something better round the corner, but refusing to live life according to what they can actually choose? If we are locked into these responses, believing that we have "no choice" but to be governed by them, we eliminate the capacity for change in our lives.

They stop you from being happy, but they are so often consciously chosen.

How to get rid of them? First acknowledge that they are there. When you slip into a position where you acknowledge that you are being controlled by a negative emotion, you can choose to think something different. Focus on what you want to create, on what you want to choose. These emotions limit you; focus on what you want to choose and create instead.

To use the example of someone cutting us up in traffic, making us angry: the anger stops us from making a choice and creating something else, while, instead, we stew in anger. This gets much bigger with things like shame, guilt, etc., which can blindside us for years.

Resistance also occurs when we meet an obstacle. You can get angry with it, or frustrated by it. Or you can bless the lesson it brings and move on; focus on changing it, rather than getting angry or creating another resistant emotion. Because the more attention you are giving it through resistance, the more you are actually creating it and bringing more of it in, because you've got in tune with its vibration. So, if you are frustrated with something, your attention is being given to frustration in connection with that thing, thus bringing in more frustration connected with it.

When you practice non-resistance, you are not inviting life or people to treat you as a doormat – when you think that's happening, you just ask to create a new situation, rather than magnifying the existing one through resistance. When you let go of, say, the frustration surrounding something, you begin to create a different emotion in respect of it, and different results. When you "let go", conversely, you bring much more in.

Gandhi's power was purely passive, yet his following of over two hundred million people was massive, and he caused considerable trouble for the British Government at the time.

Recognising when we are creating more of a problem through resistance can take time. Once you recognise it, greater understanding emerges that you have been blocking what you want to come in, by thought and behaviour patterns. But you can choose to create, rather than being held captive.

Also, ask for what you want to create to come to you easily and with fun. That's right. You might have work to do, but make it easy and fun. I ask for every manifestation to come to me this way. Growth does not have to involve difficulty, unless

291

we are resistant and have lessons to learn – that's when growth is difficult, but it is not when we are open and receptive.

Blocks

"Blocks" go deeper than resistance because we can easily and consciously acknowledge when we are limiting ourselves through resistance. It's pretty obvious when we sit down and take an honest look.

Instead, we might be blocking what we want at a very deep-rooted level, of which we are not even conscious. This goes beyond our conscious mind, which we control. The problem is with our subconscious mind, blocking what we want to create.

"Resistance" is usually self-created, yet a proper "block" might be, superficially, beyond our control.

It might be that we have a deep-rooted negative attitude to money or relationships, or whatever it is that we are seeking to bring in, and, whilst we are consciously asking for these, we have actually got a lot of work to do on getting ourselves into alignment, because our subconscious mind contains some block on this area at a very deep level.

For instance, a history of abuse or poverty attitudes which lodges itself deep in our sub-consciousness, is going to take some work to clear, if we want to create good relationships or money. The same is true in all other areas where we want to create something. Our subconscious mind is made up of our emotional responses to things. If we have a negative emotional response deep-rooted in there, it affects our ability to get into emotional alignment with having it, thus blocking it from coming through. We have limited control over this; these negative responses are just "lodged" in there. But because the subconscious is communicating with "Source", the subconscious mind is sending out the signal that determines our manifestation, however hard we are working with our conscious mind to get something different.

For instance, these subconscious blocks could be things that have happened to us in this lifetime, that require some "clearing" out of the way.

What if the limitations might be carried over from previous lifetimes? We have even less conscious knowledge of those. How does this work? In our current physical bodies, we don't realise that we are eternal, and so a "contract" which we make in one lifetime can be binding in future lifetimes. These can, for example, be marriage contracts, or vows of poverty or chastity "forever more". These contacts made in one lifetime can carry over into later lifetimes, like the one you are living now, so new relationships and money might be hard to come by in a later lifetime after we have bound ourselves to one person or to a poverty-consciousness in a previous lifetime. Sometimes we have unknowingly already tied our own hands before we have even got here.

Whether the limitation exists in this lifetime or a previous one, the effect is the same. It blocks our ability to get into emotional alignment and receive what we are asking for.

A deep-seated block can be very hard to clear. This includes blocks we have created or allowed, or those that are buried in our subconscious, or ones we have carried over from a previous life time.

There are various alternative ways of dealing with these. Some are listed below that work for me. Go with whatever resonates and appeals to you:

1. Write it down. You might be conscious of whatever is blocking you, for instance it might be a person. Write everything negative down about this situation or person on one bit of paper. Then, on another piece of paper, write down

everything that you want to bring in, or is good about this person. Burn the piece of paper containing the negatives, and release that negativity on its way, with love. Keep the piece of paper with all the good bits on, and thank them for being in your life. This symbolic "letting go" can be extremely powerful, and it releases all the negativity that holds you back. We have dealt with cord-cutting earlier in the Chapter headed *"What we give our attention to"* and this is another way of achieving the same severance.

2. Meditation. This is something you can do on your own, or with the help of a selected track on *You Tube* or something similar, for whatever situation you want to clear. There are some very good ones and there are some that clear soul contracts from previous lifetimes, if you think that it goes that deep. You can be released from these contracts if you choose to be. At the very least, meditation will clear the mind of a lot of the thoughts that distract us from focusing on what we want. You have no resistance when your mind is clear. This process of just clearing the distracting thoughts out of our mind is very important, so that "Source" can hear what we really want.

3. Hypnosis. This is something that has worked very well for me. If you are concerned about listening to tracks on *You Tube* on your own that deal with tricky clearing issues, and feel more comfortable with a professional, then this is a possible route. We referred earlier to reconditioning the subconscious mind. This is doing the same, but involves getting help from others, sometimes professional help. It can be helpful to find a hypnotist who understands the *law of attraction*. There is also a branch of hypnosis called neuro-linguistic programming, or NLP for short. It is a way of re-structuring the thought process, helping you overcome limitations that have been put there. There are many misconceptions surrounding hypnosis, and

many people might be concerned about "re-writing" their mind. I've had this done twice and found it amazing in both circumstances. You are in control, no one can compel you to do anything you don't want to do; you are just getting a "leg-up" and help from a professional in order better to create the thought conditions which will help you achieve what you are looking to manifest in your life. There are many successful company CEOs or other people in life who rely on techniques like this to help them maintain a positive frame of mind. It's more common than you think, particularly among successful leaders.

4. Reiki is also an effective clearing tool. We have energy centres in our body, called chakras, that relate to key areas in our life. They cover our connection to (i) our soul; (ii) our intuition; (iii) our ability to express ourselves; (iv) love; (vi) ego, determination and our sense of self; (vi) sex and relationships; and (vii) grounding in the physical world, such as our relationship with money. There are seven of these energy centres. Some are arguing that we are moving to the twelve-chakra system, but let's stick with seven at the moment. Blocks or imbalances in these can have effects on our physical life. So it's easy to see how a block in the expression chakra can affect our ability to vocalize what we want in life. Or blocks in our love, sex and relationship chakras will affect those areas of our life. Or a block in our grounding chakra can affect the material things in our life, like money. A Reiki practitioner can help "clear" these blocks, and, once cleared, we can create and receive things more easily. Access Bars® are also an effective clearing tool. This simply involves massaging key points on the head that act as "delete" buttons that clear away our limiting thoughts and beliefs, allowing us to create and receive. Both Reiki and Access Bars® don't just act on the level of this

physical life, they also work at a deeper level, and remove blocks from the subconscious or previous lifetimes. I have been attuned to Reiki and also give and receive Access Bars® treatments. Both are amazing, and can make a massive difference to well-being. There will be practitioners of other therapies, but these are the ones of which I have had direct experience, and which have made a massive difference to my life.

5.   Past life regression (which can be done under hypnosis) can be a useful tool to try to find the reason for a block in a past life, and clear it. In these sessions, you will usually visit the lifetimes which are relevant to the problems you are experiencing now. Plus, you can have tremendous fun with the realization that, perhaps, you were once a nun during the middle ages, or Henry VIII. Or a Hartlepool Granny. What could be more fun?

6.   Release previous soul contracts. Go on, just ask to be released. You entered them when you didn't know what you were doing. You didn't realise that you were binding yourself in perpetuity. Ask to be released. It's that easy.

I've found that, when using these techniques, not only is the mind much clearer afterwards, but my ability to create and receive increases significantly. As blocks are removed, things just come into my life where, previously, they were "stuck" because I was blocking them. On the subject of getting "stuck", or "nothing is happening", life is always in motion; it can't get stuck. Two things are happening, either: (i) pieces are being moved into place, so wait; or (ii) you are thinking the same thoughts and getting the same results, hence nothing is moving until you change your thoughts. You'll know which one is right when you ask.

For me, all of these methods are simply life-enhancing, and feel really good anyway. I am not frightened of any them, but simply curious to keep lifting the veil. They never cease to give me answers or insights. You can find the right one for you.

If you are frightened by any of these things, is fear the blocking emotion holding you back from creating and receiving the life you want? If you are sceptical, is scepticism of your ability to play with infinity stopping you creating and receiving?

Morality and karma

Here's a difficult one: the fact that you are honest, and jolly nice to everyone, does not ensure your success.

That's a hard one for people to grasp. They are taught that, if you work hard and are honest, success will follow.

It will, if you actually believe that success will follow, because you've got into alignment with success coming your way, and you expect it as a reward.

But working hard and being honest without expectation of success will not in and of itself bring success. In other words, there is no natural reward for virtue. Many people find that a hard concept to grasp, because we have always been taught that success is the reward for virtue. Nope.

But if "Source" instead responds to what we ask for, irrespective of its virtue, then can't we use this philosophy to "immoral" ends?

Yes. This is happening in the world around us every day, as "Source" responds equally to what people are asking for, good or bad, because they are in alignment with what they are asking for, whether that is good or bad.

It's a rather depressing thought that morality doesn't come into this. That "Source" is simply a mirror for "us", for better or for worse. We are here to make choices, and the manifestations of those might not be the ones of which other people approve, or might cause harm.

But what about karma? If someone acts "immorally", doesn't this come back to haunt them? Well, only if they expect it to.

Good and bad karma only exist to the extent that we expect "good" or "bad" things to come out of our "good" or "bad" actions. If you do something "wrong" and *expect* something nasty to come back at you, it will, because you have created the expectation that it will – you've given your attention to it, so it will manifest. But if you expect to get away with it, you just might.

This implies that it's a bit of a free-for-all with no countervailing force – that life is simply *Lord of the Flies*.

Well, not quite.

We have discussed the existence of "Source" as the source of all love and abundance. It's there when we ask for it, and it is powerful when we ask it to intervene. Also, when we are connected to its energy, we feel great.

But we are also free to make our own decisions, contrary to that energy.

But in an infinite Universe, is there really any reason to act immorally to the detriment of others in obtaining what we want?

To take an example, if someone asks "Source" for a hundred pounds today, "Source" might well respond by giving them the chance to mug an old lady as she walks away from the bank with a hundred pounds in her handbag. "Source" has responded to their request.

But why do that? If there is infinite supply, is it possible for us to obtain what we want without disadvantaging someone else?

To ask for something – and let's use our, "I need one hundred pounds today" example – and to ask for that, "to everyone's highest good and in divine order", allows "Source" to manifest the opportunity to obtain one hundred pounds that day without hurting anyone – for instance, by giving the opportunity to do a job.

That is a more satisfactory outcome for all sides. You will notice that I added in "to everyone's highest good and in divine order" in a standard request for something, and this is the reason. So here, as in life, it is our responsibility to act morally in the choices we make.

How we ask for things will yield different results, and we are responsible for our own moral compass.

There simply isn't the need to hurt anyone else to obtain what we want, when we consider that "Source" can respond to us in infinite ways that we consider "moral". Plus, anyone with any understanding or connection to "Source" energy knows that its wonderful energy is inconsistent with wanting to control others, or acting from motivations of hatred, or to cause harm.

The presence of immorality or evil or violence is usually a failure of the imagination to obtain what we want in other ways. Anyone acting from that perspective does so because they have to obtain something by force, by trickery, illegally, or violently, because they believe, from a limited perspective, that there is a lack of the thing they want, so it must be obtained by those means. But that perception of "lack" or "shortage" can only create more lack and shortage, for them anyway. Because they act from this perspective, and, at some level, know it's wrong. They then create their own karmic feedback, and the negativity is later reflected right back at them. Hopefully, by this stage, the point has been made that we don't have to obtain anything from that limited perspective. Those whom we consider immoral or evil are simply disconnected from the unlimited love and abundance that is "Source". Or more simply, they are disconnected from themselves.

Why favour a "moral" approach in how we manifest things? Because we are also at our most potent in attracting what we want when we have our connection to "Source", and are consistent with its energies which are light against the dark.

However we also need to suspend some element of judgement on what we consider evil or immoral or hurtful acts.

The example of Churchill was given earlier. Some might, from a moral perspective, consider him a warmonger, but there is an equally valid point of view that, even at his worst, his earlier failures (like the Dardanelles campaign, which saw the death of many) offered many lessons to achieve what we needed him to achieve later.

One party leaving a relationship might hurt someone else, but that action might be necessary for both parties' growth or expansion. Sometimes, the worst things that happen to us open the door to something wonderful. That's why, even when we are given a hard knock, thanking "Source" for the lesson and being non-resistant, suddenly opens the door to something wonderful, which we would block if we just sat there cursing and resisting it.

Also, consider what the consequences will be if you seek to create something that affects another's free will. We've given the example of a broken relationship. One party might want to get back with the other one, and, through various means "manifest" a getting back together. You can hope for that, and both parties might decide to do that voluntarily, but trying to force it back together by restricting the other party's free will is not going to work. If we are coercing someone against their will, and we suspect it's wrong, it will come back to bite us.

Also, this is hardly "getting into alignment" with what you imagine a good relationship to be if one party is coerced. The bad energy will kill the relationship. This happens in all situations where we interfere with another person's free will – the destructive energy created usually rebounds. If someone voluntarily walks away from something you want them to do, just accept that the situation you want them to be a part of is not true to them. We go back to refining our list. Ask "Source" to send someone with all the qualities that you liked in that person but, in this case, manifest a person who also voluntarily chooses to be in the situation which you are offering. And see how much better that energy is!

But it's still a bit of a free-for-all out there. You've got people manifesting stuff from all sorts of skewed perspectives. No wonder things look a mess. Even if it is a bit of a free-for-all out there, you can create things from a much better place, which will make a difference the more people do it.

And you can always protect yourself from the actions of others, if they are trying to bring things in which harm you. How? You can ask "Source" to protect you, if someone else is trying to manifest harm against you. Just ask "Source" for protection, if you happen to be that granny one day walking out of the bank with a hundred pounds. The possibilities in using these forces in our life really are endless, and may require some suspension of moral judgement.

Judgement

Ahh, judgement. One of the arguments levelled against the *law of attraction* is that it encourages the more judgemental sides of our personality.

If we are truly in control of our destiny to the extent discussed here, then the misfortunes that befall us are surely our "fault"?

I've seen some criticisms of the *law of attraction* on this basis, and I've seen some people who practice it also become hardened as a result. Some even think they are *superior* because they possess this knowledge.

Hmm… no.

Even if we have contributed to these things as a result of our thoughts and emotions, this is no reason for judgement or superiority.

If someone is having a hard time, they deserve compassion and help.

And if you are not getting the results you want, go easy on yourself, rather than blaming yourself. Judgement of ourselves simply limits our choices. Why? Because "judgement" is always placing someone in the "wrong", which limits their growth. But if we accept responsibility, we accept the capacity to change what we don't like.

We are sometimes judged because we are different, but what if being different is the reason you came here?

Judgemental people can be extremely limiting. People choose to be that way, of course. They can choose to be offended and gain power by telling someone "that's not acceptable", when, actually, they have no more than a point of view. But it's a point of view that limits them, as they think it gives them power. It doesn't. It just limits them and their capacity to create something better than their judgement or being offended.

Again, we come back to the central principle of the existence of "Source" as the source of all love and abundance. Blame, lack of compassion and judgement are not part of this philosophy.

But sometimes, if we narrowly ascribe a "moral certainty" to something, or judge a situation, we might be blocking what we want to come in. The very thing that we disapprove of, or we think will hurt us, might be the thing which we need to grow. I tend to keep an open mind, and ask "Source" if this is for my benefit or is part of my creation.

Also, when we send very strong signals or thoughts out there, they become a belief to us or a truth. The *law of attraction* then responds by sending us things that confirm our truth or belief – so we think we are "right" in our view of life, because our truths and our beliefs all get confirmed when the *law of attraction* sends a manifestation back. Not really. The *law of attraction* is just sending you more of what you are giving your attention to, being your belief or truth. But that view of life or belief which you hold might be very limiting and negative. "Events" always confirm your point of view. It's not because you are "right", though people take "events" as vindication. You are just getting back what you gave your attention to. And your belief or truth is really just a point of view. It doesn't have to have the certainty you ascribe to it. If it's a limiting point of view, question it. You might suddenly open up a whole load of new choices.

Money

On the subject of morality, some people see an obvious disconnect between spiritual philosophies, and being loaded with cash and being successful. The spiritual and the worldly do not go together, so they argue.

"Money is the root of all evil," so the old saying goes. Well money, like everything else, is just an energetic vibration; it looks solid, but it's energy. It's true of the physical coins and notes, as well as the numbers in your bank account. Money is in fact morally neutral, because it's just an energetic vibration.

303

We give it morality, for better or for worse. Money just magnifies what we are. If we are philanthropists, and give it away, it magnifies our gifts. If we are miserly, it magnifies that.

But money has no moral position in itself, so its accumulation is just the same as the accumulation of everything else which you wish to attract.

What you do with it, and the morality you imbibe it with, is up to you, as with every other choice you make.

But in an infinite, abundant Universe there is no issue with wanting abundance to lead an amazing life. There is no problem with the accumulation of lots of money and enjoying it.

Abundance, far from being in opposition to spirituality, is at the heart of it.

Of course, we can love money and not love life or people, and then problems can set in. But as the expression goes: "use money, love people". There is nothing wrong with wanting to acquire and use it to enhance your life.

Of course, many people don't acquire it, because they exist in a poverty consciousness. And not attracting money through the *law of attraction* usually has its roots in this at some level. They think that money is disreputable, a sign of greed, the root of all evil, or they think that they don't deserve to have it. These philosophies are all questionable. It's time to welcome money into your life, and to believe you deserve it (because you do) and to use it to create the life you want.

Poverty consciousness holds many of us in poverty. If you are not manifesting money into your life, it's time to let that poverty consciousness, or moral opposition to money, go. Resenting others for having money also blocks you from getting it. Envy: it's only blocking you from receiving.

If it's money you want, and you are not getting it, consider your relationship to it, and whether you are in allowance of, or resistance to, it.

As noted earlier, the Universe is infinite and always expanding, so you cannot take more than your share. Having lots of money does not deprive anyone else of it. But stop spending money, stop it being in circulation, stop its expansion, and everyone has less.

Money, like everything else in life, is something you can create by asking for it in the correct way.

Soul Mates and Twin Flames

We have touched on the subject of relationships earlier. But there is much more to say.

We all want better relationships, even at the level of just getting along with people and making life easier, or at a romantic level.

But relationships are a problem for many.

We've covered cord-cutting in the Chapter headed "*What we give our attention to*" to help with relationships with difficult people. Give it a try, to see if you can improve your relationship with them, or this exercise might mean they leave your life completely.

The other area of relationships where people have problems, and I hear it all the time, are where people want their "soul mate", and they are struggling to bring that person in.

Yet the soul mate concept is not well understood, and so the things that people are manifesting are causing them some upset on this subject.

We don't just have one soul mate. In fact, we have a number of them in our lives.

They aren't necessarily our life-long partners, living with us in perfect matrimonial bliss. They might be. But more likely, they might come into our lives and then go, perhaps never to be seen again, in this lifetime at least.

You won't always get along with them. In fact they might drive you up the wall, or become an enemy.

They might be a family member, a co-worker, lover, or even a pet.

So what are soul mates?

They are souls we make a contract with before we come into this physical existence. The contract is made to meet in this physical lifetime, and to teach each other lessons. Once the lessons have been learned, very often they move on out of our life.

It is possible to have a soul mate who is with you all of your physical life, but frequently we meet them on a "just passing through" basis.

We all know when we have met a soul mate. The connection is instantaneous. You feel like you have known them all your life, or the conversation just comes easily, or you can just see something in their eyes, some spark of recognition. That's when you meet a soul mate you like.

We can just as easily have a chemical reaction against someone when we first meet them. We don't get to dislike them over time, the dislike recognition is immediate. That can be soul mate recognition too.

All are sent as guides to offer us lessons. They will contribute in some way that shapes our lives. That is the contract that was entered into with them, before we came into this physical existence, to teach that particular lesson. Often, the lesson might be what real love looks like. That's our traditional association with soul mates, but it has that resonance because that lesson is probably the most powerful one there is. But the lessons we can learn cover every spectrum of life. Just welcome each one that comes in. Once that lesson is learned, then it's time for you both to move on, the contract has been fulfilled. The "immediate recognition" connection, whether you like them or don't, is simply the Universe's way of alerting you that you need to take note of this person, and the lessons they bring.

I've seen people ask to meet "their soul mate" and they end up with something like a cat that they have an amazing bond with. Then they sit there, hissing alongside the cat, cursing the *law of attraction* for not sending them a soul mate. Remember how we said a soul mate could even be a pet. The law isn't at fault, it's our list that's at fault, for not being specific enough (we should have asked for a human!), added to the failure to recognise that "Source" did respond, just not in the way that was expected (which is why we should keep asking "Source", if something is the manifestation of what we have asked for). Enjoy the cat, but it's probably time to work on that list again and brush up that relationship definition.

So what then is "the one" in relationship terms?

For some people "the one" might not turn up straight away, especially if they have lots of development to do. In their case they will meet soul mates throughout their lives, learn the lessons, and move on. Being in love several times, and then moving on. All part of the lesson.

Others do meet that life-long partner. That partner can be a soul mate, but there is also another level to soul mates. There is a concept of a "primary soul mate", one that involves a greater connection than with the other soul mates, but sitting at the top of the tree is our "twin flame".

The "twin flame" concept has existed for some time; Plato talks of it.

When we have a soul mate connection, we are establishing contact with a member of our "soul family".

When we meet with our "twin flame", we are meeting ourselves. As Plato describes, our soul is separated in two and we are on journey to find our "other half". The expression "other half" is really describing the twin flame reunion: two halves of the *same soul* reuniting.

Meeting a soul mate can be powerful. Meeting your twin flame, though, is pretty seismic. If we meet someone we like, we think it's explosive. But a twin flame reunion occurs on several levels - physical, emotional, mental and spiritual, as you would expect when you consider what a soul reunion would look like. For some, the intensity of the connection is simply overpowering, and one of them becomes a runner, until, in a number of cases, they are drawn back. If two twins are in physical existence at the same time, they have agreed to meet. In many cases, our twin hasn't incarnated at the same time as us, but can be reached through deep meditation and asked in.

Many people misunderstand the twin flame concept.

They think that any deep relationship is a twin flame relationship. It probably isn't, because twin flames reunions are rare, but these reunions are becoming more common.

Notice that I referred to a twin flame "union". You don't have a "relationship" with a twin flame. It's a *union*.

Twin flame "relationships" are not about 2.4 children, a house, a dog and the usual trappings. They are hard work, as they are part of a divine mission. What is that mission? Our society is built on relationships, whether romantic or otherwise, and many of them are not in a good shape.

Twin flames are templates for how a relationship should be. That is part of their divine mission, to provide that template as an example to everyone else. Twin flames don't meet perfectly formed; there are often big lessons to be learned within the relationship, by one or both of the twins, about how a relationship should function. After what is known as the "bubble love" initial meeting phase, there is usually a hard period of learning and getting rid of old ideas and templates about what relationships are supposed to be like.

This happens in all relationships to a degree. But the lessons people take away are usually the wrong ones. They draw an ego-based lesson. So when the other person doesn't behave in the way the other party's ego wants them to, the relationship suffers. And that is the essence of what twin flames are trying to teach us. To get rid of ego in relationships, and to teach unconditional love, which by definition does not involve ego, because ego creates the "conditions" in a relationship, when the union is in fact meant to be unconditional.

A considerable number of people in relationships take an ego-based approach. They actually want the other person to be an extension of their ego, and get very upset when that person does not behave as their ego wants them to. Blame sets in, and all sorts of ego games are played. Love is "conditional" on the other person's behaving in a certain way, to keep the other person's ego happy, or to provide what the other person needs the relationship for. Very often, the other party has done nothing wrong. They have just made their choices. Actually, it's the other person's controlling ego that is the problem.

Twin flames learn to let all old relationship templates go, especially ego, and "taking" what they need from relationships. When that goes out of the window, that's when unconditional love without judgment of the other person comes in. Twin flames are both the same person, after all. Finally, "you" accept "you" in all senses. That's the twin flame lesson. When you see a twin flame relationship that's gone through all the trauma and the lessons, you get it. Their purpose is to teach the rest of us.

You see how relationships are supposed to be when they walk into the room.

Why are more twins reuniting now than in the past? It's for the same reason that Reiki and other energetic healing systems are being "re-discovered", centuries after they were lost. Humanity's consciousness is rising. If things look like they are going to pot in the world, look a little closer. Spiritual movements are getting larger, and rising consciousness is happening to an increasing number of people. Just take something like yoga, rather rare two decades ago: now yoga classes are literally everywhere, and it's a spiritual as well as a physical discipline.

This rising consciousness, the rediscovery of old healing systems, the increasing number of twin flame reunions, are all part of the same awakening. The kind of people getting into things like Reiki has changed at a dizzying pace. Only a short while ago the hippy types (and there's nothing wrong with them) were into it; now people working in "grounded" careers are getting into it. I've been a commercial lawyer in the City of London for twenty years. It would have been inconceivable twenty years ago for these kind of ideas to be written about by someone doing that job. This book would not have been available in this form twenty years ago, and these ideas, that were hidden, are increasingly getting out there. The change in consciousness has been considerable in such a short space of time, and it's happening from all sorts of different directions at an increasing pace. Twin flames are one manifestation of this.

Twin flames are a fascinating subject. Want to know more? The best source on this I have found is a *You Tube* site run by two twin flames, Mel and Nicole, called Golden Ray Twin Flames. The website address is https://www.youtube.com/user/goldraytwinflames.

Oh, and the sex between twin flames is, apparently, amazing, because it's working on the physical, emotional and spiritual levels, and even the soul's higher self can get involved, so it turns into a kind of spiritual gangbang. Apparently the physical body just "gets in the way" and isn't bendy enough, or whatever, because the sex is so "out there". Yup. Sounds fun, but after that they have a serious job to do.

Relationships are often the most difficult area of the *law of attraction*. People ask for the perfect relationship, but when it shows up, it is less than their expectations.

Often, this is because they don't understand the relationship concept.

Many relationships, and love, are actually limiting. By pouring yourself too much into the relationship you can lose "you". With the wrong partner, you can subject yourself to too much of their judgement, which is also "you" destroying. To attract, or keep, a good relationship, show gratitude, caring and no judgement to yourself; then you are more likely to attract love, because that is what it is.

If some of this is new to you, your relationships might not have been great, because these are the lessons that might have needed to be learned. Successful relationships already "get it".

If you are getting some hard knocks on the relationship front, "Source" is giving you an indication of the lessons which you first need to learn yourself. As we have noted, the twin flames can go through a hell of a time before they "get it", and their relationship develops into the instructive template which it is supposed to be for the rest of us.

The "need" for the relationship can also sabotage the manifestation, because we actually doubt whether it will show up when we are "needy". If we trust that "Source" will deliver it, we stop sabotaging our own manifestation.

Is it OK just to ask for a "soul mate" and "twin flame"? I tend to the view that it's best still to write out a long list of the things you want. Does a partner have to be a soul mate or twin flame? You might be limiting your choice. If you've got your list right, you are probably more likely to manifest a twin flame or soul mate material, because of your alignment to those values, even if the person who comes in isn't a soul mate or twin flame.

Of course, if soul mates and twin flames are based on contracts, if we want to create even more choice, we can ask to be released from those contracts, and really start creating on the relationship front. Now that's novel...

But the best way by far to manifest great relationships is to become comfortable with ourselves. The lesson "Source" will send time and again is love yourself first, because, when you are happy in yourself, then "Source" will send you that which is in harmonic vibration with you.

This applies, of course, whether you are single or in a relationship. As any twin flame will tell you, the work never stops, either in attracting, or in maintaining a relationship.

In truth, we have often got to let go of our own ego to actually be in a "relationship" or "union". Try working on that, and what you create will be very different to what you have created before.

Relationships affect every area of our life. They are pretty much the bedrock of everything. Get this right, and the rest just flows...

Good luck in waving goodbye to your problem areas in creating things. In fact, *have fun* clearing them away, because it opens the door to so much.

Creating a New Beginning

Thank you for coming on this journey with me, I hope you've found it both as funny, mental and instructive as I have.

But the real journey is that ahead – the life you want to create for yourself.

At the start of Part 3 to this book, I quoted a Buddhist Monk who said to me: *"Do what you love, and if you can't yet do what you love, love what you do."*

I was attending a meditation course in northern Thailand in a temple in Chiang Mai.

It was a strange affair. I had to wear all white, but could not, anywhere, find a white meditation outfit. So someone bought me a white karate outfit. I turned up and everyone else had found perfect white pristine meditation outfits, while I looked like a clueless extra from a bad kung-fu film. One particularly bonkers monk tried to see if he could get into a mock fight with me, waved his stick about, and chased me around going, "Hiiii-yaaaaaaaa". That cry was all that could be heard, piercing the enforced silence, as we weren't allowed to talk. Plus Pug, the personal trainer with the constant erection, had injured my hip, so I couldn't get into the lotus position for meditation, so it was, all round, a bit awkward. Then we were only allowed two meals a day, the first at seven a.m., and the second at eleven thirty a.m., to encourage fasting, to aid our meditation, so, by about two p.m., starvation had set in. But strangely, amid this enforced fasting, they ran a tuck shop to which you could go to at pretty much any time, full of biscuits, crisps, chocolate, and a freezer that had one Cornetto in it. The freezer resembled the washing machine belonging to the woman in Hartlepool with the house full of knickers, as it screamed under the strain of going into full operation mode to freeze just one Cornetto. Naturally, I bought the Cornetto, to try and encourage them to turn off the freezer, for conservation reasons, and to give the freezer the chance to die peacefully. I came back the next day to find it refilled, with just one solitary Cornetto, and the poor thing continued to grind away.

We got up at five thirty a.m. each day for chanting and meditation, and that's where I met the Buddhist Monk, who thankfully wasn't the one who chased me around.

What astonished me in his talks were the parallels between his Buddhist philosophy and the *law of attraction,* although I see Buddhism as still another organised religion.

He kept re-emphasising that the past and present are no indicators to the future; that we should not live our lives by the things that have happened to us in the past. He said a number of times, "Why do you allow what someone did or said five years ago to shape your life?"

For him, the key to happiness was doing what you love doing. Finding something to appreciate each day just strengthens your bond to "Source".

And if you are not yet able to do what you love, then love what you do. And whatever situation we are in, we think we might have no choice, and have to live with it. We always have a choice. We have chosen where we are. We can also choose to change it.

Even if we dislike our lives at present, if we find ways to enjoy it, to "love what we do", the energy of our situation will change. He emphasized that any good energy which we inject into that situation would be projected back to improve it. Eventually, make the transition to do what you love, because that's what you are meant to do. Until then, loving what you do makes the transition so much easier.

I hadn't expected to go there to find any kind of validation for those ideas. But there it was – a Buddhist monk advocating *law of attraction* and positive thinking.

And naturally he just *glowed* with happiness. Because he'd created that happiness. Happiness was his own choice. Having no self-esteem issues was also his choice too, interestingly enough.

Finding that space, in the world we are in, can be difficult. Just coping, day in, day out, for many takes enough time.

Finding the space to dream about the life we want is even more difficult.

Day to day "realities" just intrude. Working-Class Hell and Middle-Class Hell, and all that...

But the monk said that, first of all, we should love where we are now. Find the advantages of it, and project some good energy into it. You might not be able to change it yet, especially if you have some obligations that need to be fulfilled. But if we hate our current situation, the Universe will simply reflect back more reasons back to hate it, so, for now, find the good in it.

Then take time to focus on what you actually, really, want. Most of us don't do that. We just exist, and try to cope with where we are now. But just for a moment, don't focus on the negatives – think about *where you actually want to be, and who you want to be. How much time do you really focus on asking the questions: (i) what life do I really want; and (ii) can I have that, please?* Most people have forgotten how to do this.

Some people think like this all the time, and have already created wonderful lives for themselves. They already know everything I have said here. But for some people, this thinking concept will be genuinely revolutionary, and all of these ideas new.

Let's recap how to ask for what you want:

1. Formulate what you want. If you are not sure, ask the Universe to help you find your way. It will respond.

2. Write it down on a piece of paper, and/or on a vision board.

3. Ask for it to be to everyone's highest good, and in divine order.

4. You should ask for what you want in the positive, no "I want... I need... I would like..." Ask as if you already have it, "Thank you for [x] in my life." Or set a deadline for when you want it to show up. Feel and express the emotion of having it as if it has already arrived.

5. Be specific. No generalities. A long list with detail is great.

6. Say it out loud or in your mind every day, morning and evening if you can, three times each go.

7. Express gratitude for it being in your life, now or at the time of your choosing.

8. Get out of the way. Don't give it any more attention than you have. Clear your mind. Don't try to control the outcomes or how it will show up. Write your list of what you want, but not how it shows up.

9. Love what you do until it shows up, and be grateful when it does.

Let's just take an example, of wanting a new job. You could ask something like this, "Thank you for my wonderful job of [x], starting on May 1, paying [£x], at [x] location, to everyone's highest good and in divine order." Add in anything else you want.

You can do this for large things, and small. All the time.

When it comes to a new direction, what feels good and right for you usually is, even if it might sound crazy to others. It's what is right *for you* that counts. Other people's truths might not be correct for you. You will know your own truth. Talk to your better self, about what you want and why you want it – it's great having that conversation with ourselves sometimes, and the Universe really hears it when we do. If something feels heavy, or your instinct says no, it's probably not true for you.

But above all, remember this. The Universe is a mirror and it's reflecting "you" back. The Universe is also infinite, and you are eternal.

Your ability to create is much, much greater than you ever thought, when you have a Universe to call on that is such a wonderful and infinite creator. And you are an extension of that; your role is as a creator.

When you make a mistake, go easy on yourself, just learn the lesson, and never hold on to it or affect your ability to create. Let things go. Always, always focus on the life you want.

And above all, we are meant to have *fun*! We've been sent here to discover who and what we are, and the main part of that is to have fun doing so. That's such a large part of what we have come here to do. And don't forget to soar and fly.

Pleasure is not in the receiving or the manifestation. It's about the feeling great, just expecting what we have asked for, of living and creating.

You are an infinite being, with infinite choices. Now enjoy making them.

Working-Class Hell. Middle-Class Hell. What on earth is that? They really don't exist.

Suggested Reading

The Secret – Rhonda Byrne

Ask and it is Given – Esther and Gerry Hicks

Working with The Law – Bob Proctor and Mary Morrissey
(audio download with written transcript)

Being You, Changing the World – Dr. Dain Heer

The Power of Intention – Dr. Wayne Dyer

Living Beyond Distraction – Gary M. Douglas & Dr. Dain Heer

Think and Grow Rich – Napoleon Hill

The Angel Whisperer – Kyle Gray